From the Esk and the Usk: Out East and Back Home

From the Esk and the Usk: Out East and Back Home

Anne Macdonald

First published in Great Britain as a softback original in 2019

Copyright © Anne Macdonald

The moral right of this author has been asserted.

All rights reserved.

No part of this publication may be reproduced, stored in a retrieval system, or transmitted, in any form or by any means, without the prior permission in writing of the publisher, nor be otherwise circulated in any form of binding or cover other than that in which it is published and without a similar condition including this condition being imposed on the subsequent purchaser.

Typeset in Galliard

Editing, design, typesetting and publishing by
UK Book Publishing

www.ukbookpublishing.com

ISBN: 978-1-913179-31-1

For my beloved children
Alex and Kate

Acknowledgements

I would like to thank my family and all those friends who encouraged me, not only to write this book (which they seemed to think was a good idea), but to finish it!

My special thanks go to Patty Macdonald, who spent time with me, checking the details of her family's history and providing me with photographs; to my children, Alexander Macdonald and Katriona Macdonald, who read through the more recent history, made some corrections, and agreed to it being published; to Angelique Gainza, who was the first person to read the manuscript in its entirety and who did not throw up her hands in horror when she had done so, but firmly encouraged me to go ahead and publish; and to Lisa Babalis who took on the task of reading it (despite her very busy life) and sent me her thoughts.

Notes

The countries of Burma, Thailand, and many cities and towns in Burma and India have changed their names since some of the events described in this book. However, I thought that to maintain the flavour of the times, I would use the names used then, and later, used to me.

Some of those names are:

Previous:	Current:
Akyab:	Sittwe
Bassein:	Pathein
Bombay:	Mumbai
Burma:	Myanmar
Calcutta:	Kolkata
Ceylon:	Sri Lanka
Madras:	Chennai
Maymyo:	Pyin U-Lwin
Pagan:	Bagan
Prome:	Pyay
Rangoon:	Yangon
Salisbury:	Harare
Siam:	Thailand
Toungoo:	Taungoo
Umtata:	Mthatha

Contents

BOOK ONE – EARLIER   1

Chapter 1: Burma Connections   3

Chapter 2: The Welsh, the Scots, the Colonial Adventurers   15

    Wills, Double-Barrels and Money   15
        The Two Jenkins

    Big Ben   16
        Charlotte and Benjamin

    Culloden, Flax and Timber   18
        The Early Gaudies

    The South Wales Establishment   22
        Vendigaid

    Montrose, Burma, the Somme   25
        Augustus and Isabella

    Gold, Gambling, and the Crash   29
        Evelyn Delahaye and Eleanor

    Opal Mining – Living in Caves   33
        Minnie and Victor

    The Black Sheep, the RAF, Smuggling at Sea,
    and an Italian Jail   36
        Cedric

Merchant Seaman at 13, Narrow Escapes, Colonial Advancement, Retirement *Arthur and Catherine*	42

Chapter 3: 'Out East' and 'Back Home' — 53

The Disappointed Dancer *Valerie*	53
Marriage, the War, a Baby, and Burmese Communists *Valerie and Glen*	55
The Seasoned Colonial *Glen*	56
Tea Gardens, Rhinos, Panthers and Snakes	66
A Canadian Idyll, a Baby Boy, and on to Thailand and Iraq	67
Baghdad: Uprisings and a Breakdown	69
'Back Home'	74

Chapter 4: Early Times — 80

A Child of the Colonies *Valerie Anne*	80
Tea Gardens	80
The Other Side of the World	81
Bangkok: Snakes, Fireflies, and Flying Elephants	83
Montrose, Rationing, the Coronation	86
Boarding School	87
Parkfield: Bad and Good Times	89
Hateful Hatley	92
Teenagers at Summerside	94
St Trinian's at School House	97
Homme House – another country	100
What next?	106

BOOK TWO – LATER   115

Chapter 5: A Mediterranean Dimension   117

    Becoming a Grown-Up – Sort Of   117
        The Ox and Cow   117
        Independence   120
        Ian James Macdonald   121
        Armenia, Armenians – and the Genocide   124
        Smyrna and the Greek 'Katastrophi'   131
        Flight into Egypt – a New Life   138
        An English Education   141
        The Suez Crisis   142
        A New Life in the UK   152
        Fun, Fun, Fun   153
        First Holiday in Greece   154

Chapter 6: People and Places   157

    Anglesey   158
    Waterville   158
    Arthur Nortje   161
    Loch Fyne   162
    Gate Crashing in Bristol   164
    Yugoslavia   164
    Swiss Connections   167
    Bath and Around   169
    France   170
        Mystery Woman   170
        Normandy   171
        Paris on the Cheap   171
        Au Pair in Paris and Brittany   172
        A barn in the Pyrenees?   178
    Harold   178
    Love and Marriage   182

Spain	185
Property Owners	186
Vera and Amsterdam	188
Eyrephort, Connemara	190
A Doctor in the House	192

Chapter 7: Across Asia — **197**

First Stop Delhi	197
Kashmir	202
Off to Nepal	208
Kathmandu and around	209
Heading East – Back into India	213
On to Calcutta	217
Rangoon	220
Bangkok and on to Singapore	222

Chapter 8: The South Pacific — **227**

Arrival	227
Rabaul – Papua New Guinea	228
Leaving Papua New Guinea	241
Oz	245

Chapter 9: London and Athens — **247**

Home Again	247
Difficulties	251
Athens, Greece and the Islands	253
Complications	264
Turkey	271

Chapter 10: Knocked Sideways — **275**
    We Were Back — 275
    1991 — 279
    Moving On. . . — 290
    A New Start — 293
    Alex's Gap Year and Uni — 294
    Kate's New School and Gap Year — 297
    A Couple More Battles — 298
        Barnet 298
        The Bradford and Bingley 301
    Kate at Uni — 302
    UCL — 304
    The Next Move — 305
    Onwards and Upwards — 307

Chapter 11: Myanmar — **320**

Illustrations

Photos

Burma	13–14
The Early Davies-Berrington Family	23
The Early Gaudie Family	26
The Later Davies-Berrington Family	48–52
Glen Gaudie and Valerie Davies-Berrington	63–65
Anne's Childhood	107–114
The Macdonald Family	147–151
Anne Gaudie and Ian Macdonald	194–196
The Arrival of Alexander and Katriona	266–270
The Next Generation – All Grown Up	313–319

Map

Southern part of Yangon city, Myanmar	326

BOOK ONE

Earlier

CHAPTER 1

Burma Connections

WE WERE ALL BAPTISED IN RANGOON: my father, my mother, and me. However, I only discovered this when I was 62, on looking through the documents and photos I had inherited from my mother.

Not only was my mother baptised in Rangoon, but she was also born there. I was born in Madras, India and my brother was baptised in Bangkok, Siam. My family, over the generations, had criss-crossed the globe, and Burma (not religion!) had played a significant role in our lives. My father, although baptised in Rangoon, was born in Scotland, as was my brother.

There is a photo of my mother, Valerie, as an infant with her Karen[1] ayah[2], taken by her mother, Catherine. She is squinting up at the sun on board the SS Aungdan, an oil tanker en route from Rangoon to Bombay.

My mother was born in Rangoon in 1920: "an European female child residing at 26, York Road, Rangoon, Burma"; the Registrar's Office given as the "Central Plague Depot". Her father, Arthur, is noted on the Birth Certificate as a Marine Officer. Having served in the Merchant Navy and the Royal Navy until 1919, he was employed by the Burmah Oil Company to run oil tankers out of their base in Rangoon. My grandmother, with her two children (my mother and my uncle) although living in Rangoon, sometimes accompanied my grandfather on board. After two years, however, my grandfather accepted an appointment to the Madras Pilot Service

---

1   Karen people: A number of ethnic groups which reside primarily in southern and south-eastern Burma.
2   Ayah: a nursemaid or nanny employed by Europeans in India or other former British territory.

and the family went to live in Madras. My mother was baptised not long before they left on 19 June 1921, at the Cathedral Church of the Holy Trinity[3].

My father, Glen, was born in Edinburgh on 13 March 1914. Shipping records show that my Scottish grandmother made the three week sea journey to Burma on her own with her newborn son, to join her husband. She left Edinburgh soon after the birth and my father was baptised three months later at the "Scots Kirk"[4], Signal Pagoda Road, Rangoon on 14 June 1914. The family returned to the UK fairly soon after this and sailed out to Rangoon again sixteen months later. My paternal grandparents, and my father, now aged one (but without his ten year old sister, who I imagine was at boarding school in the UK), and 33 other passengers, all sailed on the Henderson Line's 'Chindwin' from Liverpool to Rangoon on 22 October 1915.

My father's father, an east coast Scot, was a rice merchant in Akyab, north-west Burma, for 28 years.

Burma's pull was evidently strong. My father, in January 1934 at the age of twenty, and having been educated in England, followed in his father's colonial footsteps.

> *"A century and a quarter ago, the British annexed the last vestiges of the kingdom of Burma, what had once been mainland Southeast Asia's greatest empire. Burma was carved up by the British in three Anglo-Burmese wars (1824–1826, 1852–1853, and 1885) and for much of the nineteenth century there were two competing Burmas, a shrinking independent state in the north and an expanding colonial entity in the south. While a desperate Burmese court raced to introduce administrative reforms and to modernize with the latest Western technologies, court politics and a poorly developed economy ensured its ultimate defeat. Colonial rule created much of the "Burma" seen by the outside world today."*[5]

My father joined the trading company Steel Bros. & Co. Ltd.[6], taking up an overseas posting with their Rice Department in Rangoon in December

---

3   http://en.wikipedia.org/wiki/Holy_Trinity_Cathedral,_Yangon
4   http://www.flickr.com/photos/23268776@N03/3812885515/
5   Charney, Michael W: *"A History of Modern Burma"*
6   Steel Brothers and Company Ltd, established by William Strang Steel in 1870

1934. He joined what would have been an overwhelmingly male society, living in the company's all male staff hostel in Rangoon and making trips some distance out of Rangoon, to arrange purchases of rice from local farmers. This rice was transported to Rangoon for milling in one of Steel Bros.' rice mills, prior to it being exported. It was not all work, however; there is a photo of my father with his fellow team members in the Steel Bros. rugby fifteen in 1936. Incongruous as it may seem, rugby was played twice a week and was enthusiastically supported. Steels' headquarters had sufficient strength in numbers to field their own regular fifteen. The photo shows them kitted out in full rugby gear including knee length striped rugby socks!

I thought I would include a fascinating and maybe surprising description of colonial Rangoon provided by Michael W Charney in his "A History of Modern Burma":

". . . Rangoon was a foreign city erected on Burmese soil. It was here, to the exclusion of anywhere save for a few hill stations, that Burmese life was thoroughly pushed to one side. In its imposing architecture, its physical arrangement, its landscaped gardens, its focus on the harbour and maritime trade, the ethnic division of its population, and in many other ways, Rangoon was a mimeograph of dozens of port cities scattered throughout colonial South and Southeast Asia. A person only had to squint to be confused as to whether he or she was standing in Singapore, Penang, Calcutta, or elsewhere."

It is interesting to note that by 1937 less than 50% of Rangoon's population was Burmese: *"According to the Census of August 1872, over two-thirds of Rangoon's population was Burmese. The Burmese proportion of Rangoon's population shrank, however, and by 1937, of Rangoon's 400,000 residents, only 127,000 were Burmese. . . Most of Rangoon's immigrants came from Southeastern India and Southeastern China. . . Hindustani, for example, emerged as the lingua franca of the colonial capital and Europeans in government (and often even commercial) service, were required to pass exams in this language and not Burmese."*[7]

After war was declared on Germany, on 3 September 1939, my father was appointed in November 1939 as an Officer in 'Our Land Forces', and after

---

7   Charney, Michael W: *"A History of Modern Burma"*

training with the Burma Officer Cadet Training Unit at Maymyo, central Burma, was commissioned in 1940 in the Burma Frontier Force. He was fortunate in having left Rangoon before *"the Japanese had made a devastating air attack on Rangoon on 23 December 1941, prompting a mass exodus of 75% of the municipality's population. While Burmese were left to fend for themselves and fled to the villages, British authorities appointed "Evacuation Officers of the Indian Evacuees" to aid the Indian population that began to "walk" to India along the Rangoon-Prome Road (some 180 miles long) and then across the Arakan Mountains. The hardships of the evacuation led to the deaths of thousands from exposure and exhaustion. British Advanced Army Headquarters, as well as administrative units and all troops not assigned to demolition, withdrew from Rangoon on 7 March 1942. As Burma was to be sacrificed to the Japanese for the better defense of India, British demolition teams were put to the task of destroying much of Rangoon's economic and transportation infrastructure. The Burmese Independence Army and the Japanese took Rangoon the following day. One Burmese town after another was similarly sacrificed as the British continued to retreat toward the Indian frontier. The Japanese took Prome after the British withdrawal on 2 April, and then repulsed the Chinese Fifth Army that had only recently taken up the defense of Toungoo. Mandalay, Maymyo, and many other towns fell soon after, followed by the Arakan region, until the Japanese reached the difficult, mountainous terrain to the northwest. Topography more than British military prowess halted the Japanese advance. Burma was now a land laid waste by both sides in the war. More destruction would follow."*[8]

Julian Thompson in his oral history "Forgotten Voices of Burma" says: *"The battle for Burma was lost on 23 February 1942, early in the campaign, at the disaster at the Sittang River, when the British demolished the only bridge too early, leaving half their soldiers on the wrong side. This was followed by the longest fighting retreat in the history of the British Army, 1,100 miles, ending on 10 May when the British withdrew into Assam over the Chindwin River..."*[9]

Fighting continued and in 1944, British, Empire and Commonwealth troops successfully advanced into Burma, resulting in the Japanese retreat. Atomic bombs were dropped on Hiroshima and Nagasaki on 6 and 9 August

---

8   Charney, Michael W: *"A History of Modern Burma"*
9   Thompson, Julian: *"Forgotten Voices of Burma"*

1945, respectively, and the Japanese surrendered unconditionally on 14 August 1945. Julian Thompson again: *"Three years and eight months after the beginning of the Burma Campaign the Japanese signed the preliminary surrender arrangements at Rangoon, thus ending the longest campaign fought by the Commonwealth army on any front... The best estimate we have of casualties to the 530,000 British, Empire and Commonwealth troops in the Fourteenth Army is 9,400 killed in action and 61,800 wounded, taken prisoner or missing ... doubts still remain as to the exact numbers. Japanese figures are even more problematic... The very lowest estimate of Japanese casualties is 106,100 of which it is thought that 46,700 were killed in action, out of a total strength of approximately 400,000; a figure which itself has never been confirmed. It is impossible to guess how many of their soldiers died unseen in the hills and jungles of Assam and the Arakan, or how many bodies floated down the monsoon-swelled rivers of Lower Burma during the Japanese attempts to reach Thailand in the final months of desperate and confused fighting."* [10]

My father did not talk about his experiences during the war, but I do have some of his army records and also the obituary written about him by his company, Steel Bros. This says that he *"saw considerable active service with the Bhamo battalion in 1941/42, finally trekking out of Burma via Shwebo-Imphal in April 1942."* [11] Like many others, he contracted dysentery, from which he had to recuperate for nine months. He used to take leave in India, which must be how he met my mother. They became engaged and then married in Madras in November 1942.

This was followed by further training in India. The records show that my father was then posted to the forward areas again, in the rank of Captain, with the Chin Hills Battalion, Burma Frontier Force. When his tour of duty in the Chin Hills was over, my father returned to the Burma Regimental Centre at Hoshiarpur as a Major and Company Commander.

After leave in the UK in 1945 and his demobilisation from the army in 1946, my father *"joined the Civil Affairs Services (Burma) to be an area rice officer during the period of reoccupation of Burma..."* [12]

---

10 Thompson, Julian: *"Forgotten Voices of Burma"*
11 Braund, H.E.W: "Calling to Mind – An Account of the first hundred years of Steel Bros. & Company Ltd."
12 Braund, H.E.W: "Calling to Mind – An Account of the first hundred years of Steel Bros. & Company Ltd."

I was born in Madras on 2 June 1946. My mother told me (on more than one occasion!) that it was 109 degrees in the shade at the time. I was soon to go to Burma too. When I was approximately eight weeks old, my mother took me by boat to Rangoon. There is no record of whether she had an ayah with her to help, but essentially, she was on her own with her first baby who was still tiny, and she was having difficulty breast feeding. It is approximately 1100 nautical miles across the Bay of Bengal from Madras to Rangoon. When we arrived, my father was 'up-river' and she was told that she could not stay in the Steels Bros.' staff chummery[13] because, despite being married, she was a woman on her own! She therefore had to stay at the YWCA[14] in Rangoon, until my father's return. My mother, a strong and determined woman, managed to cope in this unsupportive and difficult environment. She told me she had to send out for tinned condensed milk for me.

All three women were remarkably courageous and strong. My maternal grandmother, never having left the south of England, and having married at the age of twenty-three in March 1918, had her first child, Peter, in November, and travelled soon afterwards to Rangoon with her husband, who was a year younger than her. She had her second child, my mother, in 1920; for some of the time living on an oil tanker journeying back and forth from Rangoon. In 1914, my Scottish paternal grandmother travelled by sea from Scotland to the Far East, on her own, with an even younger baby. My mother continued the tradition: leaving what had now become a comfortable lifestyle in Madras (living with her parents in a large house with servants, where she had lived for about three years after arriving from England), she married and then lived for a period in army tents. She then undertook a journey by sea on her own with her two month old first baby; arriving in a strange country, to find nobody to welcome her. It goes without saying that for all of them, the heat, the humidity and the strange surroundings alone, would have made life, at the very least, uncomfortable and difficult. My mother did not complain, but would relate these stories in a matter of fact sort of way, usually with a wry laugh.

My father also did not complain. By all accounts, conditions in the jungles of northern Burma during the war were beyond terrible. He experienced challenging times during his five plus years in the army there.

---

13 Chummery: a men only hostel. http://www.wright-photo.com/yangon2.htm
14 YWCA: Young Women's Christian Association – see photo

They were all young and intrepid, but above all, brave, tough, and determined.

My parents and I soon went to live in Bassein, a port about 155 miles west of Rangoon, on the Bassein River (a western branch of the Irrawaddy). A photo dated 2 December 1946 shows "Middle Mill", the house in which we lived; a comfortable looking two storeyed wooden house, with a creeper providing shade all the way round the ground floor verandah.

I was baptised, like my mother, at the Cathedral Church of the Holy Trinity, Rangoon, on 8 February 1947 and fairly soon afterwards, we went on leave to Montrose, Scotland, with a six week visit to Ireland.

We sailed back to Rangoon on the Henderson Line ship the "SS Prome", setting out on 25 November 1947 to return to Bassein. British administration had been restored in Burma since mid-1945, when my father was sent back there by the Civil Affairs Services, but Burma was to become independent in January 1948 and things were changing again:

> *"Nu[15] had argued, more vocally in mid 1947 than ever before, that during the colonial period, a small class of foreign capitalists had dominated the Burmese economy. Foreign businesses in Burma were not surprised when the government began nationalising their concerns because AFPFL[16] statements over the course of 1947 had foreshadowed this, although foreign businessmen had held on to the hope that London would negotiate with Rangoon on behalf of their interests.". . . "Winston Churchill, the leader of the Conservative opposition in the British Parliament, strongly voiced his concern regarding the fate of British businesses. Nevertheless, Labour MPs who wanted to distance themselves from colonialism as quickly as possible overrode his opposition."[17]*

Burma at this time was in a state of flux. Burma's leader, Aung San, who had managed to create unity amongst the various factions in Burma and whose AFPFL party had won a landslide victory in the elections for a Constitutent Assembly in April 1947, had been assassinated on 19 July

---

15 Nu: The first Prime Minister of Burma under the provisions of the 1947 Constitution of the Union of Burma, 4 January 1948 – 12 June 1956; then 28 February 1957 – 28 October 1958; and 4 April 1960 – 2 March 1962.
16 AFPFL: Anti Fascist People's Freedom League
17 Charney, Michael W: *"A History of Modern Burma"*

1947. Independence was finally declared on 4 January 1948, but without unity. As a result, the years following this were dominated by insurrections and civil war:

> "To make matters worse, guns, and other weaponry were everywhere whether abandoned by the British in 1942 or by the Japanese in 1945, or supplied to the men of the Burmese Independence Army...
> Communists, rightists, Karens, Mons, and a number of other groups, several of whom had begun revolt under the British and now determined to continue against the Nu regime, thus had the means available to make war on the young government...
> Among the Nu government's most serious challengers were the Communists."[18]

As a result, our time in Bassein was not to last for long. I have a newspaper article taken from a Montrose (Scotland) newspaper, which must be from 1948 since I am said to be two years old. This describes how we had to leave in a hurry:

> "Local Man Safe in Rangoon" "Mr and Mrs F A Gaudie, 28 Blackfriars Street, Montrose, have received word that their son, Mr L. G. Gaudie, has arrived safely in Rangoon. He travelled with his wife and two-year-old daughter from Bassein. Mr Gaudie is in the rice trade in charge of Mrs Tell Brothers (sic) branch at Bassein. His father received information that on August 3 the Communists had reached the outskirts of Bassein and on August 5 the British women and children sailed from there for Rangoon, spending the intervening days on a boat in the river..."

My mother had told me about those days spent on the river. It was frightening, and it must have been a relief when they finally set off on the eighteen hour or so journey back to Rangoon by boat. Once there, after farewells to friends, they left Burma, to which they would not return, and set off for India, where my father was posted to manage tea gardens in the Dooars, north-east India, close to the borders with Bhutan and Nepal.

---

18   Charney, Michael W: *"A History of Modern Burma"*

I visited Burma again with my husband, Ian, entering the country on 3 November 1973. We had been travelling in northern India and Nepal, and flew in from Calcutta en route to Papua New Guinea, where we were going to live. Our visas had been issued by the Burmese Embassy in Kathmandu and at that time a Burmese visa was restricted to a seven day visit, and specified that only certain places within Burma could be visited. There was no doubt as to where we would stay in Rangoon – our choice was, of course, the YWCA. However, it was the YMCA which offered married accommodation, so we stayed there instead. It was dirty and fairly seedy but at least we had clean sheets.

We found a city where people, despite being friendly, were unable to speak freely due to the military dictatorship in power at the time. We did manage to chat, though, with an English speaking young Burmese man working in a café, who spoke frankly, telling us he was a student, but that he had been banned from studying and that his passport had been confiscated because he had taken part in a demonstration. He seemed pleased to be able to talk to outsiders about the situation in his country. He told us about the people's poverty, rising prices and serious shortages; from rice to building bricks to fabrics; and how people could afford very little. It was particularly striking to hear of rice shortages in Burma, which before the war, had been one of the largest rice-producing countries in the world.

There was noticeable poverty. Rangoon's centre, with colonial and other buildings, was run down. The YMCA notice board included several warnings from student travellers about the dangers of bandits boarding trains and robbing passengers. One evening we were looking for somewhere to eat and were led in the dark by a helpful Indian passer-by to an Indian restaurant. Unfortunately, Ian became ill the next day. We decided not to stay in Rangoon much longer.

However, since I knew that I had been baptised in Rangoon (although I had not been told about my mother's and father's baptisms, nor my mother's birth there), we visited the Cathedral Church of the Holy Trinity and asked to see the baptism register. We were told that, unfortunately, the church's records had been lost or destroyed, and that the baptism register from those days no longer existed. How wonderful then, to have inherited those baptism certificates!

I also inherited five watercolours, which must have belonged to my grandparents. Which set of grandparents, I am not sure, but I think it most likely that my father's parents bought them. I found them when I was clearing out my mother's flat and immediately liked them. My mother never displayed them, nor showed them to me. I kept them and in due course, once I retired and had some time, I managed to identify the Burmese painter of two, if not all, of the pictures. These two are signed by M.T. Hla (1874–1946), who, I understand was one of the two earliest pioneers of Western-style painting in Burma.[19] I had the pictures conserved, mounted and framed. All five depict river or lake scenes and between them include people, boats, houses, a temple and Poinciana trees. They are delightful and hang in my hall as a reminder of my family's many connections with Burma.

---

19 Khin Muang Nyunt et al: *Myanmar Painting: From Worship to Self-Imaging*, 2006: M. T. Hla together with Ba Ohn, received instruction in Western painting techniques. M. T. Hla also received traditional instruction and undertook painting decoration for the banners and other decorations associated with Burmese Buddhist celebrations and ceremonies.

Ranard, A. *Burmese Painting: A Linear and Lateral History*, 2009: Ranard comments in respect of M. T. Hla that 'more than two dozen of his paintings have surfaced, most of them watercolour. . .' 'It is likely that most of the artist's works were acquired by colonial administrators and their families and brought back to England and Scotland in the early twentieth century. It would appear that very few of the artist's works have survived in Asia. Several paintings by M. T. Hla are found in the collection of the National Museum, Myanmar, however.' Ranard observes that twelve of the artist's paintings survive in the collection of Denison University (Ohio). Ranard reproduces five M. T. Hla paintings in his book.

My mother, Valerie, with her Karen ayah on board the SS Aungdan, an oil tanker en route from Rangoon to Bombay. 1920

Steel Bros. Rugby Football XV 1936. L. G. Gaudie end of front row, right

Rangoon office after liberation from the Japanese – 1945

My first home: "Middle Mill", Bassein, Burma, 1946

Steel Bros. Chummery (now a hotel), Yangon 2015

Anne visiting the YWCA, Yangon, in 2015

CHAPTER 2

The Welsh, the Scots, the Colonial Adventurers

MY MOTHER'S FAMILY ON HER FATHER'S SIDE was Welsh and English, and included a variety of unusual, not to say, eccentric, people. There was her father who went to sea at the age of 13; her grandfather who managed a goldmine but gambled away his money; there were grand affluent gentry; a woman who became an opal miner and lived in a cave; the unmentionable black sheep of the family, imprisoned for smuggling at sea; and a Victorian whose name became very famous. Many of them travelled the world.

On my father's side, however, a different picture: his father's family was made up of East coast Scots who worked their way from humble beginnings to a comfortable middle class life. Some took the opportunities available in the colonies, and left Scotland for most of their working lives.

* * *

Wills, Double-Barrels and Money

The Two Jenkins

Jenkin Davies lived in Swansea. Jenkin, in compliance with the Will of the heiress and last survivor of the Delahaye Berringtons of Urishay, took the name and arms of Berrington by Royal Licence in 1799. He also married Mary Morgan of Berthlwyd, one of two sisters who were co-heiresses, and then bought the other sister's half of their estate. It seems that he had a way with women and money.

In 1801, Jenkin's son, Jenkin Davies Berrington, was born in Swansea. It appears that he took after his father and also made a profitable marriage. Having been educated at Harrow and Trinity College Cambridge, in 1827 he married Charlotte Hall, sister of Benjamin Hall 3rd, after whom the Westminster clock bell 'Big Ben' was named.

In 1832, Benjamin Hall bought Woodlands Castle (now called Clyne Castle), near Swansea, and transferred the property to Jenkin Davies Berrington Senior. He bought the house for his sister Charlotte (for whom he was principal trustee), who had married Jenkin Davies Berrington Junior. The couple moved into the castle with Jenkin's father, who died shortly afterwards, in 1834. Jenkin and Charlotte's son, Arthur Vendigaid, was given the house in 1857 but sold it soon afterwards and moved to Panty-Goitre. A note of my grandfather's says *"By marrying Charlotte, Jenkin secured an injection of cash into the family"*. This was because Charlotte's mother (who had married Benjamin Hall 2nd when she was 17 and he was 23) was the daughter of Richard Crawshay, originally a London iron merchant, who became a South Wales Ironmaster, and whose estate at his death, was worth £1.5 million, a huge sum in those days. In his will, Richard Crawshay left three-eighths of his ironworks to his son-in-law, Benjamin Hall 2nd, whose son Benjamin Hall 3rd and sister, Charlotte, then benefited.[20]

* * *

Big Ben

Charlotte and Benjamin

Although I am directly descended from Benjamin Hall 3rd's sister Charlotte, rather than from Benjamin himself, I have only a little information on Charlotte, but a fair amount on Benjamin. His story is a good one, though – he became famous – and there were discoveries.

---

20   Nicholas, Thomas: *Annals and Antiquities of the Counties and County Families of Wales*: https://archive.org/details/annalsantiquitie02nichuoft. Benjamin Hall 1st, DD (1742-1825) was "a man of extensive learning and an erudite Welsh scholar". He was a Fellow of Jesus College, Oxford, Chancellor of the Diocese of Llandaff, and is buried in Llandaff Cathedral, where there is a "splendid marble monument in his memory".

Charlotte was the granddaughter of a multi-millionaire but the information I have on her, shows that she was no slouch: She had *"very kindly translated Professor Schulz's 'Essay on the influence which the legends of Wales have had upon the Literature of France, Germany and Scandinavia' from the German original into English, and that this had been published."*[21]

In relation to Benjamin, however, here are some extracts from an email from me to my friend Sarah, dated 7 November 2012:

". . . I'm writing because I have recently spent quite a lot of time and energy (and had a great deal of fun) putting together biographical notes about my family on both sides (going back to about the 1800s). I remembered that we discussed the possibility that we may be related! through some association with Benjamin Hall – after whom Big Ben was named. I thought, therefore, that I would send you (almost as is) the section on my maternal great great great grandfather Jenkin Davies Berrington (1801-1871) who lived in Wales and who married Charlotte, the sister of Benjamin Hall. My mother's maiden surname was Davies Berrington. I'm attaching a short document. The story is entertaining and I think you'll enjoy it. It would be interesting and amusing to know if/how your family fits in. . .!"

"Benjamin Hall 3rd (1802-1867), was educated at Westminster School and Christchurch College Oxford. He was MP for the united Boroughs of Monmouth, Newport and Usk 1832-7 and for the Borough of Marylebone from 1837. He was created a Baronet in July 1838; Privy Councillor 1854; President of the Board of Health 1854-5; First Commissioner of Works (originally "Chief Lord of the Woods and Forests") 1855-8; until he was called to the House of Lords as Baron Llanover of Llanover and Abercarn, 1859.[22]

Extract from "The Story of Big Ben" by Alfred Gillgrass, condensed from the booklet of the same title published by the Big Ben Council:

"The Chief Lord of the Woods and Forests, now called the Office of Works, promised "A Noble Clock, indeed a King of Clocks, the biggest and best in the world, within sight and sound of the heart of London". . .

---

21 The National Library of Wales Journal XIV: http://wbo.llgc.org.uk/en/s3-EVAN-CAS-1844.html
22 Nicholas, Thomas: *Annals and Antiquities of the Counties and County Families of Wales.* https://archive.org/details/annalsantiquitie02nichuoft

> *"At last the great clock began its service on May 31, 1859. Parliament debated the naming of the bell and there were many suggestions. The Chief Lord of the Woods and Forests, Sir Benjamin Hall, a man of immense physique[23] who was affectionately nicknamed 'Big Ben' made a long speech. As he was sinking back into his seat, a waggish Member shouted: "Why not call it 'Big Ben' and have done with it?" The House rocked with laughter, and "Big Ben" it became and has remained ever since."*

Sarah's email reply started with *"Hello Cuz! Indeed it seems that we are related!"* and she goes on to outline her direct descent from Benjamin Hall 3rd. We still enjoy the surprise connection.

* * *

Culloden, Flax and Timber

The Early Gaudies

In Scotland, William Gadie/Gawdie married Jean Duncan in 1769 in Arbroath and had three children. One of those was my great great great grandfather David Gadie. He was born in 1772 and at the age of 21 in 1793 married Ann Towns at Inverkeillor, between Arbroath and Montrose. In 1809, according to the Family Bible, their son, my great great grandfather, William Gadie/Gaudie, was born near Arbroath on the East coast.

At the age of 27 in 1835, William married Margaret Anderson (born 1815) who by then, was 20. By the time he was 32, he was an Overseer in the carding department of a flax mill in Montrose. The 1841 Census shows that Margaret, now aged 26, had four sons and the family name was spelt Gaudy. By the time of the 1871 Census, Margaret had given birth to two more sons and had died (she died in 1865 aged 50). William is listed with the name Gaudie, as a widower aged 61, and described as "formerly Flaxspinning Mill Manager", living alone in Montrose. The Family Bible documents him as the Manager of Logie Mill. Ten years later, the next

---

23 Although there are many sources that say Benjamin Hall was a very tall man, there are some which claim that he was short!

Census shows him retired and living as a boarder with a Grocer Master in Montrose, whose son, daughter and aunt also lived in the house, together with a young domestic servant. He died in 1881 at the age of 72.

It is fascinating to read a little about Montrose in those times – a very different place from the sleepy town of today: *"Montrose in the early- to mid-nineteenth century was a diverse and successful manufacturing town. The principal industry was flax spinning, and the town contained five flax mills, employing over 2,000 people. On the River North Esk, close to the town, there were an additional three flax mills, and two bleaching works. Handloom and power-loom linen weaving was also a significant industry in 1850s Montrose, employing approximately 1,400 people. The town contained three starch-making factories, two tan works, two iron foundries, two machine-making factories, a soap factory, two rope works, a shipyard, several breweries and miscellaneous workshops. Montrose was also a market town for the surrounding agricultural area, and weekly grain and produce markets were held on Fridays, in addition to fairs at Martinmas and Whitsunday. The principal exports out of Montrose harbour were manufactured goods, fish grain and cattle, and the main imports were coal, lime, slate, iron, flax, hemp and timber. In the final decades of the nineteenth century, trade and industry in Montrose suffered during an economic slump, and the population of the town fell."*[24]

It was William's second son, David, who was my paternal great grandfather. He was born in 1837, probably in Montrose. There is a photograph of him: a solid practical looking middle-aged man with a white moustache. He married Elizabeth Glen in Montrose in 1860, and the following year's Census shows him as the Census Enumerator for Montrose Division 27. In 1871, aged 34, he was a Saw Mill Clerk living at 35 Wharf Street, Montrose with his wife and five children "in a property containing four rooms with one or more windows". The next Census in 1881, lists David as a Wood Merchant, Saw Miller, employing five men and two boys, while living at 387 Crichton Place, St Andrew, Midlothian (Edinburgh). At this point, Elizabeth, 14, Julia, 16, and Harriet, 18, were all pupil teachers; all the children having been registered in Montrose except Austin Henry, 1, registered in Edinburgh. David and Elizabeth had eleven children, the seventh of whom was my grandfather, Frederick Augustus. David died in St Andrew in 1892, aged 55.

---

24   "Statistical Accounts of Scotland" Jisc-designated national data centre at the University of Edinburgh.

James Gaudie was William's fourth son and had two daughters Mary and Lena and a son, John Logie. Mary, on marriage, became Mary Henderson and wrote the following in 1968, for an interested relative (Bruce Gaudie) in New Zealand:

> "The family originally came from Arbroath, a small town 12 miles south of Montrose. One of our forbears was gardener to the Laird of an estate near there. The Laird was a strong Jacobite and joined the army of Prince Charlie, taking the gardener with him. They fought in the terrible battle against the English at Culloden Moor near Inverness at the rebellion of 1745. Both miraculously survived. The Gaudie family consisted of three daughters* and one son – William – who was the head of our family. He came to Montrose as a clerk in a Spinning Mill, and from there became Manager of the Spinning Mill at Logie. He was highly gifted, intellectually, being a good Latin, French and Italian scholar. He married in 1834 a Margaret Anderson, who belonged to Abroath. The family consisted of six sons, William, David, Edwin, James, Charles and Robert. There was a house provided for the Manager and the family were brought up there, by a very strict father. The Mill was very near to the river Esk, the hamlet consisted of a few houses and a tiny school where the family started their education. The distance from Montrose was 5 miles and all provisions had to be carried from there. All the sons were mechanically minded, I expect due to their environment. William studied engineering and settled in Dundee, died in 1914, aged 79. David** finished his education at Montrose Academy, and was subsequently Manager of a large wood business in Edinburgh. Edwin was an engineer, but was delicate and died at the age of 24. Charles, your grandfather, held a position with the Railways before setting off for Australia. He and our father corresponded all their lives, and the letters consisted of many pages of beautiful handwriting by both. Our father, James, started work as a telegraph clerk in Aberdeen and other towns, coming to Perth as assistant Postmaster to John McGregor, whose daughter he married. He was finally promoted to be Postmaster of Montrose. Our family was three, John Logie Gaudie, named after Logie! He studied Law at Edinburgh University and after taking his degrees, joined up and lost his life on the Somme. My sister, Lena, studied at the College of Art in Edinburgh and taught art in Montrose Academy."

* William had two siblings – Margaret and David
** My great grandfather.

A letter to my father from his sister Winnie, though, says: *"Great Uncle James once told me that the first trace of the Gaudies was a blacksmith who fought for Prince Charlie at Culloden. After the defeat the Jacobites were outlawed and the blacksmith had to go into hiding."* A blacksmith may well have been a more useful person to take along to a battle if you were on horseback, but we are unlikely to discover which it was, gardener or blacksmith...

By coincidence, the name of Aberdeen University's Independent Student Newspaper is 'Gaudie'. I discovered this when my daughter Kate joined the university. Both my brother and I tried to find out from the Student Union and the University the origin of the newspaper's name, but without success. The University's website[25] says: *'The Gaudie has been an iconic part of student life at Aberdeen University since 1934, celebrating its 80th birthday in 2014. The Gaudie is the oldest independent student newspaper in Scotland'*.

The word *gaudy* or *gaudie* from the Latin, generally seems to mean enjoyment or merry-making and at the University of Dundee, gaudie nights are traditional student celebrations.

However, our fairly unusual family name, along with Gowdie, Goddie, Goudie, Gawdie, Gadi, Gadie, Gady and Goodie, is said to have a different source and to be a variant of Goldie, a dimunitive of Gold, and to have appeared in Scotland in the 16th century.[26]

My brother comments on his own searches: *"In combing the Registers for Gaudie variations, the main locations have been a scatter up the North-East coast, Orkney, Shetland and Ayr, on the West coast, the last three of which were Viking settlements... Apart from that, the gaelic word gall, meaning stranger, foreigner, was applied as a name, developing into Gauld, Gall, Galt."*[27]

* * *

25 The University of Aberdeen: http://www.abdn.ac.uk/alumni/connected/gaudie-95.php
26 Black, G.F. 1946. *The Surnames of Scotland. Their Origin, Meaning and History*. New York Public Library
27 My mother bought *"The Burkes Peerage World Book of Gaudies"*. Annoyingly, the book is undated, but was probably compiled in the 1980s. It shows many Gaudie families living around the world: in Scotland, England, USA, Canada, Australia, New Zealand and France. Total households given: Great Britain: 44 (Merseyside 18 – most populous area in GB); Australia: 18; US: 14; New Zealand: 5; Canada: 1; France: 2. Total estimated households figures are higher. Total estimated population (only those with the exact name Gaudie): 279.

The South Wales Establishment

Vendigaid

In Wales in 1833, Arthur Vendigaid Davies Berrington was born to Jenkin and Charlotte. He was the only son to survive. My friends, Max and Jenny, who visited me at around the time I was starting to find out about my relatives, told me that Vendigaid is an old Welsh name. It seems that he was named after Cadwaladr Vendigaid "*a famous but rather shadowy figure in early Welsh history*".[28] Arthur Vendigaid[29] was educated at Eton and Exeter College, Oxford: a handsome man; imposing in his photograph. He married twice, his first marriage taking place in 1859 to Frances Lennox Henneage, with whom he had four children and who was said to have died of a miscarriage, having had four children in six years. Of the four, Arthur Vendigaid's eldest son, Arthur Tewdyr, after Clifton College Bristol; Oxford; and the Inner Temple; became Chief Magistrate, Selangor, and Legal Adviser to the Federated Malay States. His second son, Caradoc Charles, was drowned off the Greek island of Rhodes in 1884 "trying to save a Chinaman"(!) and was unmarried. Sadly, I have nothing further on this bizarre scrap of information from my uncle. Trevor Douglas, the third of Arthur Vendigaid's sons, also went to Clifton College, with his brother John Spencer, and became the Director of Posts & Telegraphs in India.

Prior to his uncle Benjamin Hall becoming a Peer, Vendigaid became his uncle's Private Secretary. His uncle persuaded Vendigaid to move closer to him. Woodlands Castle, which Vendigaid had inherited from his parents (and which later became a University of Swansea student hall of residence and is now luxury flats)[30] was therefore sold in 1860, and the family moved to the manor house, Pant-y-Goitre, on the River Usk.

* * *

I have driven past Pant-y-Goitre, when visiting my friends, and so had my mother and father when they were on holiday in the 1960s, when they took photos. My uncle, Peter, having settled in the USA, visited his long

---

28 Dictionary of National Biography, 1885-1900, Volume 08
29 Arthur Vendigaid used the name Arthur, but I have used Vendigaid to differentiate between him and my grandfather, also named Arthur.
30 http://www.ggat.org.uk/cadw/historic_landscape/gower/english/Gower_078.htm

Jenkin Davies Berrington 1801-1871

Charlotte Davies Berrington, wife of Jenkin, 1806-1885

Arthur Vendigaid Davies Berrington 1833-1909 My Maternal Great Great Grandfather

Ada Barbara Davies Berrington (née Lane) 1837-1912 Arthur Vendigaid's 2nd wife and My Maternal Great Great Grandmother

lost relatives with his family in 1976. Pant-y-Goitre is a Grade 2 listed Georgian manor house, built in 1776. It was sold in 1977 by Vendigaid's granddaughter, Gwendolyn.

It is a handsome house with attractive grounds running down to the river and not so long ago, it was offering "A complete weekend of country house hospitality, fly fishing and tuition". However, in January 2013, Max and Jenny (who live not far from Pant-y-Goitre) noticed in the local paper that the major part of it was for sale, and sent me the details out of interest. I could see that the interior of the main house had been well maintained but that the outside had not; despite fees of £2,790 plus VAT being charged for a weekend of fishing![31]

* * *

Vendigaid was now a widower and the story goes, according to my uncle[32], that not only did Vendigaid's Uncle Benjamin (now Lord Llanover) insist that Vendigaid should become an MP and a Liberal, which he refused to do, but his Aunt, Benjamin Hall's wife, Baroness Augusta Llanover, tried to force him to marry one of her protégées, who is said to have fallen in love with him. He refused this match, however, and his Aunt was apparently furious. Uncle and nephew then became estranged, with relations *"restored only when Lord Llanover lay on his deathbed"*. Lord Llanover had apparently considered making Vendigaid his heir, since his two sons had died and his daughter, also Augusta, had become a Roman Catholic . . . but due to this bitter quarrel, Vendigaid did not inherit Llanover.

* * *

I see from information sent to me by my friend and newly discovered distant relative, Sarah, that Lord Llanover's daughter, Augusta Charlotte Elizabeth, not only converted to Catholicism, but married a Welsh Catholic (Ivor Herbert, whose son became Lord Treowen), the family further down the line marrying into a Scottish Catholic family. These are Sarah's ancestors. We

---

31   http://www.rightmove.co.uk/property-for-sale/property-37216639.html
32   My uncle owned a series of booklets by Maxwell Fraser, the Halls' biographer, which may have been the source for these stories. See National Library of Wales Journal for detailed information on the lives of the Halls.

both wonder whether Augusta Charlotte was forgiven in the end for changing her religion and whether she received her inheritance! Interestingly, my uncle mentions that Arthur Vendigaid won the Monmouthshire Gun Club trophy from Lord Treowen of Llanarth, so despite religious differences, the families obviously belonged to the same clubs. The silver trophy cup was sold at auction at Sotheby's in London in 1972.

* * *

In 1861, Vendigaid married his second wife, Ada Barbara Lane (1837 to 1912)[33], his first wife's cousin. They had one son and four daughters, bringing the total number of Vendigaid's children to nine. It was in 1862 that his son Evelyn Delahaye Davies Berrington was born (my maternal great grandfather and the father of four children). Evelyn and all four children had very unusual stories, which you will soon read. Arthur Vendigaid became High Sheriff for Monmouthshire in 1866 and was also appointed as Secretary of Fisheries. He died on 21 December 1909 at the age of 76.

* * *

Montrose, Burma, the Somme

Augustus and Isabella

My rather grandly named (or so it seems to me) paternal grandfather Frederick Augustus Gaudie was born in Montrose, Scotland, in 1872. He married Isabella Wallace Black in September 1904 when he was 32 and they had their first child, Eleanor Winifred (my Aunt Winnie, who I never met) in July 1905. My father, Lawrence Glen, their second of two children, was born in Edinburgh in March 1914. The Gaudies called their children by their second names rather than their first, hence Augustus, Winifred and Glen, and this tradition was used again when I was named. It was after the

---

33 Ada Barbara Lane was supposedly a relative of Jane Lane. Jane Lane became famous for rescuing King Charles II in the 17th century and was rewarded by being granted permission to include the Royal Lions of England in the coat of arms of her family – something which my maternal grandparents put into practice!!

David Gaudie 1837-1892 (seated?)
My Paternal Great Grandfather

Frederick Augustus Gaudie 1872-1948
& Isabella Wallace Gaudie 1874-1960
My Paternal Grandparents

Frederick Augustus Gaudie
in the Home Guard

My Paternal Grandparents, Augustus and
Isabella (Left and Right), with friends

birth of my father, Glen, that my Scottish grandmother made the sea journey to Rangoon with him as a newborn, on her own, and my father was baptised there. I have a copy of the passenger list for SS Chindwin, sixteen months later, on the 22 October 1915 which lists my grandparents and my father, aged one, travelling again, from Liverpool to Rangoon.

I do not know when my paternal grandfather, Augustus, first went to live in Burma; it is likely that as with many Scots, the economic situation drove him to emigrate; but I do know that he was a rice merchant in Akyab, in western Burma for 28 years; Akyab (in Arakan) being the first port in Burma to become important as a rice port.[34]

Augustus may have been living in Burma when he met Isabella or he may have left for Burma with Isabella, having married in Scotland. If the latter, which is perhaps more likely, this would mean that he finally left Burma when he was about 60, in 1932, which seems about right. In 1942, when my paternal grandfather was 70, my father's engagement and wedding announcements show his parents' address as Radlett, Hertfordshire. My father had gone to school five miles away from Radlett, at St Albans School, starting in 1925; so, it seems likely that my grandparents bought a property in Hertfordshire on one of the occasions when they were on leave in the UK.

* * *

By 1947, however, my grandparents had moved back to Montrose, to 28 Blackfriars Street. There is a photo of my grandfather with a splendid white moustache, in the military uniform of the Home Guard, which he probably joined at the beginning of World War II, when he was 68. They lived in Montrose until their deaths; my grandfather at 76 in 1948, and my grandmother at 86, in 1960.

I was taken by my parents to visit my grandparents in Montrose in 1947 but I was only one year old – too young to have stored any memories of either of my grandparents from that visit. There are a couple of photos of me with my father in the garden, but that is all. However, we visited my grandmother twice in the 1950s and I have strong recollections of her

---

34 The province of Arakan came under British rule in 1826. Akyab is now Sittwe, in Rakhine State.

and of Montrose. My brother, David, was born when we were there in December 1950, but my memories are from our next visit, in 1953, just before I was taken to boarding school. My grandmother was a short, slightly round bustling figure, whose front door was approached through a porch smelling strongly of her geraniums. The smell of geraniums still brings back the memory of her house to me. When my grandmother died, my father was abroad and my mother was not informed immediately by Aunt Winnie. However, determined to attend the funeral, despite Winnie(!), my mother drove all night to Montrose by herself. She arrived just in time for the funeral and stayed, not with Winnie, but with Mary and Lena.

* * *

'Aunts' Mary and Lena, were my father's relatives, and by then, also lived in Montrose. My brother David and I visited them with my mother. James Gaudie (1840-1932), was their father; brother of my great grandfather, David Gaudie.

The Census of 1881 shows James as unmarried, living at 77, Main St., Perth, employed in the Telegraph Supply Civil Service. It seems he married twice, the second time to the boss's daughter, Jessie MacGregor, in Perth in 1886. He had three children: Mary, Lena and John Logie. He was Montrose Postmaster when he retired. In one of my Aunt Winnie's letters to my father, she gossips that Mary was the child of James' first marriage and that this had been kept hidden, although apparently suspected by others! As Mary's short note on the family history says, Lena (pronounced Leener) studied at the College of Art in Edinburgh and then taught art at Montrose Academy. She married Wilfred Smith Cox. Mary married John Henderson but does not mention her own life. After taking his degree in Law at Edinburgh University, John Logie enlisted in the Army in Montrose (Private S/40219 1st Battalion Black Watch) and lost his life in action at Flers, on the Somme, on 25 September 1916 aged 22. Mary and Lena lived together in a large terraced house in Montrose with a sloping garden at the back with a fine view, and we enjoyed our visits.

* * *

I visited Montrose on my way back to London from Aberdeen in the early 2000s, having visited my daughter, Kate, at University. I was delighted to see my grandmother's house just as it had been, although there had been a bigger garden originally, before she sold part of it. The town was very sleepy, no longer the booming town it had been in the 1850s, nor the booming oil town it had become in the 1970s. I passed the old, tall and disused buildings of a couple of local newspapers and remembered my father telling me that Montrose, Arbroath and Dundee were well known for the three 'J's: Jam, Jute and Journalism. I visited the local Museum and the War Memorial in Montrose Park, on which John Logie Gaudie's name is remembered.[35]

* * *

Gold, Gambling, and the Crash

Evelyn Delahaye and Eleanor

Ten years before my paternal grandfather Frederick Augustus Gaudie was born in Scotland, my Welsh maternal great grandfather, Evelyn Delahaye Davies Berrington was born in Abergavenny, Monmouthshire, to Ada Barbara, Vendigaid's second wife. Evelyn must have been quite unconventional and something of an adventurer, since at the age of twenty, he left his very comfortable life in Wales, to travel the world in search of gold. His older step-brothers had already set the trend for the young men in the family to travel to the colonies, so it was probably quite natural for him to travel the world. It is clear, however, that he was not interested in the usual colonial administrative career, but preferred to strike out on his own:

---

35 I saw Jeremy Paxman's series "Britain's Great War" on BBC1 television early in 2014, when I was surprised to see a section on someone called Norman Gaudie (from another branch of the family), a railway worker and forward in Sunderland Football Club Reserves. In contrast to John Logie, it seems that he is known for having been a Conscientious Objector (a 'Conchie') and for being one of a group called the Richmond 16. The 16 were imprisoned in the spring of 1916 in Richmond Castle for several months. They were then sent to France, where still refusing to fight, but now under military discipline, they were sentenced to death by shooting. This sentence, when announced, was immediately commuted to ten years' penal servitude and most of the 16 spent the rest of the war in British jails. Marjorie Gaudie, Norman's daughter-in-law, says that he was in Aberdeen, breaking stones. http://www.ppu.org.uk/coproject/cotestimony1.html

An extract from "The Anglo-African Who's Who and Biographical Sketch Book"[36] describes him as follows:

"BERRINGTON, EVELYN DELAHAY, A.I.M.M., F.R.C.I., F.S.A., is the son of A. D. Berrington, late Secretary of Fisheries. He was born March 6, 1861, at Pant-y-goitre, near Abergavenny, and was educated at Clifton Coll. and Geneva Univ. Mr. Berrington has been connected (sic) with gold mining since 1882 in various parts of the world. He was in Venezuela 1882-3, in Florida, U.S.A.,1884-6, and in Johannesburg 1887-8. He joined the pioneer force into Mashonaland in 1890, and was in Johannesburg and Matabeleland from 1894 to 1899. He acted as manager to the Lomagunda Reefs, Ltd., and the Ayrshire Mine in Mashonaland from 1899 to 1903. He married, June 2, 1894, Miss Eleanor A. Witterton."

Sadly, I have no information on Evelyn's early travels, which I have no doubt would have made for some more good stories, but the year of his birth was 1862 and he married Eleanor Witterton in Johannesburg on 2nd June (my birthday) in 1894, when he was 32 and Eleanor 29. There is a copy of their marriage certificate in Afrikaans, which notes that he was born in Monmouthshire, England (considered part of England at that time) and Eleanor in Caernarvon, South Wales in 1865. Eleanor's father was also at Clifton College, Bristol. There is a photo of an attractive young Eleanor and a leather bound 'Common Prayer & Hymns book' embossed with the initials E.A.W. on the front and signed in ink on the fly leaf "Eleanor Witterton 31/2/91". My uncle wrote that Eleanor had visited relatives in Cape Town and her sister in Port Elizabeth, which is presumably when she met Evelyn.

* * *

Evelyn and Eleanor had four children. All four, perhaps because of the somewhat flamboyant role model provided for them by their father, but probably, too, in order to cope with the family's straitened financial circumstances, became fiercely independent, pursuing highly unusual lives.

---

[36] http://archive.org/stream/angloafricanwhos00will/angloafricanwhos00will_djvu.txt

Arthur John, my maternal grandfather, their first child, was born in November 1895 at 33 Upper Hill Street, Port Elizabeth Cape Colony, South Africa. Arthur's birth certificate gives his father as *(sic)* Everyn Delehay Berrington, Bakery Manager at Umtata, born in England and aged 33 years. His mother is given as Elenor Berrington, formerly Witterton, born in England, aged 31 years. The 'Informant' is given as C. M. Witterton, Aunt. The 'Davies' part of the name does not appear. Umtata is about 300 miles north east of Port Elizabeth and was a military post for the colonial forces in 1882. The town itself was founded in 1883 and became the leading administrative centre of the area.[37] More of Arthur later.

In the late 1890s, Evelyn and Eleanor left South Africa and went to the Ayrshire Gold Mine at Lomagundi, Rhodesia, where Evelyn worked as Manager. Alice Minnie was born in 1897, but a year later, "the Boers were becoming troublesome"[38] and Evelyn sent his family back to England.

Six years later, in 1904, Evelyn returned to England to collect his family and take them back to Rhodesia. They sailed in the German ship Kron Prinz to Beira in what was then Portuguese East Africa, now Mozambique. From Beira they went by rail, under construction, to its terminus, and then by bullock cart to Lomagundi and the Ayrshire mine – about 80 miles from Salisbury. There are some fascinating sepia photos of the journey, including a picture of the train; a hotel in Salisbury covered in Union Jack flags; and one of Eleanor with my grandfather Arthur aged about nine and their second child Alice Minnie aged about seven, on the back of a bullock cart. In the same year (1904), their third child, Cedric was born.

I have a gold medal from the 'Pistol Club, Salisbury, Rhodesia', engraved 'Club Championship, Won by E. D. Berrington, 1906'. Salisbury was presumably the social centre for the region – I wonder how long that journey by bullock cart took and how often it was made.

* * *

Unfortunately, Evelyn's health failed and he retired from the Ayrshire Mine Co. in 1907. He and the family therefore returned to England, breaking their journey at the fashionable resort of Menton in the South of France,

---

37 Nelson Mandela was buried in 2013 at Qunu, approx 20 miles from Umtata
38 Boer War: 1892-1902

to avoid the English winter. They leased a villa – the Villa Palmosa – and apparently set about enjoying themselves. Here, despite his failing health, it seems that the mild weather, the exciting environment in contrast to the life in Rhodesia, and possibly the availability of plenty of French wine, enabled Evelyn to recover sufficiently to lose all his money at the gaming tables. . .!

When the family arrived back in the UK with very little money and no income, Evelyn's father, Vendigaid, came to their rescue financially. They were therefore able to lease a comfortable (and presumably very newly built) Edwardian house at 53 Victoria Avenue, Surbiton – a house very similar to the one in which I and my husband and children lived for some years in Muswell Hill, North London. Arthur was then sent to Ellery Park Boarding School, which it seems was in Wallasey, Cheshire. Unfortunately, Evelyn's health deteriorated, but he underwent surgery and made a good recovery. As a result, and presumably keen to earn a living again, he decided to undertake another commission with the Ayrshire Mine Co., and prepared to return to Lomagundi. Before leaving, however, he wanted to say goodbye to his parents and set out for Pant-y-Goitre, the family house in Wales. Sadly, he never made it; dying of a heart attack on 3 July 1908 in the Charing Cross Hotel, with Eleanor at his bedside.

* * *

Evelyn died at the age of 46 and Eleanor gave birth to their fourth child, Victor Ralph, after his death. Eleanor, a single parent now, with four children, had little means of financial support. Due to the lack of funds, Arthur had to leave school, and in 1908, almost immediately after the death of his father, joined the Merchant Navy. Eleanor and the three children went to live in Hoylake/Liscard in Wallasey, Cheshire after the outbreak of war in 1914. This is about 8 miles from where Arthur had been at boarding school, which suggests that Eleanor had family there. Later on, in 1951, Cedric gives his address as Liscard, Cheshire, so he continued to use Liscard as his base after his mother's death. I have no way of knowing how Eleanor survived her financial difficulties, but it is possible that her father-in-law, Vendigaid, who died on 21 December 1909, a year after his son Evelyn had died, left his daughter-in-law Eleanor something in his Will. Her own family may well have helped also. I have a Visiting Card printed "Mrs E D Berrington, 3 Marine Parade Hoylake" with "Wednesdays" printed in the top left hand corner. There is also a photo of Eleanor in her late forties or so, taken by a photographer from Market Street, Hoylake. Neither of these indicates that Eleanor was left entirely poverty stricken.

Eleanor lost her husband just after the turn of the century, when she was 42 and had four children to raise by herself, one of them newborn. In addition, she took what seems with hindsight, to have been a hasty decision (very soon after Evelyn's death), to send her eldest child away from the family at the age of 13; a decision she must surely have regretted later. Hers must have been a tough and difficult life, both in Rhodesia and in England. Eleanor died at the relatively young age of 57 in 1923.

* * *

My uncle Peter relates that Minnie and Victor, after their mother Eleanor's death, visited Arthur (their older brother) and his wife Catherine (my grandparents) in 1924. Their brother, Cedric, who was not with them, would have been twenty at that stage and had presumably already struck out on his own. My grandparents were on leave from Madras and on holiday with my mother and my uncle. My uncle, who would have been six at this time, but possibly met Victor again later, described Victor as "a lively, good-humoured youth".

* * *

Opal Mining – Living in Caves

Minnie and Victor

Four years later, in 1928, Minnie, now thirty-one and her brother Victor, twenty, with no longer anything to keep them in England, decided to emigrate to Australia.

Minnie was in Adelaide when she accepted her brother's invitation to take the Afghan Express 600 miles north, to join him on a trading van in the outback. It did not take long for them to decide that they would start mining opals at Coober Pedy, South Australia and Minnie decided to stay when her brother left.

Her life involved living in a cave in remote opal fields (living in a tent was too hot), and there are photos as well as a number of photocopies of articles about her. One of these is from "The B.P. Magazine"[39] dated 1st March 1932. It was clearly unusual for a woman to be living on her own in such a place and in such circumstances – and the articles do not indicate the presence of other women – but she was clearly admired among the miners and seems to have been regarded by them as their equal.

Another article says: "This wonderfully plucky girl is practically the only woman among some 150 men of various nationalities, from whom she receives the utmost chivalry." . . . *"Having acquired an expert's knowledge, Miss Barrington* (sic) *classes and values her opal, and negotiates with the buyers herself. With clever fingers she even cuts and polishes her own stones."*

Four years later she was running the store: *"To my surprise the store was presided over by a slim dark-eyed girl, who had come out to the fields four years ago from London with her brother, and had stayed on, digging. . ."*

Minnie also wrote some serialised articles in an unknown publication (of which I have copies) entitled *"The Girl Opal-Miner"*, in which she explains that she had been working in London as a typist. *The summary says: "Miss Berrington had always loved opals and forthwith – on a combined capital of exactly eleven pounds, plus complete ignorance, the two "new chums" determined to become opal miners!"* Minnie writes: *"Want was my master for many years . . . my brother and I were on board the steamer Bendigo, bound for Australia. Our home had been broken up, and he and I decided to try our luck Overseas."* During her time in the opal fields she not only owned a car and later a truck, but also learned to ride camels – often used for prospecting.

She also wrote a book about her experiences called "Stones of Fire" which I read a long time ago and have recently re-read, thanks to friends, Lisa and Tom, who kindly found a First Edition[40] for me. Minnie refers to her brother, Victor Ralph, as 'Roger' throughout the long article mentioned above, and in her book. Victor, having started out mining opals with Minnie at Coober Pedy and Five Mile, left the opal fields and, according to my uncle, *"raced motorbikes on cinder tracks, established a radio repair service and handled satellite radio communications at the Rocket Range at Woomera"*. Minnie also lived at the Andamooka opal field for some time. However, although making just enough to live on, she never made any significant money from her opals and wrote: *"Even as I sit in my tent,*

---

39   Published quarterly by Burns Philp & Co. Ltd., Sydney
40   Berrington, M. D.: *"Stones of Fire"* First Edition July 1958

writing these last few lines, that eagerly-anticipated trip Home looms once more on the horizon of hope... That eagerly-awaited one thousand pounds may yet materialize, though I must confess that a quarter of it would see me making for England! So many of the things I have ardently longed for have come to me, directly or indirectly through opal, that I should not be at all surprised if my beautiful 'birth stone' presently forged yet another link in the chain of 'coincidences,' and enabled me to come Home on a visit!"

* * *

Later, Minnie and Victor both enlisted in the Services during World War II, Minnie in the Australian Women's Army Services and Victor in the Royal Australian Air Force. There are photos of them in their uniforms and a handwritten note from a Staff Sergeant of the Australian Military Forces, Don Finch, which says *"Dear Miss Berrington, Your devotion to duty and good work has been an inspiration to this section. I do thank you most sincerely for all you have done for me"*.

Minnie returned to Andamooka when the war ended but finally left the opal fields in 1949 when she was 52, for health reasons. She ran a post office in an isolated outpost in South Australia, which may also have been at Andamooka. There is a letter dated 29 November 1949 from the District Postal Inspector of the Postmaster-General's Department in Jamestown, South Australia: *"I wish to thank you for your services at one of the isolated outposts and am sorry you find it necessary to leave. I trust you will soon be fully restored to health. Should you be through this way at any time do not fail to call at the office."* She then settled at the town of Ouorn[41] on the edge of the Outback with Victor, who died of a heart attack aged 61, on 4 March 1969. It is unclear when she left Ouorn, but later, when she was 71, she went to live in Magill, South Australia, where she remained until her death at the age of 103 years 6 months in 2000/01.

* * *

---

41 The Ouorn District is in the Flinders Ranges of South Australia and became known as Quorn.

Minnie had a friend in Magill, called Mary Wiley, who knew her by her first name Alice rather than Minnie. Mary Wiley wrote to my mother saying that Minnie had made it back to England at least once, but that the cold had been too much for her arthritis, so she had returned to Australia. Mary Wiley sent various objects of Minnie's to my mother, including a small white embroidered pillowcase with the name tape "M. Berrington" and a handwritten ink note saying "Given to M in 1908" – the year of her father's death, her brother's almost immediate departure for the merchant navy, and her brother Victor's birth.

* * *

The Black Sheep, the RAF, Smuggling at Sea, and an Italian Jail

Cedric

Cedric was born in 1904, seven years after his sister Minnie's birth and in the same year that Evelyn came back to England after six years, to collect his wife and two children to take them on that difficult journey back to Lomagundi and the Ayrshire Gold Mine. His father died when he was 4 and his mother when he was 19.

There is very little information on Cedric in my uncle's accounts of the family and no mention was ever made of him by my mother, despite the fact that she kept a letter and newspaper articles which featured him. There is not much doubt that Cedric was the black sheep of the family and it seems that it was deemed best to keep quiet about him. If my mother had only told me about his life and adventures, rather than keeping them a secret, we could have laughed a lot.

* * *

The first thing I discovered about Cedric among my mother's papers, was sad. It was a letter from Angela Naylor of 1 Barber Court, St Pancras Road, Lewes, East Sussex. She wrote to my mother Valerie on 1 November 1988, having first spoken to her by phone some time beforehand. Previously, she had also spoken on the phone to my maternal grandmother, apparently at length, but my grandmother died two years before Angela eventually wrote to my mother. Angela was seeking information about her own mother and enclosed a copy of her own birth certificate which she had received only three years before, and which registers her birth as 3 September 1935 at the Orchard Croft Nursing Home, Windsor Lane, Slough. Angela's father is given as Cedric Lister Berrington, Radio Company Representative of Greenfield, Windsor Lane, Slough. Her mother is given as Nora Winifred Barry, Hairdresser, of Greenfield, Windsor Lane, Slough. The baby was registered 24 days later on the 27th September. Angela says in her letter that she understood from my grandmother that Cedric was in poor health, and asks whether there is a chance he might confide in my mother about what happened to her own mother. At this point Angela would have been 53. She says the reason she writes is because she wants to know if she has inherited any medical conditions. This sounds like a pretext for trying to find out anything she possibly could about her mother, which is entirely understandable. Angela says *"Please answer my letter Mrs Gaudie – it has taken a long time to reach this point in my search"*. There is no sign of any further correspondence and I suspect that my mother might not have replied. Had she done so, I feel she would have made a note of it, or even have made a copy of her letter, which she frequently did. It is a sad story, since it seems likely that Angela was brought up in an orphanage, and never knew either her mother or father.

* * *

I discovered a little more about Cedric from the London Gazette, the official journal of the British Government, which includes several announcements about him, the first concerning his business activities in 1930, when he was 26, and the later ones confirming his training and status as a pilot as war was breaking out:

London Gazette 25 March 1930:

NOTICE is hereby given that the Partnership heretofore subsisting between us, the undersigned,
  Richard Palgrave Simpson Ladell and Cedric Lister Berrington, carrying on business as Wireless, Gramophone and Photographic Dealers, at 5, Belle Vue-parade, Wandsworth Common, in the county of London, under the style or firm of "RADIOCRAFT" and "THE BATTERY

DISTRIBUTION COMPANY," has been dissolved by March, one thousand nine hundred and thirty. All debts due to and owing by the said late firm of "Radiocraft" will be received and paid by the said Richard Palgrave Simpson Ladell, who will continue the business under the style or firm of "Radiocraft," and all debts due to and owing by the said late firm of "The Battery Distribution Company" will be received and paid by the said Cedric Lister Berrington, who will continue the business under the style or firm of "The Battery Distribution Company."—Dated this 19th day of March, 1930.

R. P. S. LADELL.(154) C. L. BERRINGTON.

Cedric's daughter Angela (who wrote to my mother about her parents) was born when Cedric was 31 in September 1935.

Surprisingly, a C D Berrington is mentioned as a Witness at my parents' wedding, so it seems that Cedric visited Madras in 1942.

Copies of the London Gazette in 1939 and 1940 announce Cedric's commission as a Pilot Officer on probation; his appointment to the rank of Flying Officer on probation; and then his appointment as a Flying Officer.[42]

* * *

The newspaper articles that my mother kept, show that Cedric probably followed in his brother Arthur's footsteps and went to sea when he was young: In1950, his American second mate wrote: *"His 47 years have been packed with adventure. As a boy he sailed round the world as a radio operator in tramp steamers. Throughout the war he flew with the RAF rising to the rank of squadron-leader, afterwards, flying with BOAC*[43] *until the plane in which he was wireless operator crashed into the Persian Gulf. Cedric was one of the two survivors. Then in 1946, he bought the 73 ton yacht "Sunshine", which for*

---

42 The London Gazette 2 May 1939: "The undermentioned are granted commissions as Pilot Officers on probation. 25th Apr. 1939: Cedric Lister BERRINGTON." London Gazette 6 February 1940: "The undermentioned Pilot Officers on probation are confirmed in their appointments and promoted to the rank of Flying Officer on the dates stated: 2nd July 1939: Cedric Lister BERRINGTON (73079)." London Gazette 2 July 1940: "Flying Officers: Cedric Lister BERRINGTON (73079)."

43 BOAC: British Overseas Airways Corporation: the British state-owned airline created in 1940 by the merger of Imperial Airways and British Airways Ltd which continued operating overseas services throughout World War II.

two years was to be the only home of his pretty wife Hughie and their four-year old son Anthony."[44]

Cedric is said in this article, to have bought this boat in 1946 when he was 42 years old, but it seems likely that it was 1948 – two years after the war ended. He says he first set eyes on her in Casablanca, where he went from England after two years of post-war flying with BOAC. The story set out below started on 27 May 1950, so he must have lived on board with his wife and son for a couple of years or so before these events. I thought it worth including several sections of the newspaper articles, since they are very entertaining.

The Daily Express Monday 22 January 1951[45] has a front page story:

"Skipper (freed from jail) keeps his 7,000,000 cigarettes.

Skipper Cedric Berrington of the schooner Sunshine, walked out of Genoa's Marassi jail last night and said "I'm going to sue the Italian Government for £25,000." Berrington, ex-RAF squadron leader and now aged 47, was fired on and arrested by Italian Customs men on May 25 (1950) last as he neared the Italian coast with a cargo of 7,000,000 cigarettes. He has been in jail for eight months. He was taken ashore on a charge of smuggling and jailed. On July 28 he was fined £131,000. He appealed. He pleaded that he was fired on, attacked, and boarded 14 miles out at sea – two miles beyond territorial waters. The Italian court upheld his claim and last night its order to free him was telephoned to the prison governor.

Just Soup

Skipper Berrington, grey-haired, 5ft 10ins tall, stretched out on a settee in his Genoa hotel and said:- "Life in Marassi was ghastly. I lost a lot of weight. What can you expect on a diet of soup twice a day – and nothing else? It was a perfectly legal trading job. I headed for Genoa on radio instructions. Then my set broke down and I couldn't check back. But I stayed outside the territorial limit. When the first shots were fired, I didn't know if I was being attacked by pirates or police. I didn't see any flags. There certainly is a lot of smuggling going on in these waters. But no

---

44   Sunday Empire News 17 September 1950
45   Daily Express: Monday 22 January 1951

contraband was ever carried in Sunshine. I was shot up for 40 minutes before I struck my colours. The Customs gave the cigarettes, worth £20,000 back to me today, but I can't decide whose they are. The people who chartered me in Tangier to take the cigarettes to Malta and Marseilles claim them. So do the consignees. Meanwhile, I'm just about broke. I had a slap-up meal when I left the prison today – hors d'oeuvres, fish, ravioli, wine, cognac, coffee, cigars. . . It was terrific after eight months of prison minestrone. That left me with £15. When that goes, I haven't a bean until freight dues are paid. My boat sank on January 4 when I was in prison. She was full of bullet holes. I mean to sue for loss of the ship, eight months' trading time – and my eight months in jail."

The *Sunday Empire News* 17 September 1950 ran a long story by Lee St Lawrence, Cedric's American second mate, a roving reporter who spoke Arabic, who had asked Cedric for a job: "*Only I can tell the story. I am fighting to free an innocent man, condemned by a foreign government to long imprisonment for a crime he did not commit. . .*"

The boat was apparently an old sailing vessel which had been trading out of Tangier, carrying tea, wood, asphalt and other odds and ends. According to Cedric and Lee, the crew included a Parisian doctor who had thrown up a good practice to follow the call of the sea, who was first mate; Lee himself as second mate; Mario the mechanic from Trieste, and ten Arabs; 14 in all, including Cedric.

About the trial, he writes: "*The main witness for the prosecution was the captain of the Italian Customs boat. It was proved that he had no instruments in his craft to take readings with sufficient precision to judge the distance of 11.7 miles to which he swore. In fact, he could not have read the simplest navigational instrument, even if he'd had one. He had judged our distance from the shore by eye alone. Yet the judge accepted his evidence in the face of our own carefully calculated sextant reading. Our counsel Advocato Machiavelli* (you couldn't make it up!), *revealed that two days after our arrest the Chief Customs Officer had circulated a secret letter ordering that incidents like the 'capture' of the Sunshine were not to be repeated.*"

He claims that he laid the following information before Foreign Office chiefs: "*An Italian who had his name in Berrington's notebook paid £500 to a Customs official to have the page destroyed. And it was quietly made known to us that if the right people were paid the small sum of 10,000,000 lire (£5,000) the trial would be dropped.*"

Another short article in *The Express* (no date):

"Accused of smuggling nearly a ton of American cigarettes into Italy in his 73-ton yacht Sunshine, an Englishman was fined £127,000 at Genoa today. Tonight, 37-year old (sic) Cedric Lister Berrington, of Liscard, Wallasey, Cheshire, is in jail hoping that the owners of the cigarettes, said to be in Tangier, North Africa, will pay the £127,000. The Sunshine, which is registered at Gibraltar, was sighted, flying the British flag, off the coast at Genoa on May 25 by an Italian Customs torpedo-boat. When the Sunshine refused to stop, the torpedo-boat fired over her bows with two machine-guns. Then after a chase, the yacht was taken into Genoa harbour where the cigarettes were found on board. Berrington's defence was that the Sunshine was stopped illegally outside Italian territorial waters. An Italian, Antonio de Biasi, of Genoa, said to have organised the smuggling at the Italian end, was also fined £127,000. Berrington and de Biasi have appealed."

On January 15th the Appeal was upheld and Cedric was released on January 16th 1951.

Cedric wrote three further articles himself in the *Empire News*[46] after his release. The articles are dated 28 January, 4th February, and 11th February 1951 and give his serialised and detailed account of the actions of the Italian Customs, his experience of 8 months in prison, and the proceedings of the Trial and the Appeal. The last article is headed *"My release came 16 days too late"* – his boat, which had been riddled with bullet holes, sank in Genoa Harbour 16 days before he was released.

* * *

I noticed recently that my mother's address book includes an address for Cedric in Weston Turville, Buckinghamshire, so I asked my uncle, aged 96 and living in California, whether he had any information on what Cedric did next. He had no further information, but did know that Cedric had died, also aged 96, in Woburn Sands, Buckinghamshire (21 miles away from Weston Turville) on 18 September 2000. It would be interesting to know whether Cedric met Arthur, Minnie or Victor after he became notorious in the media.

---

46 Empire News: 28 January, 4 February, 11 February 1951

Merchant Seaman at 13, Narrow Escapes, Colonial Advancement, Retirement

Arthur and Catherine

As we know, my maternal grandfather Arthur John, was born on 26 November 1895 at 33 Upper Hill Street, Port Elizabeth, Cape Colony, South Africa. His father, Evelyn Delahaye, was a Bakery Manager in Umtata at the time (the administrative centre for the area), having married Eleanor Witterton the year before. A short while later, Evelyn and Eleanor left South Africa and went to the Ayrshire Gold Mine at Lomagundi, Rhodesia, which Evelyn managed. Two years after Arthur's birth, his sister, Minnie, was born and about a year after that, because of the political situation, Evelyn no longer felt it safe for his family to remain in Rhodesia, and he sent them back to England.

At this point, Arthur would have been about three. I have no record as to where they lived in England for the six years before Evelyn returned in 1904 to collect them and take them back to Rhodesia. I never heard mention of this period of Arthur's life, despite what must have been a gruelling journey, first by ship to Portuguese East Africa, then by rail and finally about 80 miles by bullock cart, some of which he must have remembered. His sister Minnie would have been about seven and Eleanor pregnant with Cedric. Here was another strong and indomitable woman, about whom I know little.

Arthur's father, Evelyn, became unwell and retired in 1907, by which time Arthur would have been twelve. As a result, the family returned to England, deciding to stop en route in the South of France, to avoid the English winter. It was here, despite his poor health, that Evelyn seems to have recovered sufficiently to lose all his money at the gaming tables. How all this affected Arthur, we shall never know. The culture of the times may well have meant that the children were kept in the dark about what was happening. Arthur's father died a year later.

* * *

It was 1908 and Arthur was thirteen. Due to his father's death and his mother's consequent lack of funds, he had to leave school, and at this very young age, he joined HMS Worcester, where he trained for a career at sea for three years. In the following two years he served as an apprentice in merchant ships all over the world. Losing his father and being uprooted and sent away from his mother at such a young age must have been a tremendous shock. He had to fend for himself.

In August 1914, aged 19, he was called to service in the Royal Naval Reserve in HMS Armadale Castle patrolling the South Atlantic out of Cape Town. The Armadale Castle was requisitioned as an armed merchant cruiser in the Royal Navy on 2 August 1914. From 1916-19, he was on North Atlantic convoy duty and on 1 March 1918, his ship, the HMS Calgarian, was torpedoed and sunk off Rathlin Island, in the Irish Sea (2 officers and 46 ratings were lost). He told my uncle that he had been trapped under the keel and dislodged only when a heavy piece of debris struck him. He was one of the lucky ones; he and other survivors were rescued and taken to Larne in Northern Ireland before returning to England. I have three of his medals: The 1914-15 Star, which was a campaign medal of the British Empire for service in World War I. This is engraved "Mid. A J Davies-Berrington R.N.R." Recipients of this medal also received the British War Medal and the Victory Medal and I have these too. All three medals are attached to one large pin, each with its own ribbon. I also have a pair of my grandfather's epaulettes from Goode's (Portsmouth) Ltd Naval Outfitters.

* * *

With surprising speed, only five days after the Calgarian was sunk and his narrow escape, Arthur was in Southampton, marrying Catherine Louise Isworth. The marriage took place on 6 March 1918, at Wymering Church, Cosham. Arthur was 22, a year younger than his new wife who was born on 11 May 1894. There are a couple of wedding photos and the Marriage Certificate. This gives Rank or Profession of Arthur John as Lieutenant RNR. Their fathers' names are given as Evelyn de la Haye Davies-Berrington and Walther James Isworth with Witnesses Edward George Saxey and Janet A J Isworth. Although there are photos of Catherine's parents, I have almost no other information about her background except for a page of "The Court Journal"(!) which gives Catherine I Isworth as the third daughter of the late W J Isworth and Mrs Isworth, Commercial Place, Portsmouth.

Catherine's birth had been registered in Kingston, Surrey (the fee for registration set out as "not exceeding three-pence") and her mother's maiden name was McLean. I understand that her mother came from Inverness, Scotland. Arthur and Catherine's first child, Peter (my uncle) was born on 21 November 1918 in Long Ditton, Surrey. This may well explain the rushed marriage. In the wedding photos, Catherine's face is already soft and full.

* * *

After the war, in 1919, Arthur was appointed by the Burmah Oil Company to run oil tankers out of Rangoon and Catherine and Peter went with him. My mother, Valerie Catherine, was born there on 8 August 1920.

They were in Burma for about two years. Since family was not included in the crew, Catherine and the children lived in Rangoon, the main BOC base, but sometimes accompanied Arthur on board.

They all left Rangoon in 1921, when Arthur accepted an appointment to the Madras (India) Pilot Service, based on shore, which gave him much more time with his family. There, he served in increasingly responsible positions until he retired as Port Conservator. Quite an achievement for someone who was thrown out of his home to fend for himself at the age of 13, with very little education. He and Catherine lived in Madras for 27 years.

* * *

In 1924, the family took six months' leave in England. (It was usual then, for there to be three year intervals between long leaves.). This was when Arthur's sister Minnie and brother Vincent visited them, four years before they set off for Australia.

There is not much further information on Arthur and Catherine's time in Madras, but there are photographs. These show their large, solid and imposing two storey house with a three storey square tower at the front. The drive passed under the ground floor porch in the tower, so that anyone arriving would be in the shade as they got in or out of the car at the front door. There is a photo of their glistening 1940s Fiat which they named 'Biddy', together with their Driver. The house was surrounded by an extensive garden, including lawns, which must have needed a great deal of watering. They feature my mother, looking cool and relaxed in a deckchair with her dog next to her, and my grandparents, both wearing topees (pith helmets); my grandmother smoking, with their dachshund and her puppies.

The interior of the house is spacious and comfortably furnished, with well made locally produced reproduction furniture in teak or walnut and sometimes rosewood. The elephant gong (presumably people were called for dinner?) which now belongs to my daughter Kate, features in the dining room, together with one large and two small silver comports[47] on the dresser, which my grandfather must have inherited and which were auctioned at Christie's in 2010.

There are also photos of my grandfather on the 'office trolley' in Madras harbour, a small vehicle running on rails, on which he is sitting, being pushed along by two Indians. There is also a photo of the grand-looking Adyar Club, to which they belonged. The Club was founded in 1890 and gave membership to women as well as men; however, it was a Europeans-only club, and surprisingly, only started admitting Indians as members in 1960.[48] In addition, there is a certificate showing that on 18 September 1942, Lt Commander Arthur John Davies Berrington, RVR, joined the Freemasons at the Freemasons Hall, Madras, India . . . a fact never mentioned – of course!

* * *

On 31 January 1948 Arthur retired as Port Conservator and on the same day, sailed on the SS American Mail for Vancouver, British Columbia, Canada, where he and Catherine were met by their son. Peter had left Calcutta for Vancouver in 1947, and was working for a retired Group Captain from the Royal Canadian Air Force on a farm at Cobble Hill on Vancouver Island. Arthur and Catherine rented an old house at Quamichan Lake near Maple Bay until Peter moved to Victoria to sell real estate, when they moved to another rented house in a small community 30 minutes' drive west of Victoria. Arthur tried to write. He also tried, unsuccessfully, to sell real estate. Later, he accepted a job as Secretary of the Victoria Yacht Club but this came with only a nominal salary. They were living off capital.

---

47 Comport: Dish for sweets or fruit
48 Muthiah S: *Madras Rediscovered* (2004)

In 1950 my mother, father and I (aged four), visited Arthur, Catherine, Peter and his wife Betty (who he had married in 1949), in Canada.

By 1955, when Arthur was 60 and Catherine 61, their financial situation had not improved and they decided they would have to give up in Canada and return to England "*where the socialist government had implemented state retirement schemes*" and so they sailed from Vancouver. My Uncle Peter summed up their situation: "*After he was thirteen, my father was without a father and, in his chosen career, without a surrogate either. However well HMS Worcester had trained him for life in the Merchant Marine, it imparted no financial instruction whatever and, on his constant sea voyages, he was without contact with the most rudimentary business transactions. So, he arrived at retirement inadequately and hopelessly unprepared at the most vulnerable period of his life.*"

* * *

Back in England, Arthur and Catherine took on the running of a small post office in Slough, Buckinghamshire in order to earn an income. Unfortunately, this not only demanded unexpected expenditure on repairs but entailed exhausting work. They therefore moved to a more rural post office in Wooton, Northamptonshire, which it was hoped would prove less demanding and more enjoyable. However, it was not a success and they decided, finally, to retire. My uncle writes: "*Living in the colonies for thirty years with servants, clubs and an active social calendar had made them, at their ages, totally unsuited to that kind of life.*" I remember visiting them as a child at both these sub-post offices and having fun being behind the counter. However, I also remember thinking how strange it was that they were living in these random places, and also understanding that they were unhappy.

Later, they bought an old single storey house in Ropley near Alresford, Hampshire, which they named 'Springhaven' after their house in Madras, although it could not have been more different. I think they were quite comfortable finally, after the trials of being postmaster and postmistress, and I visited them there too, with my mother. We used to help keep the garden in some sort of order by cutting the grass (sometimes the grass was too long for the mower and we had to take scythes to it) but mostly, I remember the boredom of sitting around the dining table while the 'grown-ups' talked. Even then, I could not believe that the family's coat of arms (including the royal lions of England!) had been made up on a wooden plaque and was hanging in the hall. My grandparents, unlike my mother, were pretentious, and my mother's relationship, particularly with her mother, was a dutiful one. My mother spent a great deal of her time and energy helping them and also providing them with additional financial support, but often felt her efforts were unappreciated. She was quite clear that her parents' favourite had always been, and continued to be, her brother Peter, who writes at length in his own family history claiming every possible 'grand' connection.

* * *

Arthur died aged 78, on 12 December 1973. With considerable help from my mother, Catherine bought a small modern house in sheltered accommodation in Cuckfield, Sussex and my mother drove the long journey to visit her at least every two weeks. Catherine died at the age of 92 on 4 February 1986. Both Arthur's and Catherine's cremated remains are interred in Plot 155/23 at Park Crematorium, Guildford Road, Aldershot, Hampshire.

Eleanor Anne Davies Berrington (nee Witterton) wife of Evelyn Delahaye Davies Berrington My Maternal Great Grandmother

Eleanor Anne Davies Berrington (nee Witterton 1866-1923), widow of Evelyn Delahaye Davies Berrington My Maternal Great Grandmother

Arthur John Davies-Berrington 1895-1973 and sister Alice Minnie Florence Davies-Berrington 1897-2001 My Maternal Grandfather and Maternal Grand Aunt

Bullock wagon en route to the Ayrshire Mine. Eleanor Anne and children Arthur John and Alice Minnie Davies-Berrington in the back. Late 1890s

*Arthur John Davies-Berrington
1895-1973 (my Maternal Grandfather)*

*Catherine Louise Davies-Berrington
(née Isworth) 1894-1986
(my Maternal Grandmother)*

*Walter J Isworth
Catherine Davies-Berrington's Father*

*Janet Isworth (née Maclean) at
Inverness Catherine Davies-
Berrington's Mother*

Arthur John Davies-Berrington and Catherine Louise Davies-Berrington (née Isworth) – married 6 March 1918

Valerie Catherine Gaudie (née Davies-Berrington) 1920-2008 (my Mother) and Peter Davies Berrington 1895-1973 (my Uncle)

My Maternal Grandparents Arthur and Catherine Davies-Berrington's house Madras, India

Arthur & Catherine Davies-Berrington (my Maternal Grandparents) with Valerie (my Mother) & Peter (My Uncle)

Catherine Davies-Berrington with children Valerie and Peter on board ship en route to India leaving UK after declaration of war – 1939

Arthur and Catherine's Fiat with driver (lascar) and dog, Madras, India

Catherine & Arthur Davies-Berrington
My Maternal Grandparents in Madras, India

Reserve Ambulance Drivers – My Mother Valerie Catherine, 2nd Row from right at the front, and my Maternal Grandmother, Catherine Louise Davies-Berrington, same row at the back

CHAPTER 3

'Out East' and 'Back Home'

The Disappointed Dancer

Valerie

MY MOTHER, VALERIE, WAS BORN OUT EAST and baptised Out East; she married Out East; gave birth Out East; and lived Out East for a large part of her life. Most of her stories and reminiscences about those times started with the phrase: 'When we were Out East'. . .

I have already talked about my mother's birth on 8 August 1920 in Rangoon, registered at the Central Plague Depot; followed by her baptism there on 19 June 1921, and her trips as an infant on an oil tanker based in Rangoon. Her family moved to Madras, India, when she was about a year old in the second half of 1921.

* * *

Valerie was sent to St Hilda's School near Ootacamund in the Nilgiri Hills, south west of Madras, but at what age I can only guess. Her brother Peter also attended this school until he was eight. The school still exists(!)[49] and their website says: "*The school was founded in 1892 by the Sisters of the Church from Kilburn, UK, to cater to the educational needs of the protestant European communities.*"

---

49   St Hilda's School: http://www.sthildasooty.com

I see that it is approx 560 km from Madras to "Ooty" and to get there by road currently takes ten and a half hours, so they were boarders – probably from the age of four and a half or five. . .[50]

In 1924, when my mother was four, Arthur, Catherine and the children went on six months' leave to England. Arthur's mother, Eleanor, had died the year before.

My mother was sent to boarding school at St Dunstan's Abbey, Exeter, in 1927, when she was seven years old. Her school holidays were spent with her brother Peter, when they stayed with a family at a farm in Cornwall. This family later bought a small hotel in Newquay, after which holidays were spent on the beach, surfing and swimming in rock pools. Other holidays were spent with their parents when they were on leave (when they rented various houses), or with family friends.

Arthur and Catherine were on long leave in England in 1939, staying in a house in Rake, Hampshire and there are photos of this time. On 3 September of that year, war was declared on Germany, and my grandfather Arthur received a telegram and had to leave immediately for Madras.

Valerie enjoyed and was good at dancing, tap dancing, drawing and playing the piano and had plans to go to The Ginner-Mawer School of Dance and Drama in London, where, as their leaflet of the time says: *"students are equipped for the teaching profession or as stage artists"*. Very sadly, however, for her, this was not to be, since her father insisted that due to the danger of impending war, she and Peter must leave England, and join their parents in India.

Catherine, with Peter and 19 year old Valerie, sailed to India some weeks later.

Peter had passed the necessary exams to train for the Indian Imperial Police and was due to join them, as were 16 others also on board. They sailed from Liverpool in the SS City of Venice in convoy for Bombay. Peter joined the Police Training School in the Sikh Fort at Phillaur in the Punjab, where he was taught languages, law, administration, field tactics and riding, after which he was posted to various locations and to the North West Frontier.

My mother was about 5′8″; she was attractive; slim; a brunette; with blue eyes, a soft English rose complexion and a warm smile. She had the finest

---

[50] Ysenda Maxtone Graham's 2016 book "Terms & Conditions: Life in Girls' Boarding Schools 1939-1979" relates that Ann Leslie went to this school at the age of 4!

possible hair, which she described as the bane of her life and which she dealt with by having her hair permed into soft waves.

For her, it must have been a matter of joining the social round in Madras, although both she and my grandmother did also join up and train as Reserve Ambulance Drivers during the war. My mother became a member of the Madras Amateur Dramatic Society and took part in productions. She visited Srinagar, Kashmir, with her mother, staying on a houseboat on Lake Dal and making the trip up to the hill station of Gulmarg. She also visited the Hill Stations of Ootacamund (where she had been at school) and Nainital, not far from Nepal, with its large lake and altitude of nearly 7000 ft. She had a black cocker spaniel called Rumble of which she was extremely fond and about which she often talked. There are plenty of photos of her life in Madras and on trips with her parents; she was a good looking, smiling and relaxed young woman.

* * *

Marriage, the War, a Baby, and Burmese Communists

Valerie and Glen

I do not know how or when my mother met my father, Glen, but they became engaged in 1942 and married towards the end of that year, on Saturday 19 November 1942 at St Mary's Church, Fort St. George, Madras.

The wedding invitation was from Lt-Cmdr & Mrs A. D. Berrington of 2 Springhaven Road, Harbour, Madras. The newspaper announcement gives Lawrence Glen as "only son of Mr & Mrs F A Gaudie of Hertfordshire, England, to Valerie Catherine, only daughter of Mr & Mrs A J D Berrington of Madras and Monmouthshire. The marriage certificate gives 'Residence' for both as Madras and 'Rank or Profession' for Lawrence Glen as 'Captain, Burma Frontier Force'. Witnesses were R D Dennison(sic), C D Berrington (Cedric, the black sheep, now 38, must have been visiting Madras) and C Burns. A quote from the Rev. Canon J G Caldicott in the Church Newsletter said: "It is not for a hardened old bachelor like myself to say how charming the bride looked, for this was well done by Sir Robert Denniston[51]..."

---

51 Peter later married Betty Denniston in Canada. Betty's father was a cousin of Sir Robert Denniston.

Photos show a relaxed couple on honeymoon in India – in Ooty, 'Queen of Hill Stations'; my father very thin, having recently recovered from dysentery, and my mother looking casual but fashionable, in her 1940s dresses and 'slacks'.

After their honeymoon, my father was sent back to the Chin Hills Battalion, and my mother returned to living with her parents for a while. Her lifestyle there continued much as before and included a visit to her brother in Amritsar. After his tour of duty in the Chin Hills, my father was posted to the Burma Regimental Centre at Hoshiarpur in the north eastern Punjab, India, as a Major and Company Commander. He was given 28 days' leave from 23 January 1944, after which my mother returned with him to Hoshiarpur. This was a rear headquarters, behind fighting lines. Life there must have been quite an experience for my mother. It must have been awkward at times, too. They lived in army tents and slept on charpoys (beds made from wooden frames with woven rope bases). My mother told me of one occasion about which she laughed: she was lying in a bath trying to cool off, when the bath tent collapsed around her! I do not suppose there were too many women there either! After a while they were provided with a house to live in, of which there is a photo, under which my mother has written *"Army Days 1944 – our first brick house"*. They lived there until they went on leave to the UK in 1945, when my mother would have met her Scottish in-laws for the first time. On their return, my father was posted to Burma as an area rice officer.

* * *

The Seasoned Colonial

Glen

Glen, my father, was born at 1.45pm on 13 March 1914 at 106 Gilmore Place, Edinburgh (District of Morningside), Scotland. His Birth Certificate gives his Father (Frederick Augustus) as "Rice Merchant (Domicil: Akyab, Burma)" and his Mother as Isabella Wallace Gaudie. The informant on the certificate is given as Isabella W Gaudie, Mother.

It seems that Augustus was in Burma at the time his wife was giving birth in Scotland. As we know, Glen's mother, Isabella, set out for Rangoon very soon after the birth, with her new baby, and my father was baptised on

14 June 1914 at The Scots Kirk, Rangoon. The Baptism Certificate gives Akyab as their 'Abode' and Frederick Augustus's occupation as 'Merchant'.

They must all have returned to the UK on leave about a year later, since shipping records show that on 22 October 1915, Augustus, Isabella and Glen sailed again to Rangoon. The Passenger list, which shows "Names and Descriptions of British Passengers Embarked at the Port of Liverpool" (in total numbering 36) on the Henderson Line ship "Chindwin" bound for Rangoon, includes:

Mr F A Gaudie, Rice Merchant, aged 43;
Mrs F A Gaudie, Housewife, aged 34, and
Master L G Gaudie, Child, aged 1

The Country of Last Permanent Residence is given as "British Possessions", Country of Intended Future Residence given as Burma, travelling 1st class.

It seems likely that Eleanor Winifred, my father's sister, who would have been ten, had been left at a UK boarding school.

My father was sent to St Albans School in England as a boarder in September 1925, at the age of eleven. I do not know where he went to school prior to this. In December 1929, when he was nearly 16, he passed his School Certificate exam with credit and a year later, in November 1930, passed his Territorial Army Officers Training Corps exam. In March of the following year, he enlisted in the Infantry, in the Territorial Army, London. I have a medal dated 1928 (when he would have been 14) for the quarter mile relay, which looks as though it is from a Hertfordshire Athletics Club. There are also four other sporting medals of his: one for running in 1932 and three for shooting in 1933 and 1934. In 1932 he joined Union Cold Storage Co. Ltd., London, and in the spring of 1933 gained the London Chamber of Commerce, Higher Commercial Education Certificate in Spanish.

My father was 5'10", good looking, with a straight nose, a moustache, sandy hair and blue eyes. His army record describes his complexion as 'fresh'. Later on in life, he became a large man – somewhat overweight – who lost most of the hair on top of his head. He sometimes wore a tweed cap. He smoked cigarettes and a pipe but latterly only a pipe. I realised only recently, on watching some of my mother's ciné films, what a protective and tender father he had been to my brother and me when we were small.

He joined Steel Bros & Co. Ltd on 1 January 1934, for which company he would work for the rest of his life[52].

Initially, he had a *"short period on the export side of the London office"* until 8 December 1934, after which his overseas service began. He was posted to the Rice Department in Rangoon and discharged from the Territorial Army. After this, in 1935, he spent six months working at Indo-Burma Petroleum Co. Ltd.'s Calcutta branch, until he was sent back to Burma *"for a season in rice at Moulmein"*. Then in 1936, came two years in the finance department in Rangoon. It was during this time, that he played in the Steels' Rugby Football XV. He was then sent to Bassein for the off-season in 1938 and also had a short spell at the Thaton office of the Jungle Buying Section.

When war broke out in 1939, my father joined the Burma Officer Cadet Training Unit at Maymyo. He completed his training in February 1940 and was commissioned in the Burma Frontier Force where he *"saw considerable active service with the Bhamo battalion in 1941/42, finally trekking out of Burma via Shwebo-Imphal in April 1942"*.

My father's Army records show that on 10 November 1939 he was appointed by George the Sixth as an Officer in 'Our Land Forces' as a 2nd Lieutenant. His Army Book gives his Personal Number as ABRO45, the Nature of Commission as 'ABRO' and Regiment or Corps as 'Burma Regt'. His Military Identity Card Number was 053171. He is listed (along with my godfather, Malcolm Freshney) in the Section "1937-1948 – the War against Japan" under "Appointments" in the on-line Anglo-Burmese Library.

ABRO was "The Army in Burma Reserve of Officers". *This "was a British colonial army formation of volunteers that saw service during the Second World War in South East Asia (particularly India and Burma)... Appointments, promotions... were approved by King George VI and published in the London Gazette... ABRO did not serve as a single fighting unit, but were distributed across the British/Indian fighting formations, including the Burma Regiment, The Burma Rifles, the Kachin Levies and the Chin Levies. ABRO ceased to exist on 4 January 1948 – the day of transfer of power to Burma."*

ABRO mainly consisted of civilians, of whom there were 1617; 54 of whom were killed. In 1939, when my father joined up, he was one of 61 who

---

52 The quotations which follow are from the Obituary on my father in Steel Bros. Magazine and from the book "Calling to Mind – An Account of the first hundred years of Steel Bros. & Co Ltd." by H E W Braund.

joined from commercial and technical roles – Steel Brothers is listed as one of the organisations from which these civilians came.[53] In 1940, The National Service Act made it obligatory for European British subjects of military age to join up.

My father's address in his Army record is given as c/o Imperial Bank of India, Dehra-Dun and later as c/o Imperial Bank of India Hoshiarpur. His Innoculations Register is included, which lists smallpox; typhoid-paratyphoid; tetanus-toxoid; cholera; and yellow fever; and the various promotions he was given are also listed, often as Acting or Temporary ranks – Capt, Major, Lt-Col. It also notes 28 days' leave given from 23 January 1944 with free travel warrant. My father's Will is also included, although this was not signed until 17 January 1945. It gives his address as 'The Mercantile Bank of India Ltd., Calcutta', and he leaves everything to my mother.

His Record of Service shows:

In Ranks: 14 London Regt. (T.A.) from March 1932 to Oct 1934
Burma Frontier Force 1/4/40 to 20/7/42
4 Buregt (*ie Burma Regiment*). 1/10/42 to 8/2/43 (*NB: He married 19 Nov 1942*)
Chin Hills Bn. 8/2/43 to 4/12/43
To be Coy Comd. 8/2/43 to 10/2/43
To be O.C. Rear H.Q. 10/2/43 to 27/9/43
To be 2 i/c. 27/9/43 to 9/10/43
To be Offg Comd. 4/11/43 to 13/11/43
To be 2 i/c 4/11/43 to 13/11/43
To be O.C. Rear H.Q 13/11/43 to 4/12/43

This list is incomplete. He was not released from the army until 1946.

My father must have experienced challenging times and appalling conditions during his years in the jungles of northern Burma. He never discussed the war; occasionally, though, he would lightly pass on tips, such as how to remove a leech from your body using a lighted cigarette. In Julian

---

53   The Anglo-Burmese Library: http://www.angloburmeselibrary.com/the-war-against-japan.html

Thompson's oral history "Forgotten Voices of Burma" Lieutenant Michael Marshall writing about an incident in October 1943 says:

"Every one of us had forty to fifty leeches hanging off us, and we spent a good half-hour removing them. Some leeches can go through lace holes in boots. The most fearsome were elephant leeches, some six to nine inches long, in flooded chaungs[54] and rivers. We took them off with a lighted cigarette." Private Dick Fiddament says: *"That part has the heaviest rainfall in the world. It comes down in a solid sheet. You think to yourself, if it doesn't stop soon beating against my poor skull, I'll go insane. The whole area becomes a quagmire. Combined with the rain, you've got the humidity, and you're sweating – the straps of your pack, your rifle sling, and anything else you are carrying tends to chafe and rub. Your skin becomes all tender and raw. Your feet, however tough and hardened, are saturated and become sore with constant rubbing, however well your boots are fitted."*

Julian Thompson describes the conditions: *"The terrain and climate in Burma challenged both sides, particularly in the monsoon when the rain sheeted down almost incessantly: clothing, webbing equipment and boots rotted and fell apart and the men could be soaked for days on end. In Assam and western Burma, men and animals were tormented constantly by sand flies, ticks, mosquitoes and leeches. Dengue, typhus, malaria, cholera, scabies, yaws, sprue and dysentery were endemic."*

And Major Dominic Neill says: *"At first light the CO passed through my position and warned me to take Snowdon East. He reminded me that the position was to be taken regardless of cost."*

"After nine months of recuperation and further training in India he was again in the forward areas, in the rank of captain and with the Chin Hill Battalion, B.F.F. His tour of duty there over, he returned to the Burma Regimental Centre at Hoshiarpur (near Lahore) as a Major and Company Commander."

There are a couple of interesting photos. One from 30 April 1945: "Group photo of officers and VCOs[55] of Trg. Bn Burma Regtl Centre"

---

54 Chaung: Burmese for watercourse or minor river, could be as narrow as a ditch, or wide enough for small craft, particularly near the coast.
55 A viceroy's commissioned officer (VCO) was a senior Indian member of the British Indian Army.

taken at Hoshiarpur. My father the senior officer, centre, front row: Major L G Gaudie. Another dated May 1945: Passing Out of No. 1 Group 'Boys' Coy. Burma Regimental Centre, May 1945. My father the second most senior officer, left, front row: Major L G Gaudie.

* * *

After my parents came back from leave in the UK in 1945, my father *"joined the Civil Affairs Services to be an area rice officer during the period of reoccupation of Burma and on demobilisation was identified with the specialist Calcutta organisation at that time on contract to procure and supply foodgrains for the employees of the Indian Tea Association in West Bengal and Assam."*

"The Civil Affairs Service – Burma (CAS-B) came into being in February 1943, with the appointment of a Chief Civil Affairs Officer." This officer was delegated with *"full authority to conduct . . . the military administration of the civil population in these territories." "Later, in 1945, the CAS(B) authority and purpose were changed to include civil relief."* In November 1944, there were 66 Civil Affairs officers operating in Burma and by May 1945, there were 1915[56] of whom my father was one.

My father's Release Notice from the Burma Army is dated 21 January 1946 and says "Struck off duty on the forenoon of the 26/3/46 on proceeding on 6 months' release leave pending local release".

* * *

I was born on 2 June 1946 at the Lady Willingdon Nursing Home in Madras, Madras Presidency, and was taken by boat by my mother to join my father in Rangoon when I was about eight weeks old. This was when my mother was not allowed to stay in the all-male hostel usually lived in by my father, because he was 'up-river'. This, despite being a married woman with a very young baby. The matter was obviously resolved on my father's return to Rangoon and they remained in Burma for about a year, before going on leave to the UK. We visited my father's parents in Montrose,

---

56 The Anglo-Burmese Library: http://www.angloburmeselibrary.com/the-war-against-japan.html

Scotland, and took a six week holiday in Foynes, Ireland. My mother told me that the fresh eggs available in Ireland were a real treat after the shortages and post-war rationing in Scotland. Apparently, her mother-in-law had been just a little too keen on cooking 'smokies' for dinner![57]

My father, my mother and I sailed back to Rangoon 1st class on 25 November 1947 from Greenock, on the Henderson Line ship "SS Prome", with 42 other passengers.

My Uncle Peter returned to India in 1947 after only one home leave, just before independence. However, when it became clear that Great Britain would leave India, he applied to various immigration authorities and decided to go to Canada. In September 1947 he sailed as Purser on the SS Lake Winnipeg from Calcutta (the ship was not licensed to carry passengers).

In 1948 my mother, father and I returned to Bassein. That was when we had to flee the Communists; after which we finally left Burma.

* * *

---

[57] Arbroath smokies are a type of smoked haddock – a speciality of the town of Arbroath. Made using traditional methods dating back to the late 1800s. Haddock are salted overnight and then tied in pairs using hemp twine and left overnight to dry. They are then hung over a triangular length of wood to smoke. This 'kiln stick' fits between the two tied smokies, one on either side. The sticks are then used to hang the dried fish in a special barrel containing a hardwood fire. The top of the barrel is covered with a lid and sealed around the edges with wet jute sacks. This creates a very hot, humid and smoky fire. The intense heat and thick smoke is essential if the fish are to be cooked, not burned, and to have the strong, smoky taste and smell expected. Typically in less than an hour of smoking, the fish are ready to eat. https://en.wikipedia.org/wiki/Arbroath_smokie

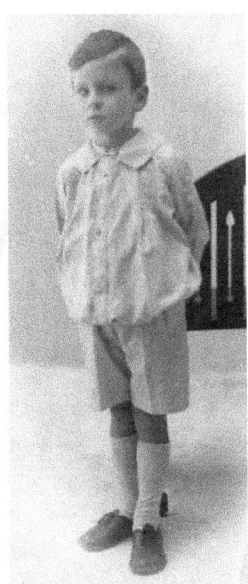

*My Father, Lawrence Glen Gaudie,
born 1914 in Edinburgh, Scotland*

*Lawrence Glen Gaudie 1914-1971
My Father*

*Valerie Catherine Davies-Berrington
My Mother*

*Valerie Catherine Davies-Berrington
and cocker spaniel Rumble*

Lawrence Glen Gaudie and Valerie Catherine Gaudie (née Davies-Berrington) married at St Mary's Church, Fort St George, Madras, India 19 Nov 1942

Valerie Catherine and Lawrence Glen Gaudie on honeymoon in Ooty, India

Major L G Gaudie (Centre). Officers and Viceroy's Commissioned Officers of Training Battalion, Burma Regimental Centre, Hoshiarpur, India, 3 April 1945

My Mother Valerie Catherine Gaudie and Valerie Anne Gaudie – born 2 June 1946

Lawrence Glen Gaudie 1914-1971 My Father

Tea Gardens, Rhinos, Panthers and Snakes

We went to live in Tondoo in the Dooars, India, close to the borders with Bhutan and Nepal, my father managing tea gardens. We were to be there for about two years. The year before, in 1947, India had become independent, and my parents were therefore no longer colonials, but expatriates. This was never mentioned by my parents as having had an effect on them. It seems to have had little impact on their way of life – the life led for years in numerous tea gardens managed by foreigners. This was largely perhaps because my father was in India in a commercial rather than in a civil service, police or military capacity. In addition, the tea gardens were located in the remote north east of India, well away from the Pakistan border, where major violence had erupted at partition in 1947.

There are photos of their first house, and later a second 'Sha o Goan' and a third, 'Bhalabarri' – all in the Dooars[58]. In 1949 we moved to the Longview Tea Estate, Darjeeling[59]. There are photos of me wearing crisp little white cotton dresses with capped sleeves, being watched over by my ayah, playing with a spade and enjoying the company of our white Siamese cat. There is also one of me on a visit to Darjeeling, sitting on a small pony named Peter Pan, with my ayah Lakshmini nearby, holding my mother's handbag for her while she takes the photo.

Steel Bros. had an office in Siliguri to which my father would be driven from the tea garden by his driver; over an hour's drive. The unmade road went through jungle, and my father told me that on one occasion when they were driving along, he was startled to see an Indian rhinoceros emerge from the jungle and start charging at the car. The driver had to accelerate (as much as is possible in a 1948 car on an unmade road) to outstrip the rhino, which charged alongside and after them for a while. I understand that Indian rhinos can run at speeds of up to 55 km/h for short periods and males are about 12ft long and weigh about 2,100 kg!

The area was remote and the lifestyle isolated, particularly so for my mother. The nearest neighbours were miles away. My mother was fond of telling me how each evening she and my father would hear a black panther calling as it passed the house on its way to a waterhole to drink. She also

---

58   http://www.dooarsonline.com
59   http://www.discoveringtea.com/tag/longview-tea-estate/

told me about the time she got up in the night to find a large venomous and dangerous snake – an Indian krait – curled up around the lavatory in the bathroom. There was apparently a sluice hole in the floor of the bathroom up which the snake must have come into the house. She woke my father and they managed, somehow, to get rid of it. My father always wore Burmese Shan pants at night instead of pyjamas, even in England. He called them bombies. *"In the Toungoo Hills, the Bwè and other tribes usually wore a shorter smock, with all kinds and variations of stripes, which would hardly reach to their knees. They covered their legs with baggy Shan "bombies" or pants, usually black in colour"*.[60] My father's bombies were made of pale cream silk with a wide fine cotton band at the top which he tied and turned over.

On leaving the tea gardens, my father was presented by the Indian staff at the office with a farewell document inside an ornate Indian silver scroll container dated 10 June 1950.

* * *

A Canadian Idyll, a Baby Boy, and on to Thailand and Iraq

On the 5 July 1950 we set off to take a holiday in Canada. A Passenger List shows us travelling 1st class from Bombay to London, my father aged 36, my mother 28 and me 4. Now my father is described as a 'Mercantile' and our address is given as my parents' bank in London. From there we travelled to Liverpool and on 2 August 1950, sailed 1st class to Montreal, on the Canadian Pacific Line ship SS Empress of France.

We went to visit my grandparents and uncle, who by now were living on the west coast of Canada. We travelled on the Canadian Pacific Railway, which at that time was transcontinental and ran from Montreal, across central Canada and through the Rockies, to Vancouver. The journey took about three days. I remember that the train had large picture windows from which passengers could enjoy the spectacular views. We visited my grand-

---

60 Bombies: See Burma Pamphlets. No. 8 The Karens of Burma, by Harry I Marshall. First published in May 1945 by Longmans, Green & Co Ltd. for the Burma Research Society.

parents in Victoria on Vancouver Island where they were living, and we all had a holiday at Yellow Point Lodge on the beautiful coast of Vancouver Island, where we stayed in wooden cabins next to the sea. The weather was fine; we went on boat trips; and my father and uncle fished for salmon.

Three months later, on 7 October, we returned to Liverpool from Montreal on the same ship, to visit my Scottish grandmother; and two months after that, on 18 December 1950, my brother, David Glen, was born in Montrose.

Steel Bros. say that in 1951, my father had a *"Short break from Calcutta, when he did a relieving job with the Siam Rice Agency at Bangkok."* On 9 March, therefore, my mother, my three month old brother and I, sailed from Southampton on the P & O Line ship "Corfu" to join my father in Siam.

On 14 July 1951 my brother David Glen was baptised at Christ Church, Bangkok, Siam.

The country of Siam, after a bloodless coup had taken place in 1932 against the absolute monarch, introduced a constitutional monarchy with parliamentary government, and in 1939, changed its name to Thailand, the new name meaning 'Land of the Free'. It was re-named Siam again from 1946-48, after which the name reverted to Thailand. However, my parents (and probably the other colonials) continued to call the country Siam.

Siam had been an ally of Great Britain in World War I, but in 1941, when the Japanese landed forces in Thailand, permission was given by Thailand, after negotiations, to allow the Japanese to advance towards the British-controlled Malay Peninsula, Singapore and Burma. Then, in 1942, Thailand declared war on Britain and the US; although the Thai ambassador in Washington refused to deliver the declaration to the US government! At the end of the war in 1945, Thailand was compelled to return the territory it had seized from Laos, Cambodia and Malaya and the exiled king returned. In 1946, however, the king was assassinated and in 1947 there was a military coup by the war-time pro-Japanese leader, and the military retained power until 1973.[61]

The country we arrived in, therefore, was a military dictatorship, stable while we were there. However, student riots in 1973, well after we had left, brought about the fall of the military government and a period of

---

61   BBC Asia: 'Thailand Profile': http://www.bbc.co.uk/news/world-asia-15641745

instability ensued. By 1991, seventeen military coups had taken place since 1932.

We were in Thailand for about two years. We lived in a comfortable, modern house with a large garden, at the bottom of which there was a klong (an artificial canal) with servants living in a separate building alongside the main house. I remember quite a lot about Bangkok which I shall talk about later.

All four of us went on leave at the end of the two year period, on 10 April 1953, sailing via Hong Kong to Liverpool. We stayed in Hong Kong for a short visit full of excitements (caught on my mother's ciné film), such as going on the Peak Tram funicular railway to the upper parts of Hong Kong, and visiting (and patting) the ancient giant tortoises.

Once we got back to the UK, we spent most of this leave in Montrose but we also rented a large Austin car and toured Scotland for a couple of weeks. I remember this quite well. I was due to be left at boarding school at the end of this holiday.

My father left the UK before my mother, who stayed behind to settle me into my new boarding school, Malvern Girls' College in Worcestershire. My father *"Returned to the Calcutta organisation and remained until mid-1956"*.

My mother rented a small flat in Malvern for herself and my brother during this settling in period. It was at the top of a large house in Malvern, owned by a chiropodist whose surgery was on the ground floor. Leaving me at boarding school, and having made arrangements as to where I would spend my holidays – with appointed guardians – my mother sailed from Liverpool to India with my brother, now 3, on 15 February 1954. They sailed on the Anchor Line ship 'Caledonia' bound for Calcutta via Port Said, Karachi and Bombay. My mother, now 33, gave her address as the Doncaster Hotel.

* * *

Baghdad: Uprisings and a Breakdown

All three of them left India and went to live in Iraq in 1956. My father had been *"Posted to Rafidain Developments Ltd., Baghdad, Iraq, an engineering associate with main activity the import and servicing of mechanical agricultural equipment, of which concern he was appointed general manager within a few months and for the next eight years this was to be his calling. An able, down-to-earth executive, liked and respected by everyone, and possessed of a grand, infectious sense of humour all of his own, he did a great deal for Rafidain Developments Ltd in that period."*

Rafidain Developments had been set up in 1952 as a subsidiary of Spinneys, a trading company set up originally by a First World War English ex-cavalry officer, in the Levant, Jordan and Iraq. *"After a chequered start the company was taken over by Steels and traded prosperously for a number of years until 1967 when, under a newly promulgated law, it had to be sold to Iraqi interests".* A quick online search shows that Spinneys has morphed into *"The premium supermarket retailer in the Middle East".*

By the time my parents arrived in Baghdad, the state of Iraq had existed for only 36 years. Prior to that, the area had been governed for four centuries by the Ottomans and was then *"carved from three provinces of the Ottoman Empire and created under British aegis as a mandate."*[62]

Phebe Marr in her book "The Modern History of Iraq" says: *"Despite Britain's long-standing interests in the Gulf, the British had no intention of occupying the Tigris and Euphrates Valleys at the outbreak of the First World War. However, when it became apparent late in 1914 that Turkey, Britain's traditional ally, would enter the war on the side of the Central Powers and was mobilizing at the head of the Gulf, Britain decided to occupy Faw and Basra to protect its strategic interests and communications and its oil fields at the head of the Gulf. On 6 November 1914 the troops landed at Faw, and by 22 November they had moved up to Basra. In March 1917 they took Baghdad and in 1918 they occupied Mosul. The British wartime conquest of most of the Iraqi provinces was complete..."*

Interestingly, it was at just this time (1918-1921) that my maternal grandfather was running oil tankers out of Rangoon.

In1920, two years after the end of the war, the San Remo conference assigned Britain a Mandate for Iraq. This led fairly soon to an anti-British revolt, suppressed by the British after about three months. The British then installed a monarchy, signing a Treaty with Iraq which included a Constitution. However, *"in June 1929 a newly elected labor government in Britain announced its intention to support Iraq's admission to the League*

---

62 Marr, Phebe: The Modern History of Iraq, 2nd Edition

of Nations in 1932 and negotiate a new treaty recognising Iraq's independence." ... *"In November 1930 ... the treaty ended the mandate but retained British influence. Britain leased two bases and retained a right to all Iraqi facilities; British "advisers and experts" remained. In return, Iraq was to receive military training, equipment, and assistance from Britain ... in October 1932 Iraq was admitted to the League of Nations."*

My father told me of three military coups which took place in Baghdad during the eight years he was there. On one occasion he was playing golf when he heard gunfire and headed for home. On another, he was at home when a loud rumbling drew him to the window to see a large tank passing by next to the house. He also told me that after at least one of these coups the most senior members of the ousted regime were decapitated and their heads displayed over the city gate.

This prompted me to find out more. Phebe Marr's book describes the turbulent period from 1930 to 1964 as one of frequent, often violent and bloody uprisings, insurgencies, rebellions and coups. Many factions and groups were involved, including the Kurds and the army. The 1941 coup, at the beginning of the Second World War, resulted in the second British occupation of Iraq. Unrest and instability were a constant.

My parents arrived in 1956, two years before the *1958 "revolution"* which: *"designed to reform and modernize Iraq, instead brought a decade of instability and military dictatorship."*...*"The result was a constant attempt to overthrow the government in power – from within and from without. Between 1958 and 1968, there were four changes of regime and countless failed coups."*

The first of these was the military coup on 14 July 1958 which finally overthrew the monarchy. *"At about 08.00 am, the king, the crown prince, and the rest of the family left the palace and assembled in the courtyard. There a young captain opened fire. Others joined in, and they were killed. This ended any hope of restoring the Hashimite dynasty in Iraq. Nuri*[63]*had managed to escape but was recognized in a street in a local quarter in Baghdad as he was trying to escape from the house of a friend disguised in a woman's black cloak. He was shot dead on the spot. His body was taken to the Ministry of Defense and quietly buried in a cemetery that night."* ... *"The first pronouncements of the revolution, promising freedom and an election, had inspired confidence,*

---

63   Nuri: Repeatedly Prime Minister from 1930-1958.

but Arif⁶⁴ soon urged the liquidation of traitors. Uncontrollable mobs surged through Baghdad. The body of Abd al-Ilah⁶⁵ was taken from the palace, mutilated, and dragged through the streets and was finally hung at the gate of the Ministry of Defense. Several Jordanian ministers and US businessmen staying at the Baghdad Hotel fell into the hands of the mob and were also killed. Finally, Qasim⁶⁶ imposed a curfew, which brought some order out of chaos but did not entirely end the barbarities. The day after Nuri's burial, his body was disinterred by the mob and also dragged through the streets. The overwhelming majority of Iraqis regarded these deeds with horror and disgust. They caused irreparable damage to Iraq's international reputation and marred the revolution's image in the minds of many of its own people."

And my father had lived in Baghdad through all this! With hindsight, his understatement is amazing. It must have been dangerous to be in Baghdad, even if you were a foreigner, and must also have been just a little alarming. He did not mention the possibility of leaving the country, although that must have been considered. But it did not end there...

The next events took place a year later, in 1959. Firstly, there was a revolt in Mosul, in the north of the country, after which the leaders of the revolt were brought to trial and executed. This then led to an attempt on the life of the Prime Minister. *"In the spring of 1959, a group of young Ba'thists, including Saddam Husain, were selected to train for the assignment. The plot was to shoot Qasim as he passed through Rashid Street in his car on 7 October. In fact, the attempt was botched and failed in its objective."* ... *"Some of the Ba'thists managed to escape to Syria, including Husain, but 78 others were rounded up... Some were acquitted; others were given the death sentence and imprisoned. None of the death sentences were carried out."* Then, in the south of the country, in Kirkuk, a bloody battle took place at a rally, with at least 30 killed and 100 injured.

The final coup that took place before my father left Iraq, when he retired from overseas service, occurred on 8 February 1963 – the fourteenth day of Ramadan.

---

64   Arif: An army officer and key figure in the overthrow of the monarchy in 1958. President of Iraq 1963-1966.
65   Abd-al-Ilah: Crown prince and regent of Iraq 1939-1953.
66   Qasim: Army officer, leader of the 1958 revolution that overthrew the monarchy. Prime Minister 1958 to 1963 when he was overthrown and killed by the Ba'th.

"Once again, a new revolution was announced over the radio, while supporters in the air force bombed the Ministry of Defense and a number of airplanes and the runway at Rashid Camp. It was at the Ministry of Defense that the heaviest fighting took place. Qasim had taken refuge in the heavily fortified building, with a few of his loyal followers. The battle at the ministry raged all day. Most of the army outside the capital apparently remained neutral. Meanwhile, the Communists took to the streets to resist for two days of bitter fighting. In encounters with the army, the Communist demonstrators were mowed down by tanks but not before killing a number of soldiers. Finally on 9 February Qasim asked for safe conduct out of the country in return for surrender. His request was refused. Instead, he was dragged before a hastily assembled group of military and party leaders and summarily interrogated about his failures. He and three associates were shot on the spot and their bodies displayed on public TV. The Qasim era had come to an end."

My father left Iraq not long after this – in 1964, just as nationalisation laws were being passed; although it was not until 1967 that Rafidain Developments itself had to be sold to Iraqi interests.

My father was on his own for most of his time in Iraq since my mother had returned to England for health reasons; initially without my brother, who was brought back to England by my father once my mother's treatment was over. My father, however, returned to Iraq after this on his own, and although, of course, he had the usual periods of leave in England when we were all together again, he must, surely, have been lonely.

* * *

The reason for my mother's absence, was that not long after moving from Calcutta to Baghdad, when she was about 37, she had a mental breakdown (she had shown symptoms of psychiatric problems three years earlier – on our Scottish trip in 1953). I have no idea what sort of symptoms she displayed in Baghdad, but she told me, resentfully, much later, that she had been *"sent back to England from Baghdad by air, on my own, leaving David behind"*. She told me she was met at the airport by an ambulance and men in white coats, and was put on a stretcher and taken to Guy's Hospital in London. My mother never discussed her treatment with me, but I suspect she was given electroconvulsive therapy. I contacted Guy's & St Thomas'

Hospital under the Freedom of Information Act, asking for information on her treatment. Unfortunately, however, they were unable to provide me with any information, since they retain medical records for 25 years only. Once she had been discharged, my mother was provided with somewhere to live and given a job for a while, working in a café in Knightsbridge, which, from the way she talked about it, she enjoyed. Despite whatever treatment she was given at Guy's, my mother had to cope with psychiatric problems for the rest of her life. She suffered from paranoia, had conversations with imaginary people and blamed a 'machine', all of which she believed were working against her. She habitually talked and sometimes shouted to herself, although she was generally sufficiently aware of her symptoms to control herself in public or in other people's company, although there were exceptions to this. Considering this disability, she managed, nonetheless (and rather admirably) to live a relatively normal but lonely life.

* * *

'Back Home'

My mother did not return 'Out East' but stayed 'Back Home' to use another of her well worn expressions – the word Home invariably spoken with an implied capital 'H'.

My parents took the decision that although my father would continue to work overseas, my mother would remain in the UK. This must have been in about 1958 and it was decided that we would stay in a small hotel in Devizes, Wiltshire, and look for rented accommodation nearby. It was while we were there that I found out how much fun it was to climb trees. However, attempts were made to stop me from doing this because the local children I was playing with, were apparently 'not the right type'. I rebelled against this as often as I possibly could. This was the beginning of a long period of living in rented accommodation, while my mother searched for a house to buy, with my father joining us when he was on leave.

Later, we lived in various parts of England in rented accommodation, but firstly, we rented half a house in the country, not far from Devizes. The house was called 'Barley Hill', in the village of Poulshot and David went to a small school in the nearby village of West Lavington. My brother and I enjoyed our life in this house with its big garden. We made friends in the village, too, with whom we played 'cowboys and Indians' in the garden, and my father helped me to learn how to ride a bike (I remember wobbling around and finally landing in a ditch full of stinging nettles).

In 1959 my brother joined 'Hillstone', a prep school also in Malvern, and I would see him sometimes as I was walking with a school group to our sports fields. He would also be on his way to his school's playing fields; he and his friends looking like wasps in their yellow and black horizontally striped rugby shirts. Heaven forbid, however, that we should ever have been allowed to speak to one another on these occasions!

Our next home was a small dreary residential hotel in Maidenhead, on the Thames in Berkshire, where we stayed for some time. My mother was good at and enjoyed drawing and used to drive from there to nearby villages to sketch them. She loved JMW Turner's paintings, and occasionally visited exhibitions in London. Apart from looking for a house to buy, it is difficult to imagine how she filled her time during our school terms. After this, she rented a flat for a couple of years in Amersham, Buckinghamshire; my father still coming Home on leave to these various places. My parents' relationship wherever we were living, was always difficult and tense.

She was a loving mother, despite everything. It is sad to think of her having to give up the possibility of an independent and creative life on her father's say-so when she was 19, and then, having found a role as a wife and mother, living in lonely isolation in various outposts of the colonies, and sending her first child away to boarding school in England at the age of seven. I suspect it was heartbreaking. When my own children were seven, I used to try and imagine how my mother could have gone through that. It is hard not to think that these experiences must, at the least, have contributed to the psychological problems she experienced later.

There were very few, if any, English or International schools in India then, and it was the norm for colonial families to send their children to boarding schools in the UK. Long leaves (say, six months) were the norm, too, since the journey itself, by sea, both to and from the UK, took so long. This meant that younger more junior colonial staff might not take leave except after three or more years and would therefore not see their children for very long periods. I like to think that if that kind of banishment became necessary nowadays (unlikely, I know), mothers might decide to go with their children, or preferably, both parents might return Home. That would have been unthinkable, however, in any colonial community at that time.

My parents' relationship, at least after my mother's breakdown, was characterised by my father's resigned acceptance of my mother's difficult and irrational behaviour, not that she could help it. He had to live with this full time whenever he returned to the UK, but never raised his voice to her, despite her frequent ranting. These rants, which had gone on for years, included accusations about 'other women' (we could not go out for a meal without my father apparently meeting the eyes of a woman on the other side of the restaurant) and paranoid assertions about everything from her clothes being altered, to her cooking being interfered with by unknown persons gaining access to our flat or house (occasionally known persons such as neighbours were accused to their faces, much to my horror and embarrassment). Perhaps my father had had affairs with other women when he was Out East – I shall never know, but I am fairly sure there were no such affairs in his later life. His regular response to my mother was to heave a huge sigh and say *"have it your own way"*, a sad and depressing situation. As for David and me, nothing was ever talked about, and on occasions when the rants became public – as happened sometimes – in a hotel, walking down a street; we suffered humiliation in silence and put up with it.

In those days very few people discussed mental illness and our family was no exception. Despite not getting to know my father well, because we were so often in different parts of the world, my father did once tell me when I was on my own with him that he and my mother loved each other despite how it seemed. However, when he tried to comfort me on one occasion in front of my mother (I was crying, saying how I hated it when they argued), she accused him of *"currying favour"*. If only my mother's problems had been properly addressed by us, she might have lived a much easier and happier life.

In 1964 my father *"Retired from overseas service and took up a position with H.G. Sanders and Sons Ltd., of which he became Company Secretary two years later and was still so when he died. On return to the UK Glen and his family settled down in the village of Yateley, Surrey, where he could indulge his great keenness for gardening"*.

Finally, in early 1965, a house called 'White Lodge' was bought in Yateley, Hampshire. It had taken my mother well over five years to find a house and I have a feeling that my father issued some sort of ultimatum in the end to get her to take a decision. White Lodge had a large garden and my mother loved gardening and took real pleasure in planting flowers, shrubs and fruit, all of which she did in a small way, taking photos of the plants sometimes, my father doing the majority of the gardening. She also had an excellent eye for colour and design and enjoyed deciding how to decorate and furnish the house. She made wonderful cakes, marvellously decorated, and was a good, if traditional, cook; always using excellent ingredients. Each year in February, when the Seville oranges were in season, she cooked pounds and pounds of delicious marmalades (orange, grapefruit and 'trinity' – orange, grapefruit and lemon) which, because there was so much of it, had to be stored in the attic for the year's consumption. The food she produced was a source of great pride to her.

My mother liked, as she saw it, to be very feminine. She used to take a long time getting dressed and 'putting on her face' or 'titivating' herself. My father always made breakfast before he went to work, while she got dressed. Even back in England, she would still sometimes change for dinner. She generally preferred to use euphemisms rather than call a spade a spade. Later in life, it seemed she was almost incapable of being on time, and was invariably in a great rush, convinced she had a great deal to do. At one time when we were in Yateley, she took a job as a book-keeper in a small company, which was a brave decision since she must have found it very difficult, never previously having had a job, except for the short term one in the café in Knightsbridge. Unfortunately, sadly, and somewhat predictably, it did not work out.

My father worked hard and gardened in his spare time, which he really enjoyed and, of course, gardening meant that he could escape from the house. He was also a prolific reader. He told me that as a child he had been made to listen on Sundays to the Bible being read aloud for hours. He had read all of Dickens amongst other classics, including, of course, Rudyard Kipling, and enjoyed reading the Blackwoods Magazines read by many in the colonies, which he kept. Something my parents both enjoyed, but only very occasionally – usually when David or I put on the record player – was listening to music from the thirties – they both loved Glenn Miller, Satchmo and The Inkspots, to which they had obviously danced in happier times. They also listened to the radio; to some music programmes – my mother loved Chopin piano pieces; to the ten o'clock news; and to 'Round the Horn' which made us all laugh. However, trying to discuss anything serious with my parents was almost impossible since their views were reactionary and entrenched. They never owned a television. There was an open fire in the sitting room and something I loved to do when I was visiting them in Yateley, was to curl up in a chair in front of the coal fire and read.

FROM THE ESK AND THE USK: OUT EAST AND BACK HOME

In March 1969 (the year I married Ian) my father *"Became the Managing Director of Sondes Place Research Institute, and in paying tribute to him we have to say it was indeed tragic that he should not have been spared to see the full results of his determined approach to a very challenging assignment."*

My father developed significant lumps on his arms and shoulders. On visiting Yateley one weekend, my husband Ian, who was a medical student at the time, was asked by my father, what he thought the lumps were. Ian told me what a difficult moment that had been, because my father watched him closely. Ian's impression was that they both suspected the worst. The GP's diagnosis, however, had been that it was gout, since my father had suffered from severe gout most of his adult life. Very sadly, it turned out to be cancer of the lung and my father died aged 57 on 27 August 1971, six weeks after being admitted to the Canadian Red Cross Memorial Hospital, in Taplow, Berkshire. My mother suggested that Ian and I should wait to visit him in hospital until he improved. As a result, we arrived in Taplow just too late. My mother met us at the station and told us, white faced, that he had died that morning. His cremated remains are interred in Plot No. 49, Row 120 at the Park Crematorium, Guildford Road, Aldershot, Hampshire.

* * *

After my father's death, my mother found that she was entirely capable of managing her affairs herself, even though this involved vast amounts of correspondence. She would make copies of her handwritten letters by using carbon paper. She sold 'White Lodge' for considerably less then she had expected, because the ground floor was riddled with damp. She then came to live with Ian and me in Muswell Hill, north London, while she looked for a flat for herself. Unsurprisingly, this took a long time. Finally the situation became difficult and we had to encourage her to go. While she lived with us, she did not offer to help us by babysitting or even cooking supper, but that was just how it was. She rose to the situation eventually, however, and bought herself a flat in Sanderstead, Surrey, just south of Croydon. Her priority was not the sensible option – to be near her daughter and grandchildren in north London – but to find a flat which had sufficient space to take her large pieces of furniture; which by then she no longer needed.

The situation was frustrating from the start, but there was no persuading her to change her priorities. She insisted on being in 'the right type of property.' The flat, of course, turned out to be a bad buy – it was dark; old fashioned; the neighbours were largely unfriendly; and on more than one occasion, her flat was badly flooded by the primitive plumbing upstairs.

The result of this move was that it became difficult to see her often. My brother and his wife and three children were living in Scotland and she managed to visit them once. However, she liked it when she was visited and was thrilled when her grandchildren, Alex and Kate, came with me to visit her – when she would get the giggles with them and positively sparkle over tea and cakes.

Later on in life when she needed active support, I made a four hour return drive across London to visit her which I did every two weeks (just as she had done with her own mother).

My mother suffered the indignities of old age, becoming frail and needing help with the basics of her life, despite being a hugely determined and indeed, obstinate woman. She had a horrible experience when she was mugged at her front door, and after lying injured in the cold, managed with her usual determination, to crawl across the road to a neighbour for help. Later, her back gave way and then she had a fall, breaking her wrist, on both occasions being admitted to hospital.

I made the necessary arrangements for care to be provided at home – short visits three times a day – but could not help feeling guilty and sad that I was unable to do more for her. However, as a single parent with a full time job and two children, I was limited as to what I could do.

Her carers did not 'care' for her and she was admitted to hospital again when I found her at home dehydrated. She told me that the carer had refused to pass her a cup of water, saying that it was not her job. I visited her in hospital and found that she was unable to eat properly because of her broken wrist. She did not recover. My brother also visited her, just before she died on 5 March 2008, aged 87.

Despite both their lives ending sadly, my parents lived such very full, unusual and varied lives, travelling extensively and experiencing so much: if only they had communicated a lot more of all this to their children. . .

CHAPTER 4

Early Times

A Child of the Colonies

VALERIE ANNE

* * *

Tea Gardens

A LARGE AND TERRIFYING ANIMAL was on the other side of the tea bushes. Keeping as quiet and as still as possible, we crouched down and waited, holding our breaths. I was about three and with my ayah, in remote north eastern India. We were tense and scared. The animal moved on.

This is my earliest childhood memory. I asked my mother a few years ago what sort of animal it would have been and she was fairly sure it must have been a wild buffalo. Wild buffalo are about 10ft long and 6ft high; they weigh from 700 to1200 kg and have enormous horns – the largest horns of any animals of this type.[67] No wonder we hid, held our breaths and waited for it to go away, and no wonder it stuck in my memory.

My mother had taken me from Madras to Rangoon by sea as an 8 week old baby in 1946. Later, we took a holiday in Scotland, when my father's parents met their new granddaughter for the first time, after which, we

---

67   Wild buffalo have been listed as Endangered on the IUCN Red List since 1986.

returned to Burma. However, in 1948, soon after our return, we had to flee the country in a hurry. It was after this that we went to live in India and my father, instead of working 'in rice', began to work 'in tea'.

We lived near the borders of Bhutan and Nepal for about two years; my father managing tea estates. I do not remember much about this time, since I was very young, but in the photos I look happy. There are photos of good sized, comfortable looking single storey houses surrounded by rudimentary gardens running into the tea plantations; tea bushes in hedge-like lines; my father and I sitting on the house steps; the two of us on the back of an elephant about to descend a steep slope in the tea gardens, with the mahout[68] sitting in front of me; me crouching down with the mali[69] in the garden having a serious chat – I was told that I spoke Hindustani in those days; I was usually wearing crisp little dresses and the whitest of white socks with Clarks sandals. In one photo, my cotton dungarees even have knife-edged creases down the front. My favourite toy was clearly Peter Panda, who features regularly; there was a very pretty cat, a Siamese; and I owned a tricycle. We made a trip into Darjeeling, where I had a ride on a pony called Peter Pan, and there are a couple of photos of the breathtaking views from there of the Himalayan mountain, Kanchenjunga, third highest mountain in the world.

* * *

The Other Side of the World

We set out from Darjeeling for a holiday in Canada. There is no record of how we reached Bombay, over 1400 miles from Darjeeling, but it seems likely that it was by train. However, nearly a month after leaving the tea gardens, we sailed, in July 1950, from Bombay to London. From there we travelled to Liverpool and took another ship, this time to Montreal. After that, it was a train journey right across Canada to Vancouver, where we met my grandparents and uncle, who were living on Vancouver Island. Quite some journey, especially then.

---

68   Mahout: person who rides and is in charge of an elephant.
69   Mali: gardener

On many occasions, we travelled on ships back and forth from the UK to the Far East, as a result of which, my memories of these journeys are made up of a hotchpotch of various experiences at different times. The things I remember are random: playing deck coits; sailing along the Suez Canal; stopping at Port Said[70] at the northern end of the Canal where the gully gully man came on board and entertained the passengers, particularly the children, with magic tricks – producing eggs from all over the place, including from behind my ear; the ship being surrounded by lots of small boats with Arabs selling leather and other goods – people haggling loudly over what they wanted and throwing money down into the boats, the goods then being hauled up to the deck in baskets.

I have very few memories of Canada: spectacular views of the Rockies from the train, but rather more mundane memories, such as feeding ducks in the park, and my grandfather driving his car round and round and round a roundabout in Victoria, for fun. Had I ever seen ducks in a municipal park before, or even a roundabout? We all went off to Yellow Point, a holiday camp on the western shoreline of Vancouver Island, where we stayed in wooden cabins, went on boat trips and where my father and uncle caught salmon. There are photos showing beautiful unspoilt beaches and woodland.

Three months after this, we returned to the UK to stay with my Scottish grandmother. My mother was due to give birth and two months later, on 18 December 1950, my brother, David Glen, was born there. I was now four and a half. My father's six month leave was coming to an end so he left for his next assignment, which was to work in Bangkok. We followed him later, when David was about three months old. We travelled via Malta, Aden, Colombo and Singapore. We stopped in Singapore for a couple of days, and stayed at the original Seaview Hotel, a luxurious 1900s hotel (now re-vamped) located by the sea.

* * *

---

70   Port Said was a cosmopolitan community. Referring to this, Rudyard Kipling reputedly said "If you truly wish to find someone you have known and who travels, there are two points on the globe you have but to sit and wait, sooner or later your man will come there: the docks of London and Port Said".

ANNE MACDONALD

Bangkok: Snakes, Fireflies, and Flying Elephants

Bangkok swims into focus a little more, since I was there for two years, from the age of almost five to nearly seven. The house we lived in was large and modern for the time, with two storeys, a balcony, a terrace with a small water-lily pond, some attractive shrubs, and a garden with a klong[71] edged by bright orange wildflowers.

I understand that there are over 200 species of snake in Thailand, so maybe it is not surprising that some of the first stories that come to my mind are about snakes. My bedroom was on the left at the top of the stairs and had a high window. For some reason, I was always scared that there might be a snake under my bed and I used to take a running leap at my bed to make sure I was safe – luckily, there never was! However, just before my bedtime, our night watchman would go into the garden and collect fireflies for me in a jam jar. Fireflies have lights that flick on and off in the dark and they would be set free in my bedroom once I was in bed. It was wonderful and I loved it! I can remember it still. Next to the house, and fenced off, was a large field full of rough grass where water buffalos grazed occasionally. One night, when the night watchman was standing close to the fence and the long grass, leaning over to catch fireflies for me, he was bitten by a snake. Pandemonium broke loose and my father immediately drove him to the hospital, where he was treated. What kind of snake bit him, I do not know, but fortunately, he survived, and made a full recovery. Lying in my bed, though, I could hear the servants, whose living quarters were below my window, blaming me. I remember my sense of unfairness and upset about the whole situation.

Coincidentally, we all visited the hospital in Bangkok to see the snake pit which the hospital maintained. We watched as men went into the snake pit, caught one of the snakes (a banded krait) by the head and the tail and then gave it a dose of white fluid via a plastic funnel put into its throat. (Was this some kind of medication, I wonder?). The snakes were presumably the source of the anti-venom that had saved our night watchman. There is still a snake farm in Bangkok, a modern one, which seems to be quite a tourist attraction. It *"was the second snake farm in the world to be built... This is a working snake farm where they breed snakes in order to extract venom for*

---

71   Klong: Artificial canal or natural stream

anti-venom production. There are over 200 species of snakes in Thailand, over 60 of which are venomous, so it's essential for all hospitals to have anti-venom available."[72]

On another occasion, I was playing in the garden and disturbed a snake. I ran away at speed; terrified; convinced it was chasing me. I ran in a zig-zag, as I believed I should. Maybe it came after me for a short distance – maybe it was a cobra – maybe I had been reading too much of the Kipling Rikki Tikki Tavi story – who knows? – but whatever happened, I still feel as if I was chased! Anyway, snakes were around and a significant part of our lives, as, of course, they had been in India.

Another exotic creature in our lives was a chameleon, which we could watch closely as it sat on the climbing shrub growing up the side of the house.

When the rains came, the garden would flood. There is a photo of David (walking by now), standing in the flooded garden, holding hands with me. We are both wearing wellie boots, underpants and vests. Bangkok is hot and humid. Temperatures can reach 35°C and humidity 76%.

From the photos and my memories, our lives certainly seemed fun – we had an inflatable pool on the balcony and friends came to play. Our Thai ayah, Soonee, was always there, as was my mother. Birthday parties were celebrated in style, and there was always the British Embassy Fête – for which we dressed up. We had elephant rides – six children all at once with the mahout at the front, walking round the Embassy drive; we had trips in a rowing boat on the lake – no sign of life jackets; and I was still wearing white socks and sandals. I also went to school in Bangkok, about which I remember nothing – however, there is a photo of me playing an angel in a school nativity play. My father was driven to work each day in his short sleeved shirts, long shorts, long socks, and lace up shoes; and was driven home again each afternoon by his driver.

My parents held occasional lunch parties at home for friends and my mother also played mah-jong with friends.[73] I still have my mother's mah-jong set in its case. I have never learned to play, but the mother of one Kate's Chinese school friends in London, is an expert player and used to play regularly for money.

---

72   Bangkok Snake Farm: http://www.bangkok.com/magazine/snake-farm.htm
73   Mah-jong originated in China: it is played with a set of 144 tiles decorated with Chinese characters and symbols.

I did have one other unpleasant experience in Bangkok, which I remember well. It was decided that I should have my tonsils removed and I was taken to the hospital by my mother. However, she was not allowed to come with me to the ward, and I was duped into going with the nurse by an invitation to 'come and look at the trains'. Standing up on the bed, in a small room, I was able to look out of a window at a not very busy goods yard and I soon realised I had been conned. The tonsillectomy seems to have gone as planned, but I had no visit from my mother for at least three days – she was simply not allowed to visit me. My mother told me many years later, that I refused to speak to her or anyone else for a week afterwards.

As a family, we liked exploring, so we went on trips and visits. We visited temples: the Marble Temple; Wat Arun; Wat Pho; and the Emerald Buddha Wat, all large significant temple complexes. We also took a boat trip along the main river, the Chao Praya, and into the klongs; along the sides of which people were living in houses on stilts. We saw the floating markets on the klongs, too – no tourists then. There is a photo of a Thai Royal Golden Barge on the main river, which must have been quite a sight; these vessels are now housed in a museum.

On one occasion, we visited the docks and watched elephants being loaded on to ships – huge canvas slings were put under their bellies by the mahouts and they were hoisted high into the air, swinging from side to side. An extraordinary sight. They were given sugar cane to keep them happy and calm. It was important, therefore, to stand well back! Once they were on board, the elephants walked freely on the ship, under the care of their mahouts. We also went away for a break to a beach resort, called Saeng Sebai, where my mother and a friend, also with children, rented a bungalow close to the sea. Soonee, our ayah, came too, and my father joined us occasionally.

In 1953, it was time for us to take leave granted to my father after over two years in Thailand, and my parents decided to visit Hong Kong and then to sail home on one of the new Blue Funnel Line ships, the SS Peleus (built in 1949). The Peleus carried 35 passengers and called at Singapore, Penang and Colombo. Our visit to Hong Kong was marked for David and me, by our trip to see the "Several Hundred Year Old Tortoises". Both Hong Kong and Penang[74] had funicular railways, both of which provided us with spec-

---

74 The Penang funicular was built in 1923 and was 87 years old before it was closed for upgrading in 2010.

tacular views. I remember the panoramic view of Hong Kong. In Colombo, David and I are pictured on a beautiful sandy beach at Mt Lavinia. I see there is a luxurious looking "British Colonial theme hotel . . . located on a breathtaking beachfront in *Colombo,* Sri Lanka" called the Mount Lavinia Hotel[75], and I am fairly sure that is where we stayed.

We arrived in Scotland in early summer.

* * *

Montrose, Rationing, and the Coronation

We arrived in Montrose and stayed once more with my grandmother Isabella. We spent most of our time with her, but also toured Scotland for a couple of weeks, in one of those large round Austin cars – an A70. My brother was three and I was seven and due to go to boarding school at the end of our holiday. We stayed in rural hotels, had picnics in beautiful countryside and visited the Trossachs, Loch Ness, and the Highlands.

Most of the holiday, however, was spent in my grandmother's house. It was a semi detached house with two storeys in a quiet residential street. It was built of pink granite and had a sitting room with a coal fire, a dining room where we had all our meals, and a garden. There was a solid fuel range in the kitchen, into the bottom oven of which my grandmother would put a dish of oats and water each evening, which magically (it seemed to me at the time) became porridge by morning. I was sometimes given bread with beef dripping, which I really liked. The baker delivered fresh warm baps to the front doorstep each morning and the milkman delivered orange juice as well as milk. The newly elected Labour Government had taken on an emergency welfare responsibility; it provided milk for babies and orange juice and cod-liver oil for children, to supplement post-war rationing. I was made to have a spoonful of cod liver oil every day.

My mother complained that my grandmother was forever cooking Arbroath smokies for us but no doubt they were plentiful and cheap. I would go with my mother to the butcher, a cheery man with red cheeks, who would always give 'the bonnie wee lass' our ration of meat. We would

---

75   Mount Lavinia Hotel: www.mountlaviniahotel.com/

also visit Woolworths on Montrose's wide High Street, where I spent my pocket money – which was either a farthing, or included a farthing coin – I can't remember.[76]

My grandmother (who I called Grandma) used to make sure I was ensconced by the fireplace in the sitting room each afternoon to hear 'Listen with Mother' on the radio. I listened with enormous pleasure and excitement to 'Alice in Wonderland'. I remember my grandmother standing at the sink in the kitchen and quoting to me from Lewis Carroll, particularly 'The Walrus and the Carpenter', which I enjoyed reading to my children when the time came. There is a photo of David and me making jam tarts at a table in the garden.

My grandmother's house was close to Montrose Basin, a vast area of mud when the tide was out, around which we would occasionally walk (this inland tidal lagoon is now a Nature Reserve). I have strong memories of huge pale sandy beaches on the nearby coast too, where we would sometimes go for the day with friends. There were jelly fish the size of dinner plates on those beaches, which I am ashamed to admit, we cut up with our small spades and threw at each other, until I was hit in the eye. . .

I would visit the family opposite, who had a daughter a little older than me. When the biscuits were passed round, I was invariably told by her father that I must have hollow legs.

The Queen's coronation took place on 2 June 1953 and a television was hired so that we could all watch it. I had not watched a television before, nor seen the queen, nor seen a coronation coach. That day was my birthday, so a very exciting and special day indeed.

* * *

Boarding School

My father left the UK before my mother, who stayed behind to settle me into my new boarding school, Malvern Girls' College in Worcestershire[77].

---

76 4 farthings = 1 penny, 48 farthings = 1 shilling, 960 farthings = £1
77 Malvern Girls' College no longer exists. In 2006, MGC merged with St James's, which prior to that, had merged with The Abbey and Lawnside. The newly merged school was refounded as Malvern St James (MSJ). http://www.malvernstjames.co.uk/

My father *"Returned to the Calcutta organisation and remained until mid-1956"*.

My mother rented a small flat at the top of a large house in Malvern for herself and my brother during this settling in period.

Malvern was and is famed for its connections with the composer Edward Elgar, who lived much of his life around Malvern and of whom there is a statue in the town. It is also famous for its spring waters (about 12 million litres of which were processed per year at Colwall and distributed worldwide until 2010); and its range of beautiful bald hills, which were designated an Area of Outstanding Natural Beauty in 1959. The nine mile spine of the Malverns includes the Worcestershire Beacon (1,395 ft) and the Herefordshire Beacon (1,109 ft), the latter surrounded by Iron Age earthworks known as the British Camp. The main town of Great Malvern, with its 11th century Priory, is built on a very steep slope.

In the 19th century Malvern's spring waters, which became widely known for their health-giving properties, led to Malvern developing as a spa town. Hydrotherapy clinics were set up there in the middle of the century and by 1855 there were 95 hotels and boarding houses! By 1865, over a quarter of the town's 800 houses were boarding and lodging houses.[78]

By the end of the 19th century, however, the spa industry collapsed in Malvern, which left many hotels no longer viable. These buildings were then acquired for use as private boarding schools, and education became the basis of the town's economy. By 1865, the town had 17 single-gender private schools, increasing to 25 by 1885. Malvern Girls' College (MGC) was founded in 1893 and in 1919 acquired the Imperial Hotel, the largest building in Malvern, situated conveniently (for all those boarders with their trunks), very close to the railway station.

I clearly remember being left at boarding school by my parents. I was seven years old. I was upset, despite not really understanding how long it would be before I saw my parents again. At that stage of my father's employment, leave was usually granted every three years, and I have some recollection of realising this. However, the fact that my mother and brother were living in Malvern for the first five months of my schooling, and I would have seen them occasionally and spent the first Christmas holidays with them, must have made a significant difference. There are photos of

---

78 Hembry, Phyllis May: *British spas from 1815 to the present* (1997)

the Malvern Hills covered in snow and my small brother standing in thick snow in the garden of the flat my mother had rented.

Leaving me at boarding school, and having made arrangements as to where I would spend my holidays – with appointed guardians – my mother sailed from Liverpool to Calcutta with my brother, now 3, on 15 February 1954.

It was two years later, in mid-1956, that my parents and my brother left Calcutta and went to live in Iraq, and it was after this, that my mother was sent back to England because she was unwell. She did not return to Baghdad, and although I do not know how long my mother's treatment lasted, nor when my father flew back to the UK with my brother, it must indeed have been about three years until I saw my parents again.

* * *

Parkfield: Bad and Good Times

My first experience of boarding school was at Parkfield – the junior section of 'MGC'. Parkfield was a large detached Victorian house (probably one of those buildings mentioned earlier, originally built as a hotel). It had an extension, and was surrounded by a large garden. Not only did the school look Victorian, but, as I was soon to find out, it was run along strict Victorian lines. The regime was harsh in many ways, but there were some good times, too.

Life was tough at Parkfield and many girls suffered from homesickness. One of my friends would cry in bed every night and sadly for her, also had a bad time in the holidays with her guardians. She was very unhappy.

We slept in dormitories. In the mornings, we had to strip back our beds and roll the covers up into a sausage at the foot of the bed. The beds had to look neat and were inspected at this stage. After breakfast, we had to make our beds with strict military precision – with hospital corners – and the beds were inspected again. We also had to visit the matrons in the dispensary each morning, to declare whether we had "been" (ie opened our bowels) or not the day before. If not, we were given a spoonful of syrup of figs. Syrup of figs was rather popular though, which must have resulted in record numbers of constipated children being recorded in the books! One of the worst things we had to contend with, however, was that, once in bed, we were absolutely not allowed to get up to go to the lavatory. This rule resulted in girls being so terrified of getting caught out of bed (the corridors were patrolled) that I remember cases of girls deciding to urinate in their beds rather than risk the wrath of a matron.

I do not remember having a bath at Parkfield, but presumably we did have them, in which case, as in the middle school, these would have been rationed on a strict rota. Outside the dormitories, there were sets of pegs, on which were hung laundry bags. We wore white underpants, called linings, and over these, wore another pair of large maroon or navy cotton pants with a pocket. The number of times we had to put our linings and liberty bodices[79] (compulsory wear) into these bags was also rationed – it was certainly not every day and I think maybe twice a week! Our uniform, which we took to school in our personal trunks at the beginning of each term, was set out in a detailed list – 3 pairs of this, 2 pairs of that. It was compulsory to have everything on the list. We wore skirts held up by braces, and long sleeved shirts and ties; there were double breasted overcoats and round wide brimmed maroon felt hats.

Before meals we each had to show our hands – the backs and palms, for inspection by the deputy matron, and had to ask "Please may I go?" We sat at medium sized tables, with a member of staff at the head of each one. It

---

79   Liberty bodice: a cross between a corset and a vest – thick, sleeveless, with reinforced cotton seams rather than bone. The Spring 2014 issue of the 'Liberty' (Liberty, the National Council for Civil Liberties) newsletter celebrated the 80th anniversary of Liberty. It "approached some of the greatest writers and liberal thinkers of the day and asked them to write a piece on the idea of 'Liberty'. Esther Freud wrote a piece entitled 'Liberty': "When my mother was young she used to wear a Liberty Bodice. It was tight and itchy and was to be worn whatever the weather, whatever her complaints. She was at a convent, and the idea was that somehow the Liberty Bodice would keep her safe, and chaste. The Emancipation Bodice some called it, a reminder it had been designed to liberate women from the heavily boned and firmly laced corsets that had once been in fashion. But my mother didn't want to be safe, or chaste. It was the tail end of the 1950s and she wanted to escape. As soon as she could she left her convent, left Ireland, left her family. Not long after she met my father in a club in Soho and by the time she was twenty she had two children, a name she'd changed herself, and her grandmother's wedding ring, to ward off hostility. But one afternoon as she waited at a bus stop with her toddler and a new baby in a pram, she was spotted by an acquaintance of her parents. Within a week she had a letter. 'You've made your bed and now you must lie on it.' But at least they didn't send anyone from the church to take away her babies, or lock her away with the Magdalena Sisters, as she'd feared. And she was free, to make her bed, to lie on it, or if she chose – to take her Liberty Bodice, or her bra for that matter, and throw it on the fire."

goes without saying that the food was not haute cuisine; the most horrible dish to my recollection, was sweet sago pudding for dessert – frogspawn, we called it. We took great delight in the occasion when the deputy matron's lack of attention resulted in her inadvertently pouring a jug of water over her plate of food rather than gravy. This same woman was mercilessly parodied – she had a very large bosom and had a habit of keeping one arm underneath it and frequently shifting said bosom upwards.

An unpleasant incident involved my oldest friend Maggie, who, like me, joined Parkfield when she was seven. I cannot remember her crime, but she was made, by matron, to stand on the top table platform in the dining hall, with her back against the wall, facing all the girls. This was to humiliate her. I remember her fury and the fact that, despite everything, she was unrepentant. Matron tried to restrain her and she bit matron's arm! We must have been a handful, but we did not deserve some of the teachers and matrons who were there.

Our punishments were various, depending on the misdemeanour. A serious punishment was to be made to sit for a certain length of time on one of the sofas near the headmistress' office. The blue sofa was farthest away from her office, but the pink one was right next to it. If you were lucky, you could get away unseen if you had been told to sit on the blue sofa, but there was no escape if you were on the pink one. Although there was no question of corporal punishment, a telling off from the head and some further punishment was sufficiently scary to mean that anyone sitting on the pink sofa was nervous and fearful. The most extreme punishment I remember was my whole dormitory being made to get up in the evening, after we had gone to bed; roll back our beds as if it were morning; get dressed; and then run circuits round the perimeter of the garden until the light was fading and we were exhausted. We then had to remake our beds before finally being allowed to sleep.

We went out for walks sometimes, when we had to walk in pairs in a 'crocodile'. When we needed to cross a road, we were all told (in military fashion) to turn and face the road. Two lines of girls then had to shuffle left and right to create the right distance between us so that 'daylight' could be seen between the two lines of girls. The command 'Over' was then given and we marched to the other side of the road, where we faced front and walked off again in our pairs. It was efficient and safe, but we were not in the army.

As a child, I almost never looked unwell (even if I was) because I had pink cheeks and generally looked fine. One year, however, Parkfield was hit by a flu epidemic, when almost all the girls were confined to bed for some time. It must have been difficult for the staff. I was very unwell and was selected with one other child to give blood samples to be sent away – somewhere? – for analysis. Despite not wanting to eat, we were served with what was considered the right food for the bed-ridden – steamed fish. I can see it now – glistening white coarse fish with small black flecks of skin. It was incredibly off-putting and I refused it, on the grounds that I was not hungry and could not eat it. Ridiculously, however, I was forced to eat it – with, I am glad to say, the inevitable consequences, which of course, created even more work for the staff.

There were some positives, though. Playing in the garden was fun – there were a couple of seesaws, but better still, there were several very large rhododendron bushes in which we made 'rooms' where we played – setting up shops to sell our mud pies decorated with daisies. In the summer we were allowed to take our rugs out into the garden, and in the autumn we made large piles of fallen leaves – into which we took flying leaps. There was an animal house in which children could keep their pets – snakes, hamsters, and mice. I did not have a pet, but remember there being a huge storm once, with thunder and lightning, and for some reason running at top speed in the pouring rain to the animal house, to see if the animals were alright. There was also a kitchen garden, and I remember very clearly hiding between the rows of bushes, pinching gooseberries.

Indoors, there were also activities I enjoyed. There was a huge craze for playing jacks (knucklebones). Most of us would sit in pairs on the floor to play. After a while we started to wear out the carpets and were provided with squares of carpet to play on. The game required some skill, but mostly practice, and was fun. Best of all, we were read to in a group on Sunday evenings – the novel 'The Secret Garden' has stayed with me from those times.

* * *

Hateful Hatley

At the age of about ten, I was moved from the relative civilisation of Parkfield to the next section of the school, in another large building, this one called Hatley. Here, the staff were not only uncaring and ignorant of how to look after and be responsible for children, but some were vicious and in at least one case, caused real harm to one of us. It was them versus us.

In the dormitories, each bed, just as in a hospital, had a curtain round it, running on a rail; we each had a small chest of drawers and were provided with a bowl for washing and an enamelled jug in which we could collect warm water. After strip washes (and I suppose we had baths, but I do not remember having one while I was there) we had to empty our bowls of dirty water into buckets which whoever was on the rota, had to carry downstairs and empty. There was the odd occasion when a girl spilled some or all of the contents of a bucket – once, all the way down the stairs – and immediate punishment would follow. If we were sick, we had to clear up our own vomit. . . However, it goes without saying that we each had to kneel by our beds each evening before bedtime, to say our prayers.

I do not remember any learning experiences either at Parkfield or at Hatley, although we must have had lessons. That, in itself, speaks volumes. I also do not remember receiving any comfort or support, either. What I do remember was the total lack of caring of the girls by the staff. The memory that most stands out, because the incident was so shocking, concerns a girl who was clearly (even to us) very unwell – to the extent that, finally, she was so weak she could not physically get herself out of bed in the morning and was bullied and shouted at by the matron until she managed (just) to push her bedclothes back. One morning, she managed, somehow, to get to morning assembly. (Morning assemblies were taken by the Head and we had to sing hymns and pray.) The girl managed to kneel down with the rest of us but was unable to get up again. The Head, standing on the platform and in front of all of us (small, demonic and spitting fury) shouted at her and bullied her to get up. We were not allowed to help. The girl had to crawl along the floor to the radiator on the wall and use this to haul herself up to a standing position. She was eventually diagnosed with polio and was not at school for some time afterwards. Amazingly, the girl returned later, to attend middle school, so either her parents had not been told how she had been treated, or did not care. She had been disabled by the polio and now had one leg shorter than the other and a hump on her back. This event so shocked me, I never forgot it and even now, I remember the girl's name.

Hatley was always cold – we were constantly hugging radiators or sitting against them – and frequently told not to do so because we would apparently get piles. The atmosphere in the school was more like how I imagine a girls' remand centre of the time might have been – not remotely like an expensive fee paying school. There were quite a few of us whose parents were not in the country, including Maggie, and for some of us, Hatley made life much harder than it needed to be. Some of us managed to tough it out, but for others, it caused great unhappiness.

We did have one or two triumphs over the staff. On one occasion, we wickedly put a mixture of ketchup and mustard on the seat of matron's dining chair before a meal. At the end of each meal, it was the habit of staff to file out of the dining hall first, before the girls, and matron wore a starched white uniform. The fact that her backside was covered in horrible smears without her knowledge, caused great satisfaction and hilarity. No-one owned up to the prank.

I can only remember two things that I even vaguely enjoyed doing while I was at Hatley: playing netball in the courts and playing bolo bat[80] in the playground.

* * *

Teenagers at Summerside

Middle school at MGC comprised seven medium sized houses full of girls in the fourth and fifth forms. The house I was in was called Summerside. I must have been about 13. We were growing up and things were becoming slightly more normal. Life was becoming slightly less prison-like, and we began to recognise life outside our houses. We were allowed to walk in small groups on our own to the main school building, where we had lessons and did sports, and we began to get to know the town of Malvern – in particular the pervasive smell of damp autumn leaves and the fact that everything was on a steep slope. Malvern (at least to us) was a town of schools, retired people and the hills. One of the schools was for boys only, but we were forbidden absolutely to speak to any of them.

On Sundays we were allowed to wear 'mufti' – 'home' – clothes. My clothes were always horrible as far as I was concerned – bought from Daniel Neal, the school outfitters, at the same time as items of uniform were

---

80 Bolo bat: a game played by hitting a small rubber ball attached to an elastic band about 3ft long, with a bat. The ball springs back and can be hit again.

bought – and I really disliked them. Some girls were beginning to be aware of fashion and one even brought in black patent leather 'winkle-picker' shoes. We often went to sleep at night with incredibly uncomfortable rollers in our hair and the next morning would back-comb our hair into tangled bee-hives. In the summer, it became the rage to wear stiff petticoats to make our cotton school dresses stick out. In order to make the petticoats stiff, we rinsed them in gelatine and hung them on the line to dry.

I do remember having baths at middle school. There was a rota and the matron would bang on the bathroom doors to make sure it was you in there and that you had not swapped your bathing slot with someone else, to get out of bathing!

At Summerside, we were allowed to keep our own supplies of butter, jams and spreads and were each allocated a locker in which to put them. We could also bring in sweets, but they had to be put in special sweet tins which were in a locked cupboard. Twice a week, we were allowed a weighed amount of these sweets. We had to queue, and in front of the deputy matron, make a selection from our tins and put them on the scales. Obviously, marshmallows were particularly popular.

We sat at long tables for meals, and strict table manners were enforced. We were not allowed to ask for anything but, subtly, as it were, had to ask our neighbours if they would like the salt, water, or whatever it was we wanted. Conversation about the 'Three 'Ds' – dirt, disease and diet – was banned!

We played a lot of sport, and although I did not enjoy hockey very much, I did enjoy lacrosse, although only managing to get into the school's 3rd team. In the summer, we played tennis and rounders and also had swimming lessons. After games, we would go back to our houses for tea. At Summerside, we were supplied with huge mounds of white sliced bread, which we spread thickly with our butter and covered in layers of white sugar. We were allowed to order our favourite dessert for our birthdays and on the whole, our food could have been worse; although I believe the food varied considerably between houses.

We also had lockers in which we kept our personal belongings. I remember a copy of 'Lady Chatterley's Lover' secretly doing the rounds. On Sundays, we were sometimes allowed to listen to records. 'Rock Around the Clock' had been popular previously, but by now Cliff Richard's 'Living Doll' was a favourite.

We were allowed only three 'exeats' per term, in other words, three weekends on which we could go out with parents, guardians or friends.

Those, like me, whose parents were not around, were sometimes invited out by friends. However, if we were to go out with a friend rather than our parents, then one day of the weekend counted as one whole exeat. How extraordinary. I have no idea why or how this rule came into force, but it does seem strange to punish even further, those whose parents were on the other side of the world. I did spend some excellent exeats with friends, however – there was a friend who lived in Pershore, whose modern house had a swimming pool in the garden. Her parents would generously invite a group of girls to join her at home in the summer term, where we ate strawberries and had a lot of fun in the pool. My guardian also took me out sometimes (just for one day) and on one occasion, I took two friends with me, which was particularly nice for me.

Later, once my mother had returned to England and my brother was at school in Malvern (from 1959), she (and sometimes my father, too, if he were on leave) would take David and I out on weekends. They would stay in a hotel in Malvern and we would go sightseeing by car and be treated to picnics and cream teas. We would travel significant distances to visit Cotswold villages, country houses, and even the Slimbridge Wildfowl Trust. My parents seemed to have no knowledge of what my schooling was like – I think they assumed that since they were paying fees for us to go to 'good' schools, everything must be fine. When I was older, I never really explained to my mother what life had been like at MGC – it seemed harsh to do so, since a great deal of hard earned money had been spent, and they had done what they thought was best for us.

I was apparently a rebellious girl (although I have no recollection of any particular misdemeanours at this stage). I was once taken into the Headmistress' room at Summerside and told by her that I would make a great leader *'if only I would lead people in the right direction'*. Maggie had been put into a different middle school house to me – on the other side of the road – and so we did not see each other very much at this stage, until, of course, we were both moved up into 'School House' in the main senior school building, and were allowed to be in a dormitory for just the two of us. . .

* * *

ANNE MACDONALD

St Trinian's at School House

There we were – apparently the two naughtiest girls in the school, about 16 years old and sharing a two-bed dormitory! Brilliant!

As far as we were concerned, the aim of MGC was to turn out girls who would go on to get married, wear twin-sets and pearls, walk the corgi, and do nothing at all unusual. Conformity was everything. Those who were particularly bright and worked hard would get to a good university regardless almost of the teaching. Most of the rest of us, however, were on a conveyor belt, being trained to become middle-class 'ladies'. Maggie and I were not good at conforming. We both hated school – its endless petty rules and the way we were treated. As a result, the school threatened to expel us more than once. It was no coincidence, I suspect, that the parents of the two naughtiest girls in the school had lived abroad and away from their children, for years on end. However, we managed to have a little fun here and there.

Our room was high up in the enormous building that was the main school (the old Imperial Hotel)[81], overlooking the main quadrangle at the back of the building. Our first innovation was to lift several of the floorboards under the beds. Here we stored a record player, supplies of cake, biscuits and other food, and the cigarettes which we smoked out of the window. We were never caught with any of these! One of our favourite records at the time, was the song "Ag Pleez Deddy" a South African song written in 1961, with the chorus 'Popcorn, chewing gum, peanuts and bubblegum' which Maggie must have been sent from Africa, where her parents were living. I cannot imagine how we were not overheard playing this. My mother, who by this time was living in England, was an ace cake maker and decorator, and supplied me with a beautifully decorated birthday cake – conveniently presented in a tin for safe-keeping under the floor.

Neither Maggie nor I worked hard. We got by. In some subjects, there were good teachers – in English, for example – but in others, they were either clever but hopeless teachers – for example in maths, or they were obsessed by matters completely unrelated to teaching, such as whether you were wearing your liberty bodice in class (if not, you were apparently causing

---

81 MGC:https://www.google.com/search?site=imghp&tbm=isch&source=hp&biw=1004&bih=500&q=malvern+girls+college&oq=malvern+gir&gs_l=img.1.0.0j0i24l9.172357.180053.2.181641.17.8.9.0.0.0.156.768.5j3.8.0....0...1ac.1.36.img..4.24.1993.m_O9hVemZW4

the classroom to smell). Many of the teachers conformed to a particular image: mostly, they had very short hair (one wore her hair in a bun) and wore double breasted, often pin-striped suits, bullet-proof stockings and laced-up brogues. One teacher, with the name Williams, spent a lot of time and energy walking along the long corridors flapping her hand at us and calling out repeatedly 'keep to the left' to ensure that there was a two-way system in the corridors (she taught Latin and we nicknamed her Latin Willy); another would walk up the stairs behind us and if she spied a petticoat showing beneath the hemline of a skirt, would (in apparent outrage) pull the petticoat down sharply and demand that the girl go to her room and take the petticoat off. One of the deputy heads of school, hair tied back in a bun, would march around school, prowling around corridors, spectacles on, hands clasped behind her back and head thrust forward, on the lookout for anything untoward. We named her The Brigadier.

We had divisions for subjects and if you were considered no good at a subject, you were simply put into the domestic science class. I was good at maths initially, and in Division 1. However, we had a teacher who was completely unable to communicate her subject and a number of people were soon moved down into Division 2. I just managed to get by for a while (by copying other people's homework) until fairly rapidly, I reached a point where I had no understanding of the subject at all. Realising that this would be exposed when it came to taking 'O' levels, I refused to take the exam. Later on in life, I was to discover that I was not entirely useless at maths. I was put in Division 4 for French and had an unusual teacher who did things differently. She decided that we would study Anouilh's play 'Antigone', based on Sophocles' play; but that we would study it in French, which I certainly enjoyed and found interesting. I had piano lessons for some time and my teacher used to rap me across the knuckles when I made a mistake. I was playing grade 5 pieces, mostly by ear, but firstly I refused to take exams and then I gave up, which I later regretted.

Our punishments were generally meted out in the form of supervised detentions and I was given many of those. We either sat and wrote lines, or had to write essays, the main point being that we were deprived of our free time.

There were some, but not many, positive aspects to life in School House. The Malvern Hills became an escape from school: we were allowed to go on walks in groups of four and went as far up and along the hills as we liked. On one occasion, we walked all the way along the ridge to the other side of the British Camp. It was freedom, and I grew to love the hills. The school occasionally organised concerts in which well known musicians played. I enjoyed these events and remember some of them well. Peter Katin played Chopin to us and Leon Goossens, the oboe player, performed on another occasion. In addition, we were taken on a couple of outings to the theatre at Stratford. We were studying Shakespeare's King Lear and were taken to see the now famous 'revolutionary' Peter Brook production in 1962 with Paul Schofield and Alec McCowan. It was very avant garde at the time, with brilliant direction and acting and a minimalist set. It made a huge impression on me.

Following this, in 1963, as a 17th birthday treat, my mother took me to the Old Vic to see Laurence Olivier, performing with Michael Redgrave and Joan Plowright, in Chekhov's play 'Uncle Vanya'. The Old Vic had recently become the home of the National Theatre. Included in the treat, was a very grown-up and delicious meal at 'Overtons', a smart well-known fish restaurant, which may well be quite different now, but still exists.

Despite these glimpses of civilisation, there is no doubt that a lot of girls at MGC hated their time there and resented the way we were treated. This manifested itself in the events of one April Fools' eve, when a group of us excelled ourselves in St Trinian's mode. We not only hauled knickers up on to the school flagpole; we made a guy and climbed up on the science block roof where we displayed it; we made a cat's cradle across the bedroom door of the Deputy Head; and glued all the breakfast cutlery to the tables in the dining hall. Our crowning achievement, however, was turning off the main electricity supply to the whole enormous building. We did this by taking a lacrosse stick down to the basement, poking it through the bars of the cage protecting the main electricity switch, and flicking the switch to 'off'. Chaos ensued.

Unfortunately, one of the girls in our group had epilepsy and (presumably) the excitement of the night's activities caused her to fit. She was taken to hospital and recovered, but we were all quite shocked.

After staff had managed to cope with the fact that they could not ring the corridor bells to wake everyone up, all the girls in the building assembled in the dining hall (coping with the cutlery situation) and were given a talking to by one of the Deputy Heads, who emphasised how serious and dangerous our actions had been, and used our friend's epilepsy attack not only to blame us, but to make us feel as guilty as possible. We were told to go into the gym to hear how we were to be punished. When we got there, those who had been involved in the events of the night were asked to put up their hands. The outcome of this was astonishing – every single girl bar one (and the majority had not been involved), put up their hands. Such solidarity! There was only one thing staff could do and that was to punish us all. We all traipsed off to various classrooms where we had to write essays on how dangerously we had behaved, and how we would never do such a thing again.

In 2013, Maggie and I returned to Malvern for a few days, where we visited the RHS Spring Garden Show and took a few trips down memory lane. We visited the main school, which although in the same building, has changed considerably since the school became Malvern St James. We talked to a teacher we came across, who was surprised at some of our stories of our time there and assured us that nothing like that had occurred during his time at the school! A new accommodation block had been built for boarders and Summerside was empty and crumbling. Maggie's middle school house, Ryall, although showing some signs of occupation, looked as if it was falling into disuse. We explored the town, visited the ancient and beautiful Priory (founded in 1085) where we used to go for Matins every Sunday morning, and, best of all, climbed the Beacon, where a gale was blowing at the top and we could hardly stand up. The view was still huge and magnificent.

* * *

Homme House – another country

In contrast to the restricted regime at school, I enjoyed wonderful holidays with my appointed guardians, Commander Kyrle and Mrs Agnes Pope, at their large country house and estate in the village of Much Marcle in Herefordshire. They had had three sons of their own, one of whom had died and two of whom were grown up, and later became high-ranking naval officers. Times must have been difficult for the Popes financially, with the expenses of a large estate, and I always assumed that this was why they took on the guardianship of girls from MGC. There were about five of us of varying ages when I arrived. I was the youngest and the last girl they took, so after not too long, there were only two of us and latterly, just me. The Popes were recommended to my parents, who did not know them previously. I was very lucky indeed, therefore, that it worked out so well. Much Marcle is about 13 miles from Malvern, but in spirit it was another country.

The estate was about 200 acres. It consisted of a large area of parkland with a path leading through it to the small church in the village. The park included a couple of ponds and the land was let out to a farmer, who grazed his cattle there. There was a long steep drive leading up from the lodge house, on the road between Much Marcle and Dymock. At one side of the house there was a large lawn with banks leading up to woodland and on the other side, through a castellated older building with a tower, an archway led to a large yard and outbuildings and the back entrance. Behind the house was a large walled garden where lots of fruit and vegetables were grown; a smaller walled rose garden; and barns which housed hens. Around this, there was more land and woodland. At the top of the walled garden was an ancient summer house which we were always told was one of a series of lookout points running across the Welsh Marches, although this may have been a little fanciful.

> *"The origins of the Homme House Estate date back to the 14th century, when it was owned by the Mortimer family. The Mortimers rose to fame through Roger Mortimer's affair with Isabella, wife of Edward II, who was imprisoned in Berkeley Castle and murdered there in 1327. The remains of Mortimers Castle lie on the edge of the Estate, adjacent to St. Bartholomew's Church.*
>
> *In the mid-15th century the Estate became the property of the crown before later being bought in 1574 by Thomas Kyrle – great-great uncle of John Kyrle, 'Man of Ross' – and stretched from Ross-on-Wye to Ledbury. The ownership is traceable thereafter through the same family links to this day.*
>
> *The origins of the current house date back to the early 1500s, when a large stone house stood on the current site. The tower is the only surviving wing and is the oldest part of the current building, dating from this period. The Kyrles were part of an influential county-wide extended family; Thomas's son and heir Sir John was created a baronet by Charles I in 1627 and was twice High Sheriff of Herefordshire. He rebuilt the house in the early 17th century after a major fire; this is commemorated by the cartouche above the front door, which bears the date of 1623 and the marital coat of arms of his parents, Thomas Kyrle and his wife Frances, daughter of John Knotsford of Malvern, Worcestershire.*

> *The house was substantially altered in the middle of the 19th century including refacing with its current red brick and stone dressings. The large bay window was an addition from that time.*
>
> *Homme House was used as a hospital during World War II; documents on display from H M The Queen and the Red Cross acknowledge the house's wartime use.*
>
> *The house is now a Grade II listed building, surrounded by an extensive garden, 100 acres of historic parkland said to have been landscaped by Capability Brown (1715-1783), and 80 acres of woodland. The house was renovated in 2001 by the present owners.*
>
> *A recently restored Grade 1 listed Summerhouse stands at the top of the two acre Walled Garden with breathtaking views of the Malvern Hills and the Cotswolds beyond.*
>
> *Architectural and archaeological analysis has concluded that the Summerhouse may be one of the most important buildings of its date and type in the region and is also of national significance. It was built very early in the 18th century, if not towards the end of the 17th century, and represents a very early example of a Gothick garden building, pre-dating Miller's work at Radway Grange in the late-1740s or Walpole's work at Strawberry Hill. The date and significance of the lantern at the apex of the roof, however, remain a delightful mystery.*
>
> *The two-storey building was constructed in a single phase and subsequently remodelled only slightly. The status and comfort of its two rooms and the spacious stair access to them suggests that it was built as a fashionable garden building for the owners of the house. It would offer suitable accommodation for both winter and summer use, a little removed from the main house and yet conveniently still within the walled garden, and may have been used as a space for 'peaceful bucolic contemplation'."*

Because Homme House is now used as a wedding venue, the above potted history and many photographs are provided on its website.[82]

The Popes provided us with a welcoming, friendly and relaxed environment in which to enjoy our holidays, as a result of which we behaved well and were happy. There were rules, but sensible ones. We called them 'Commander' and 'Mrs Pope' and they were kind to us. I must have lived

---

82   Homme House: http://www.hommehouse.co.uk/

there in the holidays for about five years and look back on that time with great affection.

When I first arrived, I was the youngest and the older girls spoiled me. The girl nearest to me in age was Merrilyn, who was only a couple of years older and we explored the great outdoors together. There were three dogs and five cats in the household, some of the cats living in the barns, and we were fond of them all. There were also two magnificent cart horses in the field immediately in front of the house and a pig sty at the back, well away from the house. That area of Herefordshire is famous for its daffodils and the grounds of Homme provided banks and banks of them in the spring. Merrilyn and I would pick bunches of them to sell by the roadside. I remember making a small fire outside, collecting elderberries and trying to make jam (with no sugar) and offering round my horrible concoction. I also remember skinning a dead mole and trying, somewhat unsuccessfully, to preserve its skin with salt. We spent a great deal of time outdoors and a large gong was beaten when meals were ready, to summon us from wherever we were. The old tower at the top of the walled garden, mentioned in the history above and now refurbished, was a mysterious place to us. We were excited to be allowed to camp out there overnight a couple of times during the summer. There was quite a view from the upper floor.

We all ate in a dining room of our own on the ground floor, not far from the enormous high-ceilinged kitchen, with its giant ranges and cats sitting up on high shelves above them, keeping warm. There was a big larder and also a utility room leading to the back door, in which game would sometimes be hung. A woman who lived in the village, came to the house each day to cook for us all. On special occasions we ate in the Library with our guardians and were allowed a glass of local perry – a cider-like drink but made with pears, produced in the village by Westons Cider[83], which is still there, and which Alex, Kate and I visited when we were on holiday once. They produce a range of the most delicious ciders of differing ages.

We had our own sitting room at the very top of the house, where among other things, we had a record player. I bought my first record and played it there – Perry Como singing *'Magic Moments'*. I had a bedroom of my own which was next door to the room of a very elderly relative of the Popes – Uncle Ernle. Someone would read aloud to him in the evenings

---

83 Westons Cider: http://www.westons-cider.co.uk/

and I would fall asleep hearing unending murmurings through the wall. My worries about what might be underneath my bed had stayed with me. I had no bedside light and continued to do the habitual running leap to get 'safely' into bed.

There was a friendly woman who lived in the house, looked after us and helped with the housework. She not only told me, but showed me, how to get rid of chilblains on your toes by putting them into a potty of your own urine! There was also a couple who lived in the castle section of the house – he worked on the estate and she was the housekeeper.

Once I became the last girl at Homme, I continued to enjoy myself, since I made two friends in the village – Janet and Joyce – both about my age. I had a bicycle which I used to ride through the park to the church, on the other side of which was the village, and I used to visit them occasionally. However, I had to take my courage in both hands to do this since the park was home to a number of bullocks. When our cook walked through the park, she was in the habit of giving the bullocks the odd apple, which meant that they were always interested in visitors. The way to deal with this, I found, was to whistle loudly and cycle as fast as I could. However, on one occasion when the bullocks followed me, I only just reached the church gate in time. I threw my bike over the gate and climbed over to safety in the nick of time, getting quite a fright.

There was an inflatable boat which we used on the ponds. With the older girls, we also swam in the ponds, which was exciting. The water was cold and eels lived in the ponds – we were sure we felt them around our feet! We used the boat as a paddling pool too when it was hot.

Commander kept hens and each year many tiny chicks were reared in a heated annexe to the house, where I visited them. I also used to go round the barns with Commander to collect the eggs. He would take these and various vegetables to the nearby small market town of Newent to sell, and I sometimes went with him in his small van.

There was a cattle market at Ross-on-Wye and we were taken to watch the auctioneering. It was interesting – the atmosphere was busy and noisy. Ross became particularly memorable because I was taken to the cinema there and saw my first film, a thriller, which terrified me. I also went to a children's party, where we played hide-and-seek, which also scared me because the house was full of large dark rooms with huge cupboards. We even went to Worcester on one occasion, biking to Ledbury and then taking the train, to see the film – 'Rock-Around the Clock' – a classic of the time.

A highlight of the year was when the local hunt had its 'meet' at Homme. The drive would be filled with horses, hunters and their hounds, and as the youngest member of the household, I was asked to help with taking the stirrup cup round to all the riders. Once the hunt had set off, we would congregate in the large drawing room facing the park and with the huge fire lit, would watch from the windows as the whole hunt – fox in front – streamed across the park. It was a marvellous sight.[84]

The other honour I was given, as the youngest, was being asked to ring the bell in the tower on New Year's Eve, to ring in the New Year. It was quite an experience, pulling the rope in the tower with Commander and then re-joining everyone in the large drawing room after midnight.

I do not know in which year Mrs Pope died, but it must have roughly coincided with the time that I stopped spending holidays at Homme, when I was about 14. Commander gave me, as a memento, a silver and garnet necklace which had belonged to Mrs Pope. I think that those five years spent with the Popes were an excellent antidote to school and probably kept me relatively sane.

Much later, on one of our holidays, I took Alex and Kate to stay in a small house I rented in a village in Herefordshire. We had a great holiday and among the many things we did, we visited Ross cattle market and Weston's cider factory in Much Marcle. We also drove up the drive of Homme House so that I could show them where I had lived. Despite explaining to the man who came out of the house (one of Commander's sons, I think, now quite elderly) he was unwelcoming, sadly, so we left. Much Marcle, a lovely village with its 13th century church, ancient (1500 year old) yew tree and black and white houses, came to the forefront of news in the early 1990s as the original home of the serial killer Fred West. I read that he was born in 1941 (five years older than me) and was one of six children. Fortunately, my friends from the village were girls. . .

* * *

---

84   Fox hunting looks rather different to me now.

What next?

The last place in which we lived before my parents finally bought a house, was a comfortable three bedroomed rented flat on the ground floor of a house in Amersham, Buckinghamshire.

Having left school in 1963 with an undistinguished academic record, I returned to living with my mother in this flat, with no idea of what to do next. My brother was at boarding school in Sherborne, Dorset and I had no friends anywhere nearby and was lonely and fed up. I would gaze out of the window at the young male journalists who lived upstairs and had a red sports car – but was never allowed to make contact. Otherwise I would occasionally go for walks in the woods on my own or go shopping with my mother. One advantage of having all this free time, however, was that I spent almost all my time reading. I had no guidance as to what might be a good read, but I was a frequent visitor at the local library where I picked anything and everything that took my fancy. We had no television at home, and I read and read.

Discussions did take place as to what I should do next and somehow or other a decision was taken that I should go to secretarial college. My parents were opposed to the idea of my going to London, which they thought of as a city of iniquity; and so it was that I went to the Oxford & County Secretarial College in Oxford.

Valerie Anne Gaudie, 6 months, Bassein, Burma

Valerie Anne Gaudie on 'Peter Pan' in Darjeeling, India

Anne with the mali (the gardener). Tea Gardens, India

*Anne, 'Pussy' and Kamalu,
Tea Gardens, India*

*Anne with her ayah, cooling off.
Tea Gardens, India*

*Elephant ride. Anne with her Father, Glen.
Tea Gardens, India*

Valerie & Glen's house in Bangkok, Thailand. Children's party.

Valerie Anne with new brother David Glen (born 1950 in Scotland), in front of Bangkok house, 1951

Anne and David in the flooded garden in Bangkok, Thailand

On Leave in Scotland, Lawrence Glen Gaudie with David Glen and Valerie Anne, 1953

FROM THE ESK AND THE USK: OUT EAST AND BACK HOME

On Leave in Scotland, Valerie Catherine Gaudie with David Glen and Valerie Anne, in Montrose, Scotland, 1953

Valerie Anne Gaudie – off to boarding school aged 7 years – in school uniform, 1953

Homme House, Much Marcle, Herefordshire. Anne's guardians' house – Anne's home in the school holidays.

Homme House, Much Marcle, Herefordshire. Anne's guardians' house – Anne's home in the school holidays.

Anne's guardians, Mrs Agnes Pope and Commander Kyrle Pope, at Homme House, on exeat with two of Anne's schoolfriends.

Anne with 'Shrimp' at her guardians' house – Homme House, Much Marcle, Herefordshire.

BOOK TWO

Later

CHAPTER 5

A Mediterranean Dimension

* * *

Becoming a Grown-Up – Sort Of

The Ox and Cow

OXFORD WAS WHERE MY ADULT SOCIAL LIFE started and also where I learned to be a secretary. It was 1964. Everything changed.

I lived in digs, which in this case, was a hostel for those attending the Ox & Cow. The house was a large Victorian building in Norham Gardens, just north of the University Parks and I shared a bedroom with two other girls (as we were still known, despite being about 18). The owners/caretakers of the hostel lived on the premises; provided us with meals; and were supposed to keep a general eye on us. They were quite relaxed about this, until a couple of weekends when I went AWOL, when they informed my parents.

The Oxford & County Secretarial College taught me shorthand and typing, at which I became very speedy. It was situated on St Giles, almost in the centre of Oxford and a short walk from our digs. When I re-visited Oxford recently, I found that the College no longer exists – hardly surprising, since most people now learn to use a keyboard from an early age and shorthand has disappeared as a desirable skill. I always found shorthand a very useful skill, however, and still use it occasionally, even now.

The grapevine worked well and we all started to go to parties, where we danced like crazy to the Stones and drank copious quantities of the cheapest Spanish red wine. We also went to 'The Forum' – a dance hall where well known groups played. Georgie Fame and the Blue Flames were there on one occasion when I went along. The setting and atmosphere in the hall had not changed since the fifties: all the girls sat on chairs around the edge of the room, with the young men standing in the middle of the room in groups, a young man occasionally plucking up courage to ask a girl for a dance. If the girl didn't like the look of the young man, she would say she was "waiting for someone", at which point the young man would feel humiliated and rejected. Likewise, if a girl sat for some time not being invited to dance, she also felt humiliated and rejected. What a scenario!

There was also the odd occasion when a group of us would drive up the A40 to spend an evening at a brand new bowling alley which had opened somewhere not far from Heathrow. I had several short term boyfriends from the university. I remember it was said that the Ox & Cow provided a rich source of available girls for the university students, along with the nurses at the John Radcliffe Hospital! There was a big chunky Canadian student from University College; the cleric's son from Keble, who had a wonderful three wheeler Morgan sports car in which I remember you had to pull a piece of string to get the windscreen wipers to work; a very good-looking young man from Pembroke who took me punting; and someone who took me to the Oxford Playhouse to see a production of "The Crucible" by Arthur Miller – a playwright whose plays I came to know and love much later. I got to know the secret ways into various Colleges. Decidedly the worse for wear, I once climbed up a rope into a window of Wadham College and was only saved from certain death by a strong wiry bloke who grabbed hold of me from the window, saving me from falling on to the pavement below. We knew exactly which bar of the railings outside St John's College was a removable false one and of course, I duly learned, although never personally used, the route over the wall into Jesus College, which landed you in the rubbish bins on the other side.

During all this, I had become friendly with a girl in the same hostel as me, whose parents lived outside Farnham in Surrey. She was quite a worldly wise girl, unlike me at the time. She was very cool, with long bright red hair, lots of pale make-up and black mascara and wore the shortest of short skirts, most of which she made herself from furnishing fabrics. She became friendly with a group of young men at St John's who were all either gay or bi-sexual, one of whom was very good looking – like a cross between Rudolph Nureyev and Mick Jagger and one of whom was obviously extremely rich – owning at least two Aston Martins. However, my friend had a boyfriend at home and regularly went to stay with her parents at weekends to see him. He was a troubled young man and we visited him in a psychiatric hospital once. She invited me to stay with her at her parents' house on a couple of occasions and we would join the group of young people who met each Saturday at lunchtime at 'The Bush' pub in Farnham. When visiting my parents (also living in Surrey), I sometimes went to Farnham for the day. It was here that I met my first longer-term boyfriend, a young man who lived with his mother near Hindhead. It was when I went to stay with them for the weekend without telling anyone where I was going, that my parents were informed that I had gone AWOL. They were angry that I had 'disappeared' but also annoyed about the boyfriend – who was deemed not to be 'the right type' – not that they had ever met him! One evening, after he had driven me back to their house after a day in Farnham, I was smacked across the face by my mother – my parents had stayed up specially to check up on me – it still shocks me to think about it.

I had a very frightening experience once, stupidly accepting a lift from a stranger in a car because it was dark and pouring with rain and I was on my way to my boyfriend's family house to go to a work 'dinner dance'(!) with him. I had a small suitcase with me. The situation became threatening, but I luckily managed to jump out of the car and walk the rest of the way along the main road with the car concerned plus one of his friends' cars, being driven very slowly up and down the road, passing me again and again. They even stopped to ask me the time. . . It was a horrible experience but I got to my destination in one piece although shaken and extremely bedraggled. What a fool I was. The dinner dance was a classic!

The relationship lasted for nearly two years. By the time it was over, I had left the Ox & Cow and was living in a rented flat with my very sixties girlfriend. I took a temp job working at the Oxfam Head Office in Summertown but soon took my first permanent job (August 1965) as a sub-editor's assistant/secretary at Pergamon Press, a publisher of scientific books and journals, based at Headington Hill Hall, Oxford. The company was owned by the infamous Robert Maxwell – looking back, I remember that if he happened to come into the office, we all had to stand up!

* * *

Independence

I was now independent and earning a wage.

After a while, my girlfriend and I moved out of our fairly basic flat and into another one, which we shared with one other girl. It was in a basement – not far from the centre – and I remember eating, on a regular basis, carrot and potato stew cooked with water and a stock cube. I also took a new job at an American engineering company in Oxford, where I became secretary to one of the directors. I worked for a delightful and energetic man and the job was a lot of fun. This, despite the fact that I sat in an office where a female colleague went to the fish and chip shop each day, bought a large portion of chips and a roll, and made chip butties with lashings of butter and plenty of vinegar, making the office stink – every day! I don't think I ever came across a more unhealthy lunch in all my working days. I was even asked to drive the company car on occasions, on one of which, the brakes failed on a hill – I narrowly avoided disaster.

Soon, however, our new flat mate decided to celebrate her birthday by having a party – on a barge – and we were invited. It was through this, that I met Ian, who I later married.

While living in Oxford, I had visited my school friend Maggie a couple of times in London. She was living in a bedsit in Tufnell Park. One night, in the early hours after a party, we walked across Hampstead Heath in the dark. I shudder to think, now, that we did that. I used to hitch-hike up to London on my own, too. However, having got a lift in a lorry on one occasion when I felt very uncomfortable, I decided that hitching should stop.

I invited Maggie to stay with me in Oxford for the weekend of the party. When she arrived, however, there were several people who had already been invited to stay at the flat for the party, so there was not enough room for her to stay as well. However, she had a childhood friend called Johnny, who was at Jesus College and she was sure he would help. The two of us went to Jesus to find Johnny and as we were going through the main gate, Ian Macdonald was coming out. Maggie had met Ian before, through Johnny, so told him what we were doing. Ian immediately offered Maggie floor space in the flat he shared with his friend Pete. We were just leaving Ian when we turned to each other thinking we should invite him to the party as a 'thank-you'. He accepted immediately and although I had gone to the party with someone else, he and I spent most of the party dancing together, particularly to Sandi Shaw's "These Boots Are Made for Walking"(!). That was in 1966 – when the Mediterranean started to have an influence on my life. It was not long afterwards that Jules, who was also at Jesus and a friend of Ian's, met Maggie through us, and they too, later married.

After the party, I received a postcard from Ian ("an official card from Jesus") which he put through the letterbox. It was addressed to "Miss Alicia Z Gaudie, 32A The Warneford" (the street I lived in had almost the same name as the psychiatric hospital in Oxford. . .). He was going to the cinema to see "The Silken Skin" and hated the idea of going on his own, especially since it was an 'X', and wondered whether I would care to go with him. If I wanted to join him, I would find him at the pub adjoining the Scala – the earlier I went, the more I could booze . . . I still have the card. I went, and on Day Three, when I went to his flat (he had cooked a delicious feast for Sunday lunch), he asked me if I would marry him! In spontaneous mode, I agreed immediately and moved into the flat with Ian and Pete.

* * *

Ian James Macdonald

Ian was studying medicine at Oxford University. He was 26 years old when I met him – a mixture of Anglo Scottish on his father's side, and Greek and Armenian on his mother's side. He was strongly attached to all things Greek, and spoke the language. He did not know, however, that he was partly Armenian, until his father told him after his mother's death. His mother had kept this a secret from her children all their lives.

Ian's father, Ernest Brian (known as Brian), was one of twins born in Cropston, Leicestershire on 27 September 1912. Brian's twin sister died young and Brian was found to have a heart murmur, resulting in his not being able to join the army later in life. The family name was Macdonald (Brian said that the family had its origins in Skye, but had become thoroughly anglicised).

Brian's mother, Alice Emily Susan, was a teacher. After a while, Brian's parents separated, and the family moved to Reading. It seems that his father was drinking heavily, and the story is that he was thrown out. Ian told me that Brian's mother favoured his younger brother, Guy James, and that Brian could not wait to leave England. Brian went to Wyggeston Grammar School for Boys in Leicester where he matriculated with honours in Latin and Greek. Brian was highly intelligent, well-educated, kindly, generous, very well informed and well read, and became a fully qualified chartered accountant. He decided to go to Egypt and went to Alexandria as a partner in a firm of chartered accountants, where he met Clio, his Greek/Armenian wife. Initially, they both lived in Alexandria, where they married, later moving to Cairo. Despite Brian's 'flight into Egypt', his mother and brother visited him there, possibly when he and Clio became engaged.

Clio's father, Athanasios Zographides, was a Greek from Adrianople (present day Edirne in East Thrace). Athanasios worked at the Royal Mint in Constantinople[85] (Patty does not know in what capacity). Clio's mother – Josephine Boudourian – was an Armenian from Constantinople. However, Josephine officially changed her name to a Turkish one: Bouzouroglou.[86] Her two brothers were killed by the Turks, so it is probably safe to assume that she did this in order to protect herself. Athanasios and Josephine married and lived in Constantinople, where all three of their children were born, each in a different area of the city, although their passports and birth certificates were registered in Adrianople: Clio (27 May 1913), Olga (15 February 1915), and Ismini (7 May 1920).

Josephine spoke Armenian, Turkish, French and not very good Greek, and Athanasios spoke Greek and French, so, they talked and wrote to each other in French.

The situation in northern Turkey, particularly for Armenians and Greeks, was highly dangerous at this time, and many were killed (including, as I have said, Josephine's two brothers). In 1915 the Turks ordered the mass expulsion of Armenians from eastern Anatolia (the start of the Armenian genocide). Thrace was an area whose border was disputed by Turkey and Greece until the signing of the Treaty of Lausanne on 24 July 1923. In exchange for Turkey giving up all claims to the remainder of the Ottoman Empire, the Allies recognised the independence of the Republic of Turkey and its sovereignty over Asia Minor, Constantinople and Eastern Thrace. Part of the Treaty involved an agreement between Greece and Turkey to forcibly exchange around one million Greek Orthodox Christians and under half a million Muslims, a huge population exchange.

It is difficult to work out the family's movements. Ian understood that the family had been in Smyrna (modern day Izmir); a city where there were

---

85   After Turkey became a Republic in 1923, the name Istanbul started to be used instead of Constantinople.
86   Ian's sister, Patricia (Patty), holds the original document.

large populations of both Greeks and Armenians. Any such move would have been made to escape the Turkish persecution and massacres taking place in Thrace and northern Turkey (of Armenians from approx 1909 and of Greeks from approx 1913).

It is unsurprising that Josephine changed her name. Josephine bravely kept her secret and her document, regardless of how terrible things became, and survived.

It is also not surprising that so little is known now about what exactly happened next in the story, since the whole matter was a secret until after Clio's death. After this, when Ismini was asked about it, she denied any connection with Armenia. . .

There is a photograph of the family at the Athenian Acropolis with Ismini in the picture when she was about three years old (Clio was not with them, since, by then, she had been collected by her Aunt Rose (Josephine's sister) and taken to stay with her and her husband in Alexandria, Egypt. On the back of the photo Ismini wrote that it was taken in 1923. The photo shows the family en route from Turkey to Egypt via Athens (there are still regular boat services between Athens and Egypt). In this photo Josephine, who, instead of being dressed as usual in the clothes of her affluent middle class, is dressed, atypically, in ordinary clothes.

How they reached Greece, we are unlikely ever to know. It could have been by travelling overland from Constantinople via Thrace, or it could have been by the shorter land journey to Smyrna and then by sea.

We know that Ismini, the youngest, was born on 7 May 1920 in Constantinople, and it was only a couple of years later, that the family fled Turkey. The limited facts available beg many questions.

Judging by Josephine's sister Rose's new surname (Haladjian), she married an Armenian, like herself. It would be interesting to know when she and her husband Paul left Turkey to go and live in Egypt, although it is easy to see that as Armenians, they may have had a more pressing need to flee Turkey than Athanasios and Josephine, who were both ostensibly Greeks. It would be interesting to know how Josephine communicated with her sister, particularly to arrange for Clio to be collected – when, and where she collected her from, are unknowns.

Had the Zographides family left from Smyrna, the question arises as to whether this was before or after the 'katastrophi' of 1922 (when the city of Smyrna was burnt down and thousands of Greeks and Armenians perished). It is tempting to think that we would know if they had survived this major event in Smyrna, but since almost nothing is known, we can only speculate. It is quite likely, however, that, at some point, they were there and left from there.

The population exchange took place in the late summer of 1923, so it is possible that the family did not flee independently before then, but as part of this compulsory exchange (when Ismini would have been 3 years old). The conditions that the 'exchangees' experienced were shocking. It was a huge operation and it does not take much imagination to realise that the elderly and young especially, suffered from the terrible travel conditions. There are many pictures online of ships filled to overflowing with refugees; lines of refugees on foot, lines of refugees in primitive ox carts, and on packed trains.

Patty was told by her father, Brian, that the family had to flee for their lives – that they had been warned they should leave urgently. He also told her that they nearly starved en route. Patty believes that, like many others, they fled on foot. Josephine contracted smallpox and Clio contracted malaria and paratyphoid, lost all her hair and could hardly stand – but when was that?

One way or another – however it was that they left – the Zographides family was forced to flee Turkey for reasons of ethnicity and religion, fearing for their lives. They clearly went through an unimaginably arduous and terrifying experience.

Since both my children are, of course, partly Armenian and interested in their heritage, and since, it seems to me, not enough is generally known about the Armenian genocide (recognised as such by 29 countries, but still not recognised by the UK), nor about the killing and the destruction in Smyrna, I continue with sections on both these major events, which it was illuminating and horrifying to research.

* * *

Armenia, Armenians – and the Genocide

> *"Armenia was the first country in the world to adopt Christianity as a state religion. The conversion and baptism of King Trdat, the royal family, the nakharars[87] and the army, together with thousands of the people, took*

---

87   Nakharars: Members of the Armenian nobility

place in the year 301 . . . and finally, in 404 he (Mesrop-Mashtots) succeeded in creating an alphabet which with thirty-six characters reproduced the sounds of the spoken Armenian."[88]

The period during which Ian's maternal grandparents lived in Turkey was acutely dangerous for Armenians.

"Having entered the First World War in October 1914 on the side of Germany and her Allies, the Turkish Government decided to exterminate the entire Armenian population in Turkey, especially in the interior of the country, and thus settle the Armenian question once and for all. . .

". . . Turkey profited with impunity by the crime of 1915 since Turkish Armenia was now completely evacuated of her population according to the original program of wholesale massacres and mass deportation.[89]

Dr Philip Mansell, in his book *"Constantinople"* writes:

"The Committee[90] *decided on a policy of extermination. In Anatolia, between six and eight hundred thousand Armenian men, women and children died during deportations, epidemics and massacres (many thousands of Turks and Kurds also died in the same region during the war). From Constantinople itself 2,432 men, the elite of the Armenian community, were deported. . . Few were seen again.*

"The 'special organization' which concerted the deportations and massacres, was run from Constantinople. Its work of destruction was well known. On 25 June the German ambassador, informed by German consuls in the East, reported that deportations had begun from areas not threatened by Russian invasion. 'This fact and the manner in which the

---

88 Kurkjian, Vahan M. *"A History of Armenia"*
89 Kurkjian, Vahan M. *"A History of Armenia"*
90 Mansel, Philip. *"Constantinople: City of the World's Desire 1453-1924"*: However, real power lay, not with the official government under Kamil Pasha but, with the Committee of Union and Progress*, led by three patriots who would dominate the government for the next ten years: Enver, Cemal and Talaat Pashas. . . Talaat, a burly former postal official in Salonica with a sweet smile, was the most ruthless of the three"

* *The group of revolutionaries which spawned this Committee in the 1890s and ultimately engineered Hamid II's capitulation, became known as 'The Young Turks'.*

relocation is being carried out demonstrates that the government is really pursuing the aim of destroying the Armenian race in Turkey.'"[91]

Chris Morris (BBC foreign correspondent and later World Affairs Correspondent) in his book "The New Turkey" writes:

"There is almost no serious discussion in Turkey about what happened to the Armenians in the last years of the Ottoman Empire. It is the biggest taboo of all.

For several centuries Armenians had lived peacefully and prospered under the Ottomans. They were craftsmen, jewellers, silversmiths and traders. But towards the end of the nineteenth century the rise of competing Turkish and Armenian nationalist movements started to create serious unrest. As the minority community, the Armenians were vulnerable to attack and tens of thousands were killed in pogroms in the 1890s and again in 1909.

Much worse was to come amidst fierce fighting on the eastern front of the First World War, when many local Armenians sided with the Russians against the Ottoman Turks. Even though Armenians fought in the ranks of the Ottoman army as well, the Armenian community came to be regarded as 'the enemy within' by hardline nationalists in the Young Turk government. In 1915 they ordered the mass expulsion of Armenians from eastern Anatolia. They believed with good reason that some Armenian nationalists were working with Russia to carve out a separate state. But everyone was made to pay.

On 24 April – the day now commemorated by Armenians as the anniversary of genocide – hundreds of Armenian politicians, intellectuals and community leaders were arrested in Istanbul. Most of them were subsequently killed. What followed in the east was almost unspeakable, but it was documented in detail by missionaries, diplomats and survivors. Men, women and children were machine-gunned in pits and ravines; rape and torture were commonplace and rivers were clogged with bodies; Armenians were taken out onto the Black Sea by the boatload and thrown overboard; sealed trains were packed with deportees who were sent to disease-ridden prison camps in the Syrian desert; others were forced to march

---

[91] Mansel, Philip. *"Constantinople: City of the World's Desire 1453-1924"*

southwards until they died by the side of the road. Kurdish tribes in eastern Anatolia acted with particular brutality, and even Turkey's wartime ally, the German ambassador in Istanbul, reported to Berlin that there was no doubt that the Ottoman government was trying 'to exterminate the Armenian race in the Turkish Empire'.[92]

In August 1920, part of the Treaty of Sèvres[93] provided for an independent Armenia, self-determination for Kurdistan and the liberation of Eastern Thrace and Smyrna. President Woodrow Wilson declared the right for self-determination of all peoples of Asia Minor. A month later, Nationalist Turkish forces attacked Armenia which was defeated and one half of which was annexed to Turkey.[94]

It is hardly surprising that Clio claimed that she was, like her father, Greek. It was only after Clio's death that Brian passed on her well-kept secret to Ian and his sister, Patty, who were both amazed and intrigued to learn more about their background.

Chris Morris goes on to say:

"Many Turks don't know any of this; they're not taught about it in school, and it's not discussed much in the media. Instead they're told about the thousands of Turks who were killed in equally atrocious ways by roaming bands of Armenian irregulars. In the eastern town of Igdur, the Armenian Genocide Memorial and Museum is not what the unsuspecting visitor might think. It was opened when I was living in Turkey in 1999, and it commemorates the deaths of local Turks. Of the Armenian dead, there is not a word. 'We are the victims,' the local governor complained at the inauguration ceremony, 'we are the ones who were massacred. But the Armenians are trying to show that the opposite is true.'

---

92 Morris, Chris. "*The New Turkey*"
93 http://treaties.fco.gov.uk/docs/pdf/1920/TS0011.pdf The Treaty of Sèvres (10 August 1920) was one of a series of treaties that the nations that constituted the Central Powers were made to sign subsequent to their defeat that marked the end of World War 1. Its ratification on 10 August 1920 marked the beginning of the partition of, and the ultimate annihilation of, the Ottoman Empire. The harsh terms it stipulated, motivated mainly by the Gallipoli Campaign, defeat of the Allied powers at the hands of the Turks, included the renunciation of all non-Turkish land that was part of the Ottoman Empire, as well as parts of Turkish land, to Allied powers.
94 http://www.ahistoryofgreece.com/venizelos.htm

It's this refusal to deal honestly with the past which is so disturbing. The Turkish authorities accept officially that 'tragic events' occurred and that three hundred thousand Armenians died in 'widespread internal fighting'. But there is not a hint of regret or remorse for the lasting trauma of it all. It was self-defence, they say, and any Turks who divert from the official line (a handful of academics and Turkey's leading novelist, Orhan Pamuk) are dismissed as traitors. Armenians maintain that the number of people killed was far higher. They insist that the death toll reached one and a half million, in an organized campaign of genocide. And most scholars abroad – with some notable and vocal exceptions – agree.

Both sides produce stacks of documents to back up their claims, and pour scorn on the forgeries of their opponents. The Internet brims with vitriol. Even the most famous quotation used in the bitter battle is disputed. Nine days before he invaded Poland, Adolf Hitler addressed his troops on the eastern front, and argued that Nazi Germany could and would exterminate European Jewry. 'Who, after all, speaks today of the annihilation of the Armenians?' eyewitnesses quoted him saying, even though the words didn't appear in the official text of his speech.

Hitler's rhetorical question is now inscribed on one of the walls of the Holocaust Memorial in Washington, DC – an awkward piece of symbolism for those who deny the Armenian genocide. Efforts to get the US Congress to recognize genocide officially have been derailed by frantic Turkish pressure, and threats to withdraw American access to military bases on Turkish soil. Every year since he's been president, George W. Bush has issued a statement on 24 April acknowledging the 'annihilation of as many as one and a half million Armenians'. It was, he said in 2004, 'one of the most horrible tragedies of the twentieth century'. But for reasons of expediency he doesn't use the 'g' word, and the diaspora feels betrayed.

Several countries have gone further than the United States. When the French parliament publicly recognized genocide in 2001 Turkey erupted in fury. The government threatened to break off diplomatic relations, universities suspended academic cooperation and France – which just happens to be home to the largest Armenian population in Western Europe – was shut out of defence tenders and other lucrative projects. The crisis soon blew over, as it usually does, and many French politicians who voted in favour of the bill say they had no intention of condemning modern Turkey. But most Turks thought that was exactly what had happened.

It's where patriotism slides across the line into prejudice. Turkey needs to discuss the bad parts of its history as well as the good, and the slaughter of the Armenians in 1915 must be at the top of the list. Politics, say the Turks, shouldn't come into it – this is an issue which should be left to the historians. But whatever the old documents and diaries say, and whatever secrets may still lie hidden in the Ottoman archives, there is no dispute about the broad legal definitions contained in the UN Genocide Convention, which came into force in 1951. It defines genocide as acts 'committed with intent to destroy, in whole or in part, a national, ethnical, racial or religious group'. It is not confined to mass murder, and it doesn't even have to be carried out under government instruction.

The conclusion isn't a comfortable one for the Turks. If Slobodan Milosovic can be charged with acts of genocide in Bosnia, and the Sudanese can be accused of genocide in Darfur, then the slaughter of the Armenians falls into the same category. But in a country where national pride is so important, and sensitivity to criticism from abroad is so acute, the Armenian genocide debate still stirs deep and lasting anger. It's as if admitting to the full severity of what happened under the Ottoman Empire would undermine the legitimacy of the Turkish republic ninety years later. It is a reminder of how history and identity are still so painfully intertwined."[95]

Philip Marsden won the 1994 Somerset Maugham Award for his book *"The Crossing Place: A Journey Among the Armenians"* in which he visits and describes the many parts of the world which make up the Armenian diaspora. After first describing some of the events of 1915, he goes on to give a positive picture of the role of Armenians in history and in the world today:

"In the interior Turkish forces began to deport the Armenians. Torkom showed me the published report of one of the only foreigners who had witnessed what these deportations really meant. Leslie David had been the American consul in Kharput. He had watched the Armenian groups come and go, and had listened to the rumours. Since it was wartime his movements were severely restricted and he had been unable to confirm what he heard. But one morning before dawn he managed to slip out of the town. He rode on to the plain of Kharput.

---

95   Morris, Chris. *"The New Turkey"*

And wherever he rode he saw the Armenians. They were casually buried in the roadside ditches, their limbs half eaten by scavenging dogs; he saw the heaps of charred bones where the remains had been burned; he saw the swollen bodies of the newly dead and in places they lay so thickly in the dirt that his horse had difficulty avoiding them. As the day wore on, David rode further into the hills. He reached the shores of Lake Goeljuk. Here, in the valleys leading down to the lake, the scene was the same: corpses scattered amidst the thornscrub, bunched together in their hundreds – at the foot of cliffs, in gorges, in the hidden folds of land. Those who weren't killed at once were gathered into convoys and driven south. These were the marches.

. . . More than a million Armenians died in the last years of the Ottoman empire, a half of Anatolia's total. The Turks had managed to do what numerous powers had tried before them: they managed to finish Armenia, though not the Armenians. In most of the world's cities you can find Armenians – Armenian newspapers in Armenian script, Armenian restaurants. In exile the Armenians are curiously resilient; only the Jews have resisted assimilation as fiercely. In the mountains of Colombia there is a small town actually named Armenia where they serve 'Antioch-style' beans.

. . . They shouldn't really exist at all. They should have been destroyed, written out of history by its worst horrors. But they have survived. Instead of a footnote to the story of these border regions, the Armenians can be read like a kind of subtext.

. . . In the library of the Armenian quarter (in Jerusalem), tacked to the wall, were the lines of the Armenian writer William Saroyan:

> *'I should like to see any power of the world destroy*
> *This race, this small tribe of unimportant people,*
> *Whose wars have all been fought and lost, whose*
> *Structures have all crumbled, literature is unread,*
> *Music is unheard, and prayers are no more answered.*
> *Go ahead, destroy Armenia. See if you can do it. Send*
> *Them into the desert without food or water. Burn*
> *Their homes and churches. Then see if they will not*
> *Laugh, sing and pray again. For when two of them*
> *Meet anywhere in the world, see if they will not*
> *Create a New Armenia.'*

> *Wondering what Saroyan meant by a 'New Armenia', and wondering what remained of the old, I said goodbye and left the monastery on a damp December evening. I headed for Venice, where there had been an Armenian community for eight hundred years."*[96]

When I visited Venice in 2006, having read about the Venetian Island of San Lazzaro degli Armeni, I made the trip by boat across the lagoon to visit the island. The island has been occupied by an Armenian Catholic monastery, the headquarters of the Armenian Mechitarist Order, since 1717, when the Venetian Senate ceded the island to them. The island was marshy then, with a few ruined buildings on it, but it was built upon and expanded by the Armenians. It has become one of the world's foremost centres of Armenian culture, housing a state-of-the-art library full of Armenian texts, funded, we were told, mainly by members of the Armenian diaspora in America.

* * *

Smyrna and the Greek 'Katastrophi'

> *"To mention the name of Sherman to a Southerner of the United States is to fill him with burning indignation. Even the most ignorant yokel knows that the name Attila is associated with untold horrors and vandalism. But the Smyrna affair, which far outweighs the horrors of the first World War or even the present one, has been somehow soft-pedalled and almost expunged from the memory of present day man."*
>
> Henry Miller: *The Colossus of Maroussi* 1941

As I wrote earlier, Ian's grandparents, a Greek and an Armenian, initially lived in Constantinople and then may well have gone south to leave Turkey via Smyrna, where there were large Greek and Armenian populations,[97] or

---

96 Marsden, Philip. *"The Crossing Place: A Journey among the Armenians"*
97 Jeffrey Eugenides in his 2002 Pulitzer Prize winning novel *"Middlesex"*, writes about two young Greeks who leave their rural mountain village above Bursa in northern Turkey, and, to escape the Turks, flee to Smyrna on 31 August 1922, arriving just before the Turks enter Smyrna on 9 September 1922 and The Great Fire takes place, in which vast numbers of Greeks were either killed, burned or drowned. They escape by pretending to be French – getting tickets to join a French evacuation ship – and eventually get to America. This section of the book, highly pertinent to this story, gives a powerful impression of those events in Smyrna.

they may have left Turkey from Constantinople via Thrace. Either way, it seems important and relevant, to include the story of Smyrna in the family history:

> "When Istanbul stood at the heart of the Ottoman Empire, it was the minority communities – Greeks, Armenians and Jews – which gave the city its unique cosmopolitan mix. The Greeks in particular were well educated, confident and prosperous. But history has been unkind, and the end of the empire hit the Greeks hard. A community which numbered hundreds of thousands at the end of the nineteenth century has shrunk dramatically. By the end of the twentieth century, there were fewer than three thousand Greeks left in Istanbul, most of them elderly, many of them poor, living on memories of the past."[98]

To provide some background, I have stitched together, in a long footnote, a potted version of a highly complex period in history, taken from various online sources.[99]

---

98   Morris, Chris. *"The New Turkey"*
99   In Turkey the decaying Ottoman Empire was continuing a policy that could be called the Turkization of Asia Minor. In 1909 the first massacre of Armenians by Turkey took place in Adana, Tarus and other towns (30,000 Armenians dead) and in 1913, Turkey committed atrocities and massacres of Greeks in Eastern Thrace, killing more than 15,000. In May 1914, the Turkish authorities at Pergamum commanded all Christians to leave the town within two hours and the terrorized inhabitants crossed over to the Greek island of Mytilini.
    Meanwhile, the first Balkan War had broken out in October 1912, with Greece, Serbia, Montenegro and Bulgaria attacking Turkey. Thessaloniki was captured and became part of Greece. In July 1913, in the second Balkan War, Bulgaria attacked Greece and Serbia, and was beaten. The two victors then split Macedonia. Mount Athos and many of the North Eastern Aegean islands were liberated by the Greeks.
    Turkey allied itself with Germany in the First World War, and the French and the British wanted Greece to join their side against Germany.
    What is known as '*To Megali Idea*' or '*The Great Idea*', a Greek concept of a new Hellenic Empire on both sides of the Aegean looked as if it might become a reality. The major powers supported it. At the 1918 Paris Peace Conference, President Venizelos of Greece lobbied for an expanded Hellas including the large Greek communities in Northern Epirus, Thrace and Asia Minor.
    In 1919, Greek troops were sent by the victorious allies to the beautiful and multi-ethnic city of Smyrna in Asia Minor to 'protect' Greek citizens. Little known to the Greeks, the Italians and Russians were selling arms to the Nationalist Turks under Kemal Atatürk and the British and French had negotiated a separate peace, realizing that the Ottoman empire was dead and the Nationalists were the new face of Turkey. After being encouraged by

Dr Giles Milton, in his book *"Smyrna 1922: The Destruction of Islam's City of Tolerance"*, includes eyewitness accounts and the memories of survivors, many interviewed for the first time. One of these was Petros Brussalis, whom he visited and interviewed in Athens. Petros was 93 years of age and according to Milton, had never quite recovered from the loss of his childhood.

> *"'Forget Constantinople, Alexandria and Beirut,' he (Petros) says. 'Smyrna before the 'katastrophi' was the most cosmopolitan place on earth'.*
>
> *... And if Petros's father cared to read a daily newspaper, he had quite a choice: eleven Greek, seven Turkish, five Armenian, four French and five Hebrew, not to mention the ones shipped in from every capital city in Europe.*
>
> *... The harbour was indeed one of the great sights of Smyrna. There were thirty-three steamboat companies catering for passenger liners arriving almost daily from London, Liverpool, Marseilles, Genoa, Brindisi, Trieste and Constantinople, as well as all the principal ports of the Levant.*[100]
>
> *... Here, too, were the city's principal banks – the Imperial Ottoman, Credit Lyonnais, the British Oriental and the Bank of Vienna. No fewer than seven countries had their own postal systems that worked alongside the Ottoman system. And there were several dozen maritime insurance companies.*

the European 'friends' the Greek army found itself isolated in central Turkey. They were defeated by Kemal Atatürk and forced to flee to the shores of the Aegean. In their wake they brought with them thousands of Greek and Christian citizens of the Ottoman empire who feared that the advancing Turks would massacre them. While the French, British, US and Russian fleets watched in the harbour, waiting to sign contracts with the new Turkish government, the city of Smyrna was burned. The disaster of Smyrna meant the end of the three thousand year Hellenic presence in Asia Minor.

In January 1923, there was a compulsory exchange of populations between Greece and Turkey. In July 1923 the Treaty of Lausanne reversed all Greece's gains of the Treaty of Sèvres. There was to be no 'Greater Hellas' with the Aegean a Greek sea and Constantinople the capital. But there were now a million and a half new Greeks in Athens and Thessaloniki. http://www.ahistoryofgreece.com/venizelos.htm

100 In 2015 I bought a DVD "ΣMYPNH" (Smyrna) from the Benaki Museum in Athens. This gives an excellent picture of life in Smyrna from 1900-1922, leading up to the "Katastrophi" and complements Dr Giles Milton's book *"Smyrna 1922: The Destruction of Islam's City of Tolerance"*.

... The waterfront was lined with lively bars, brasseries and shaded café gardens, each of which tempted the palate with a series of enticing scents. The odour of roasted cinnamon would herald an Armenian patisserie; apple smoke spilled forth from hookahs in the Turkish cafes. Coffee and olives, crushed mint and Armagnac: each smell was distinctive and revealed the presence of more than three culinary traditions. Caucasian pastries, boeuf à la mode, Greek game pies and Yorkshire pudding could all be found in the quayside restaurants of Smyrna. . . . It had the climate of southern California, the architecture of the Côte d'Azur and the allure of nowhere else on earth 'In no city in the world did East and West mingle physically in so spectacular a manner,' he (American Consul George Horton) wrote.

The city was dominated by the Greeks. They numbered 320,000 and had a virtual monopoly on the trade in the sticky figs, sultanas and apricots for which Smyrna was so famous.". . . "The Greeks had left their mark on every walk of life. Smyrna boasted scores of Orthodox churches and almost as many schools. The young Aristotle Onassis was one of the many local Greeks who attended the famous Aronis School.

. . . Adjacent to the European area of Smyrna was the vibrant Armenian quarter, home to another of Smyrna's wealthy communities. The Armenians, who numbered around 10,000 had a reputation for being diligent and conscientious. . . They were indeed 'doing well' and they had learned to enjoy their bourgeois creature comforts.

. . . The Levantines were by far the richest community in the area. Of European descent, but thoroughly versed in the ways of the Orient, they had lived in Turkey since the reign of King George III. They, more than any other community, had helped to shape Smyrna in their own image – rich, cosmopolitan and of mixed blood and heritage. . . In the dark days of the First World War, many of Smyrna's families would owe their continued existence to the Levantine magnates.

. . . Although the Turks played a marginal role in the commerce of Smyrna, they dominated the politics of the city. The Ottoman governor of Smyrna was traditionally always a Turkish national and his primary task was to represent the interests of all the different nationalities who had made the city their home. A glance at the 1913 census reveals why his job was not easy. Smyrna's Christians outnumbered the Muslims by more than two to one; his was a majority Christian city in a resolutely Muslim world. To many Turks – and especially to government *ministers in Constantinople – Smyrna had forever been the city of the infidels."*[101]

Smyrna's fortunes were about to change: after three years of brutal fighting between Greece and Turkey – fought on Turkish territory, in which Britain, and other Western powers, had aided and armed the Greeks, the Turks defeated the Greeks.

> *"Smyrna was known throughout the world of Islam for having a majority Christian population and there were concerns that the newly victorious Turkish army would sweep into the city to unleash a terrible fury on the infidel inhabitants. . . . She (Smyrna) had a Greek population that was at least twice that of Athens. . . By 1922, its Christian population included Greeks, Armenians, Levantines, Europeans and Americans. . . Yet there had been no resistance to the Turkish army and few inhabitants could really believe that their city would meet with such a fate. Smyrna had long been celebrated as a beacon of tolerance – home to scores of nationalities with a shared outlook and intertwined lives. It was little wonder that the Americans living in the metropolis had named their colony Paradise; life here was remarkably free from prejudice. . .*
>
> *. . . "There was another reason why Smyrna's inhabitants were confident that the city would be spared. In the harbour there was the reassuring presence of no fewer than twenty-one battleships, including eleven British, five French and several Italian. There were also three large American destroyers, among them the newly arrived 'USS Litchfield'. Everyone believed that these ships would deter the Turkish army from committing any excesses.*
>
> *. . . The Turkish cavalry presented a magnificent spectacle as it cantered along the waterfront. The horsemen sat high in their saddles, their scimitars unsheathed and glinting in the sun. On their heads they wore black Circassian fezzes adorned with the crescent and star. As they rode, they cried, 'Korkma! Korkma!' Fear not! Fear not!'*
>
> *. . . Their entry into the city of Smyrna on 9 September 1922 was watched by thousands of anxious inhabitants."*[102]

---

101 Milton, Giles. *"Smyrna 1922: The Destruction of Islam's City of Tolerance"*
102 Milton, Giles. *"Smyrna 1922: The Destruction of Islam's City of Tolerance"*

> "On Saturday, September 9, 1922, the victorious Turkish cavalry rode into Smyrna, the richest and most cosmopolitan city in the Ottoman Empire. The city's vast wealth created centuries earlier by powerful Levantine dynasties, its factories teemed with Greeks, Armenians, Turks, and Jews. Together, they had created a majority Christian city that was unique in the Islamic world. But to the Turkish nationalists, Smyrna was a city of infidels. In the aftermath of the First World War and with the support of the Great Powers, Greece had invaded Turkey with the aim of restoring a Christian empire in Asia. But by the summer of 1922, the Greeks had been vanquished by Ataturk's armies after three years of warfare. As Greek troops retreated, the non-Muslim civilians of Smyrna assumed that American and European warships would intervene if and when the Turkish cavalry decided to enter the city. But this was not to be. On September 13, 1922, Turkish troops descended on Smyrna. They rampaged first through the Armenian quarter, and then throughout the rest of the city. They looted homes, raped women, and murdered untold thousands. Turkish soldiers were seen dousing buildings with petroleum. Soon, all but the Turkish quarter of the city was in flames and hundreds of thousands of refugees crowded the waterfront, desperate to escape. The city burned for four days; by the time the embers cooled, more than 100,000 people had been killed and millions left homeless.[103]

Professor Marjorie Housepian Dobkin (1922-2013), of Columbia University, New York, wrote in her book *"Smyrna 1922: The Destruction of a City"*: "In September 1922, Mustapha Kemal (Ataturk), the victorious revolutionary ruler of Turkey, led his troops into Smyrna (now Izmir), a predominantly Christian city, as a flotilla of twenty-seven Allied warships – including three American destroyers – looked on[104]. The Turks soon proceeded to indulge in an orgy of pillage, rape and slaughter that the Western powers anxious to protect their oil and trade interests in Turkey, condoned by

---

103 Milton, Giles. *"Smyrna 1922: The Destruction of Islam's City of Tolerance"*
104 Housepian Dobkin, Marjorie. *"Smyrna 1922: The Destruction of a City"*: ". . . an imposing display of Allied might at daybreak on Saturday 9 September 1922. Besides twenty-one warships – two British battleships, three cruisers, and six destroyers; three French cruisers and two destroyers; an Italian cruiser and destroyer; and three American destroyers – the harbour was massed with virtually every sort of vessel that could float, from tiny Levantine caïques, to massive freighters bearing the flags of all the maritime nations on earth – except Greece. The last Greek ship had pulled down its flag and slid away before dawn."

their silence and their refusal to intervene. Turkish forces then set fire to the legendary city and totally destroyed it. There followed a massive cover-up by tacit agreement of the Western Allies who had defeated Turkey and Germany during World War I.

"... in July 1920 came the stunning disclosure that Britain and France had during April of that year secretly signed an agreement at San Remo, Italy, dividing between them Turkey's oil-rich territories. Berenger, Henri. 'Letter to Clemenceau 12 December 1919: "He who owns the oil will own the world."'

By 1923 Smyrna 's demise was all but expunged from historical memory."[105]

"In January 1923, under the Treaty of Lausanne, there was a major compulsory exchange of populations between Greece and Turkey. It was an agreed mutual expulsion based on religious identity, and involved the Greek Orthodox citizens of Turkey and the Muslim citizens of Greece. This led to there being a million and a half new Greeks in Athens and Thessaloniki. Many other Greeks fled elsewhere."[106]

"The crushing defeat of the Greek Army in Izmir (ancient Smyrna) in 1922 was accompanied by widespread killings and a massive population transfer involving well over a million people. In 1923 Greeks from across Anatolia – the merchants, tradesmen and professionals who kept many Anatolian towns running – were forced to swap places with ethnic Turks living in mainland Greece and the Greek islands. In one fell swoop, the long-established Hellenic culture of Asia Minor all but disappeared, leaving only ancient monuments and abandoned houses as a reminder of what had once been. Many of the ethnic Greeks who remained chose to convert publicly to Islam for self-preservation, and they kept their old faith to themselves."

... In Istanbul the Greeks were allowed to stay under sufferance – many had nowhere else to go, but some were convinced that their control of much of the city's commercial wealth would afford them some kind of protection. For a while it seemed to work, they kept their heads down and got on with their lives as Kemal Ataturk signed a friendship treaty with Greece. But during the Second World War a punitive wealth tax directed specifically at Greeks and other minorities in Turkey brought many businessmen to their knees, and worse was about to come. Nationalists in both countries were spreading lurid stories about the growing communal tensions on the island of Cyprus, and in 1955

---

105 Housepian Dobkin, Marjorie. *"Smyrna 1922: The Destruction of a City"*
106 http://www.ahistoryofgreece.com/Venizelos.htm

> *Istanbul was convulsed by riots. Mobs organised by the government rampaged through the city. Homes and businesses belonging to minority communities were left in ruins, and Orthodox graveyards were desecrated. Tens of thousands of Greeks fled in the following months, as the character of Istanbul began to change for ever.*[107]

* * *

Flight into Egypt – a New Life

Ian's grandparents, Athanasios and Josephine, and two of their daughters, Olga and Ismini, joined Josephine's sister, Rose Haladjian, husband Paul, and their eldest daughter, Clio, in Alexandria, Egypt, in 1923, or thereabouts.

Tragically, Ian's Greek grandfather died very soon after the family's flight from Turkey and their arrival in Alexandria. He died of food poisoning, having already survived a road traffic accident in the very early days of cars in Egypt, which left him walking with a limp. He had been run down by a taxi whose passenger was an Englishman, who forced the taxi driver to take Athanasios to hospital.

He died when Clio was 11 years old, so about 1924. Josephine was left to bring up their children on her own.

The three girls, who had been brought up speaking French, spent some time in a French convent school outside Alexandria. However, their mother soon felt that this was unsafe since it meant travelling there and back by tram, so they were sent from Egypt to a French convent school in Cyprus as boarders. Patty speculates that this may have been paid for by generous members of the Armenian community, keen to help a destitute family, especially since the children's father had died. Despite dreaming of finishing school and studying piano in Paris, Clio decided, in her teens, to leave school and get a job to help her mother, and Ismini returned to Egypt with her. Olga may have stayed in Cyprus for a while, but later, the three daughters went their separate ways.

Clio, Ian and Patty's mother, was the eldest of the girls. The family was living in their mother's flat in Alexandria and Patty told me that her

---

107 Morris, Chris. *"The New Turkey"*

grandmother, Josephine, would take in lodgers to help make ends meet. I was told that Brian was living in the same apartment block and met Clio in the lift (I remember Clio and Brian laughing about this). This resulted in Brian suggesting that he might become their lodger! Due to Brian's classical education, he could read Greek. He could also understand it, but later, on our holidays, invariably pretended that he could not and left Clio to do all the talking! Clio had a good sense of humour, was intelligent, well educated, lively, petite, rather glamorous, played the piano, and spoke several languages fluently. She must have seemed quite exotic to the young man from Cropston. In due course, on 11 November 1939, they married and Ian was born in Alexandria on 30 July 1940. Later, they moved to Cairo, where Patty was born on 19 March 1947.

Olga, the middle sister, fell in love (so it was said) with a British RAF pilot during the war, who, when he left Egypt, left Olga behind, too. Olga suffered from a broken heart, had a mental breakdown of some kind, was 'treated' with ECT, and never made a full psychological recovery. She continued to live in Alexandria with her mother until her mother's death in 1955, after which she decided to strike out on her own. She went to live in Athens, where she worked as a secretary, renting a flat and supporting herself for the rest of her life. Brian supported her throughout her life, too, by giving her regular financial help. She never married, but worked for years at Biokat Corporation, 6 Aristidou Street in central Athens, where she became well known and respected.

Ismini, the youngest, was sent by Brian to the UK at the age of eighteen (ie just as the war was starting in 1938/9), to train as a nurse. She stayed initially with Brian's mother in Leicester. However, the British declared her an enemy alien (Greece had not, as yet, joined the Allies), as a result of which, she lost her place at Guy's Hospital. However, she later managed to join the Gloucester Royal Infirmary and became a nursing Sister in due course.

She met Henryk Cygielski in Leicester and married him on 16th August 1950. Photos show that the family came over to England from Egypt, to attend Ismini and Henryk's wedding. Brian gave Ismini away and Patty, at three years old, was a bridesmaid.

Henryk was a Pole who had immigrated to the UK after fighting at the Battle of Monte Cassino in World War II – a series of four assaults by the Allies against the German Line in Italy. The Polish Cemetery at Monte Cassino holds the graves of over a thousand Poles who died storming the bombed-out Benedictine abbey on top of the mountain, in May 1944. It was common knowledge in the family that Henryk had been a recipient of an award for bravery, although he never mentioned it. This was the Polish Order of the 'Virtuti Militari' – an award given "to recognize and reward outstanding military valor above and beyond the call of duty. It is equivalent in stature to the U.S. Medal of Honor and the British Victoria Cross." His name can be found on the online list of recipients of this highly prestigious award, at the link below.[108] Patty tells me that Henryk also fought in Egypt at one time, and on another occasion, was imprisoned in Siberia.

After their marriage, Ismini and Henryk lived in Leicester, Sheffield and Dartford. Ian told me that Henryk worked at night in the steel works in Sheffield, and studied for a chemistry degree during the day. They had two daughters, Juliet and Margaret. Later, Henryk became a Director of one of the major pharmaceutical companies based in London and in due course he and Ismini bought a house in Surbiton, Surrey, where they lived very comfortably. He also ran his own small enterprise from home, translating Russian and Polish pharmaceutical journals into English. Henryk died first, with Ismini dying on her 98th birthday on 7 May 2018.

Henryk's funeral service, which I attended, was held at the Polish Catholic Church in Putney. The congregation was made up of many Polish ex-military men as well as his family. After this, Henryk's remains were taken to Poland, where a military funeral was held with full military honours. Ismini attended this ceremony and I understand that plans have been discussed to take her ashes to Poland.

Once Clio and Brian had married, they lived in Alexandria in some comfort – enjoying the cosmopolitan Egyptian lifestyle of that time, not far removed from the sort of life that anyone would have experienced in Smyrna. There was a hugely multi-cultural society (Lawrence Durrell wrote about people and their lifestyles in 'The Alexandria Quartet' and Brian told me that he had known several of the people mentioned by Durrell). They would have eaten well on an abundance of Mediterranean and Middle Eastern foods; several languages would have been spoken; Clio played the piano; Clio's clothes were handmade by a tailor who came round to their flat to do fittings; there was a woman who visited to wax away unwanted hairs(!); their flat would have been spotless (all white laundry items were invariably boiled on the stove);and Arabic jokes were recounted with relish

---

108 http://feefhs.org/resource/poland-virtuti-militari-recipients

(I remember Clio telling us what a great sense of humour the Egyptians had). It was a wonderful part of the world in which to live at that time if you had a reasonable amount of money, and they clearly enjoyed it.

James was born in Alexandria on 30 July 1940 and his birth was registered by the British Consul General there. I remember being told that when people started calling him Jimmy, his English grandmother objected, so his parents decided he would be called Ian from then on, the names Ian James appearing on his passport and all other official documents thereafter! They moved to Cairo and Ian's sister, Patricia Margaret (Patty) was born in 1947. From the age of four or five, Patty went to a French kindergarten in the district of Zamalek with Daphne, whose home was nearby. Daphne's family also moved to London later, where she became an artist printmaker and a friend of mine as well as Patty and Ian's. I have several of her works displayed on my walls. The family's life continued in much the same vein, in the sophisticated city that Cairo had become by the 1940s. The family joined the (originally British) Gezira Club where they socialised. They had regular outings to Groppi's famous ice-cream parlour – which became an important part of the children's lives! Brian played squash extremely well, and in the war years (when British servicemen were stationed in Cairo and competition was particularly fierce) I understand he became Egypt's amateur squash champion.

From the age of seven, Ian attended Gezira Preparatory School. I have his reports from Autumn Term 1947 to summer 1950 and I read that not only did he learn Arabic, but that he "forgot his gym shoes every class" in spring term 1950!

* * *

An English Education

In the autumn of 1950, when Ian had recently turned eleven, he went to England and boarded at St Hugh's School, Woodhall Spa, in Lincolnshire. He was bullied at first, until he grew tall enough to fight back, when the bullying stopped. He spent alternate summer holidays with his Aunt Ismini and Uncle Henryk (together with their children later on – his small cousins) and in Cairo. There is a photo of Ian in his school uniform, with Ismini, dated Easter 1952 – they are both in a park on a sunny day, with a baby in a pram. After that, in the spring of 1954, Ian joined Leighton Park School, a Quaker boarding school in Reading (where Brian's mother still lived) and the family visited the UK that summer. He became a good athlete (representing the school in the 880 yards in a match against Eton in March 1959), and a Prefect. He passed five GCSE subjects at 'O' level and four – History, Geography, French and a General Paper – at 'A' level before leaving in 1959. He and a friend were given a School Travel Scholarship to hitch-hike across France and Italy to Greece, staying in YHA hostels and camping. They explored the Peleponnese, ending up after two weeks in Athens – I have a carbon copy of their proposed itinerary and Ian's YHA membership cards. Mention is made of Ian having lots of friends in Athens and also an aunt. I can imagine that Olga was overjoyed to see him.

* * *

The Suez Crisis

In 1956, Clio and Brian had to leave Cairo in a hurry. (I seem to have written something along those lines elsewhere. . .)

They had to leave almost everything behind which included, of course, their furniture and their car, and were only allowed to take one suitcase of clothes and a few sheets with them. Brian did manage, however, to return to Egypt once for a brief visit, to retrieve a few of their most treasured belongings.

An extract from Hansard[109] briefly outlines what occurred:

> *"Commander Noble Her Majesty's Government have been deeply shocked by the news received through the Swiss Ministry of Foreign Affairs who had a report from their Minister in Cairo on 23rd November to the effect that all members of the British and French communities in Egypt were to be expelled within the next week or 10 days. Each person was to be allowed to take a maximum of £20 with him."*

I thought I would set out a brief history of the Suez Crisis and the events leading up to it, since it was these that forced Clio, Brian and family, to leave Egypt in a rush, to start a new life in London.

---

109 Hansard, 26 November 1956 vol 561 cc30-3

The Bodleian Library at the University of Oxford ran an exhibition on The Suez Crisis in October 2006 and summarised the crisis as follows:

"The 1956 Suez Crisis is one of the most important and controversial events in British history since the Second World War. Not only did Suez result in deep political and public division in Britain, it also caused international uproar. It has come to be regarded as the end of Britain's role as one of the world powers and as the beginning of the end for the British Empire. In future British foreign policy would be conducted in concurrence with American diplomatic support."[110]

The BBC on its "British History in depth" website sets out the main events:

"Despite anti-western demonstrations in Egypt, in January 1956 the United States and Britain had pledged funding to help finance the construction of a new High Dam at Aswan. The US, however, became convinced that the Dam project would not be a success and wanted to reduce expenditure on foreign aid.

It was also concerned about Nasser's[111] *purchase of Soviet arms. On 19 July, US Secretary of State John Foster Dulles informed the Egyptian ambassador in Washington that his government had decided that it would not provide funding for the construction of the dam.*

The British Foreign secretary, Selwyn Lloyd, followed suit and withdrew the British offer of aid. The World Bank then refused to advance Egypt a promised $200 million. On 26 July 1956, President Nasser nationalised the Anglo-French Suez Canal Company, declaring that he would take the revenue from the canal to finance his dam.

Eden, who recalled Britain's appeasement of Adolf Hitler in the 1930s, looked to military action which might result in Nasser's downfall and restore Britain's influence in the region. The United States, however, made it clear that unjustified military action would not be tolerated.

The end of the Second World War in 1945 had brought a period of rapid change. The creation of the state of Israel in 1948 was followed by

---

110 Bodleian Library, University of Oxford: *The Suez Crisis* http://www.odl.ox.ac.uk/digitalimagelibrary/
111 Gamal Abdel Nasser Hussein was the second President of Egypt, serving from 1956 until his death in 1970.

the first Arab-Israeli War and a renewed upsurge of Arab nationalism made the Middle East a volatile region.

The United States had emerged from World War Two as a global superpower and, as a former colony itself it was committed to overseeing the decolonisation of the globe. Furthermore, the spread of communism fostered by the Soviet Union was seen by the US as a threat to democracy"[112]

The Guardian's Derek Brown wrote an article in March 2001, from which I quote to continue the story:

"Nasser's nationalisation of the canal was followed by intensive diplomatic activity, ostensibly aimed at establishing some kind of international control of the strategically vital waterway. It turned out to be a smokescreen for military preparations.

In September, Nasser made a defiant speech rejecting the idea of international supervision of an Egyptian national asset. By then, the die was cast."[113]

The Bodleian Library noted:

"14 October Sir Anthony Eden holds secret discussions with French officials over a military operation to recover use of the Canal. The talks result in the formation of a plan by which Israel would invade Egypt and thus allow British and French forces to seize the Canal as an act of intervention between warring nations.

22-24 October The British Foreign Secretary, Selwyn Lloyd, concludes the agreement with French and Israeli officials at Sèvres, France. The British copy of the resulting Sèvres Protocol is subsequently destroyed on Eden's order."[114]

". . . Israeli forces swept into the Sinai desert on October 29, two days before the Anglo-French invasion, and raced towards the canal. (One

---

112 BBC History – History in depth: *"The Suez Crisis"*: http://www.bbc.co.uk/history/british/modern/suez_01.shtml
113 The Guardian.com: Derek Brown, 14 March 2001: *"1956: Suez and the end of empire"* https://www.theguardian.com/politics/2001/mar/14/past.education1
114 Bodleian Library, University of Oxford: *The Suez Crisis* http://www.odl.ox.ac.uk/digitalimagelibrary/

column was headed by a young brigade commander who would go on to become prime minister: Ariel Sharon.) In less than seven days, the entire Sinai peninsula was in Israeli hands.

British and French troops, spearheaded by airborne forces, invaded the canal zone on October 31. Their governments told an outraged world that they had to invade, to separate Egyptian and Israeli forces, and thus protect the freedom of navigation on the canal. The reality was that the British and French, in top secret negotiations with Israel had forged an agreement for joint military operations. Israel, in fact, had the most legitimate grievance of the three invaders, for since the establishment of the Jewish state in 1948, Egypt had denied passage through the canal to any Israeli-flagged or Israel-bound ships.

The Anglo-French invasion was a good deal more ignominious. Just eight days after the first airborne lands, the operation was halted under a ceasefire ostensibly ordered by the United Nations, but in fact dictated by the Americans. The Egyptian air force had been destroyed and its army mauled – though it put up spirited resistance both in the canal zone and in Sinai. There is little doubt that the invading allies, who had overwhelming military advantage, could have gone on to take undisputed control of the canal zone – albeit at a cruel cost.

The greatest irony of the operation was that it was totally counterproductive. Far from bolstering Anglo-French interests, it had badly undermined the political and military prestige of both countries. And far from ensuring international freedom of seaborne passage, it had done just the opposite: under Nasser's orders, 47 ships were scuttled in the waterway. The Suez canal was totally blocked...

... The final straw for Eden came when the Treasury told the government that sterling, under sustained attack over the crisis, needed urgent US support to the tune of a billion dollars. 'Ike' had a crisp reply: no ceasefire, no loan. The invaders were ordered to halt and await the arrival of a UN intervention force. "[115]

The BBC again: "Accusations of collusion between Britain, France and Israel started in 1956, but were denied in parliament by Eden who tried to avoid giving a clear and categorical answer. He was at last asked

---

115 The Guardian.com: Derek Brown, 14 March 2001: *"1956: Suez and the end of empire"* https://www.theguardian.com/politics/2001/mar/14/past.education1

whether there was foreknowledge of the Israeli attack and on 20 December in his last address to the House of Commons, recorded in Hansard, he replied: 'I want to say this on the question of foreknowledge, and to say it quite bluntly to the House, that there was not foreknowledge that Israel would attack Egypt. There was not.'

In January 1957, his health shattered and his political credibility severely damaged, Sir Anthony Eden, the British prime minister, resigned."[116]

The *Economist* summarises:

"*The Suez crisis, as the events of the following months came to be called, marked the humiliating end of imperial influence for two European countries, Britain and France. It cost the British Prime Minister, Anthony Eden, his job and, by showing up the shortcomings of the Fourth Republic in France, hastened the arrival of the Fifth Republic under Charles de Gaulle. It made unambiguous, even to the most nostalgic blimps, America's supremacy over its Western allies. It thereby strengthened the resolve of many Europeans to create what is now the European Union. It promoted pan-Arab nationalism and completed the transformation of the Israeli-Palestinian dispute into an Israeli-Arab one. And it provided a distraction that encouraged the Soviet Union to put down an uprising in Hungary the same year.*"[117]

---

116 BBC History – History in depth: "*The Suez Crisis*": http://www.bbc.co.uk/history/british/modern/suez_01.shtml
117 The Economist, 27 July 2006: "*The Suez Crisis, An Affair to Remember*" http://www.economist.com/node/7218678

Athanasios Zographides (right) as a young man, with his father, mother and two sisters. In Thrace?

Athanasios Zographides. In Constantinople?

Josephine Boudourian/Bouzouroglou. In Constantinople?

Josephine, Athanasios, and left to right, Ismini, Clio, and Olga Zographides. In Constantinople

FROM THE ESK AND THE USK: OUT EAST AND BACK HOME

Josephine, Athanasios, Olga and Ismini Zographides, in Athens, having escaped from Turkey. En route to Egypt. 1923?

Olga (top left), Clio (top right), Ismini (front), Zographides. Alexandria, Egypt

Josephine and Clio Zographides. Alexandria, Egypt

Clio Macdonald with Ian James. Alexandria, Egypt.

Josephine Zographides, seated. Clio Macdonald, standing, with Ian James and Patricia Margaret, in Cairo, Egypt, 1947-8

Olga and Ismini Zographides. Visiting London 1949

Ernest Brian Macdonald with Ian James Macdonald at the wedding of Ismini Zographides and Henryk Cygielski in the UK. 1950

Patty Macdonald, 3 years, bridesmaid at Ismini Zographides and Henryk Cygielski's wedding. 1950

FROM THE ESK AND THE USK: OUT EAST AND BACK HOME

Ian James Macdonald who started boarding school in the UK in 1950, with Ismini and Henryk Cygielski, 'in loco parentis'.

Patty, Ian and Clio Macdonald.

Clio and Brian Macdonald in their house in Wimbledon, London. Early 1980s?

Olga Zographides in Athens. Visited by Anne in the 2000s

A New Life in the UK

Clio and Brian bought the house at 30 Barham Road, Wimbledon, south west London, where they settled and remained for the rest of their years. By the time I knew him, Brian was a senior figure at the Dutch owned company Philips. He and Clio lived a comfortable and affluent life, with Brian visiting Holland from time to time and later, when Philips took over Pye, commuting twice a week to Cambridge. Wimbledon was not far from Surbiton where Ismini and Henryk later bought their house, so Clio and Ismini were then in constant close touch. Clio and Brian also made regular visits to Greece for holidays and to see Olga, who visited them in London occasionally too.

On finishing at Leighton Park School, Ian decided that he would like to study medicine and applied to King's College London. On 18 November 1959 (having been interviewed) he was offered a place on the 1st MB course in October 1960 and the 2nd in October 1961. The King's College Hospital Medical School also offered him a place as a clinical student to start in 1963, dependent on his having passed the first two courses at King's College.

Before going to King's, however, Ian had to wait a year, and I think this must have been when he worked for BOAC at Heathrow airport, acting as an interpreter among other things. Clio and Brian were now firmly settled in Wimbledon in south London and Ian lived with them.

I remember Ian telling me that when he started his studies at King's he simply found it just far too difficult – he had done almost no science at school and had no sciences at all, either at 'O' or 'A' level. (I wonder what the entrance criteria could have been at the time?!). Unsurprisingly, he left King's.

However, he decided to continue with the idea of doing medicine and went to Kingston Technical College, to study for 'O' levels in Chemistry and Zoology, which he passed in 1962, and then 'A' levels in Chemistry and Zoology plus a Special Paper in Zoology, which he passed in June 1963. Having now got 6 'A' levels under his belt, plus a Special Paper, he applied to Oxford University to study medicine, where he was offered a place almost immediately. I have the offer letter from The Principal of Jesus

College, which explains why; and shows how times have changed![118] So, in January 1964, at the great age of 24, Ian went up to Oxford.

* * *

Fun, Fun, Fun

We had good times with lots of friends. The Jesus College Bar and the Turl pub – the closest pub to Jesus – featured fairly significantly in our lives, as did pubs outside Oxford which we would visit occasionally: the White Hart at Witham and Dirty Dudleys at Kingston Bagpuize, whose mead was legendary. A large old green Daimler which was named "The Duchess" was bought by several friends. Journeys to Dudleys could be interesting – the back of the Duchess was huge, like a London black cab – and there were always several passengers. On one occasion one of the doors burst open as we went round a corner – fortunately, no-one fell out.

A weekend summer afternoon was sometimes spent lying on the grass at the College cricket ground with a glass of beer. An evening in the College Bar would invariably include loud singing – Beatles' songs, "Strawberry Fields" being a favourite, and songs by The Supremes sung at top volume, with David's neck veins standing out in prominent relief with the effort of reaching those top notes.

We also cooked a lot, which we enjoyed, but ate out occasionally, too – curries (there really was a guy who used to ask for the hottest vindaloo the restaurant could provide) and occasionally, for a celebration, a good Italian restaurant.

It was at the nearest pub to our flat that the landlord not only kept the key to the loo behind the bar, but also the loo paper. He was a mean and bad-tempered man, and a group of about six of us decided we would razz

---

118 Letter dated 11 December 1963 from The Principal, Jesus College, Oxford: *"Dear Mr Macdonald, I was glad to make your acquaintance yesterday, and I write to offer you a Commoner's place at this College to read Medicine, coming into residence in January 1964. As you may realize, this is an unusual time for a student to begin his course, but it so happened that one of our medical Freshmen unhappily died in the course of last Term, and consequently we have a vacancy. You are older than most of our men, and you have not had the usual school training. However, Dr Rushworth thought highly of your potential merits, and I personally should be glad to have you as a member of the College. I hope to hear from you that you can accept this offer. If so, Dr Rushworth will send you the necessary details. Yours sincerely. . ."*

him up. We went into the pub, ordered a half pint of shandy and some straws and sat round a table, passing the glass round, each of us in turn sipping the shandy through our straws. After this, each of us went up to the bar one by one, and asked for the key and some loo paper... We did not make a return visit! At no point did I tell my parents that Ian and I lived together – which we did for three years before we married.

* * *

First Holiday in Greece

When the university summer vacation arrived, Ian and I thought it would be wonderful to go to Greece for six weeks. I asked my boss if I could take unpaid leave. That was in the summer of 1966.

I was working at a small engineering company in Oxford by then: Potter & Brumfield, a branch of a large American company. It was run by a small, bright and young go-ahead senior team, my boss being one of them. He commuted in from the Cotswolds every day, was intelligent, lively, fun, and approved my unpaid leave.

It was our first holiday together and it was brilliant. We took the train to Athens: a three day journey which cost £32 return! We met Aunt Olga and (for reasons of decorum) I stayed at the XEN (YWCA) and Ian stayed at the YMCA. We decided to visit the island of Aegina for a couple of days. I can remember women bathing in the evening at the edge of the sea with most of their black clothes still on – a very few daring to expose their bras. I was naive enough to burn the exposed part of my neck and shoulders on the ferry trip across to Aegina, the resulting burns taking a long time to heal, but nothing spoilt our enjoyment.

After returning to Athens briefly, we caught a ferry to Crete, where we spent the rest of our holiday. Crete was glorious. It was unspoilt and beautiful, and only a few tourists went there. We stayed in small village lodgings on the north coast and went up into mountain villages by bus, where we were followed around by groups of children unused to visitors. Women were sitting on doorsteps making lace and Ian's Greek was a passport to our being accepted. There was nowhere to stay, but we were offered the use of somebody's front room, where we slept on the side of a cupboard for 3s 6d = about 18p. Later, we took a bus south to Omalos, just over half way across the western part of the island, to walk down the gorge of Samaria to the coast. This is now a popular walk with tourists – there is an entrance fee and opening hours; the path and various springs are maintained and there are loos and wardens – very different indeed to the isolated place it was then. We were completely unprepared – we were carrying luggage (not rucksacks); were wearing flipflops; and had no equipment such as water bottles. We stayed the night in an isolated café in the middle of nowhere on the plateau above the gorge, where we slept in the one room they had at the back where we needed a blanket because it was chilly. The café was a meeting point for shepherds and farmers from the surrounding area, one of whom (quite a character, with a large bunch of basil stuck behind his ear) discovered that Ian was a medical student and, while we were eating, asked him detailed questions about his health problems.

The next morning we set off (they gave us some dried breads (paximadia) and water). We hitched a ride in a lorry towards the head of the gorge at a height of 1230m. We walked and walked (16km from the head of the gorge to the coast) and it became hotter and hotter. We met a Cretan shepherd after a while, with long black leather boots and traditional black Cretan trousers, who assured us that there was water lower down the gorge. We explored a ghost village but found nothing, and a dry well. My feet were blistered and painful. Every time we caught the sound of a breeze in the trees, we thought we heard water . . . we had to leave our luggage behind – hidden under some shrubs. Eventually, with swelling tongues, we at last came to a stream and amazingly sensibly, given everything else, drank only little by little as we lay down recovering. After some time, we walked on and reached a tiny village on the coast. By this time, my feet were the size and shape of footballs. There was a small café in the village where we were given the best of what they had – eggs, paximadia, goat's milk and honey. Ian was then taken back up the gorge on a mule (led on foot by the mule's owner) to collect our bag – I was no longer able to walk. The village had clearly not changed much for a very long time – we watched the elderly and charming café owner in his traditional Cretan clothes, milking his goat, and in the evening, counting his money by the light of an oil lamp. He was immensely generous. We slept on the bench seats in the café. It was dark, quiet, and timeless – hugely atmospheric.

The following day, two English girls arrived, one of whom was to become a close friend and live with us later. They had found a number of plasters on the way down the path – from my feet! After that, three or four young

French people arrived. The only way out of the village, Agia Roumeli, was by sea, to some distance east, along the coast to Hora Sfakion, where there was a road and a bus. However, the weather had changed and the sea was far too rough for a boat to put out, so we all had to stay in the village for three more days. Happily, someone had a pack of cards. Then, before dawn, in the dark, with the sea calmer, we all set out in a small boat lit by oil lanterns (another timeless scene) and reached somewhere with a small road. We had been very stupid but also very lucky.

After this adventure, we left our new companions, and headed east along the north coast, visiting Knossos en route and staying at Aghios Nikolaos where we bumped into the two English girls again – Flicky and Clare. We played tavla (backgammon) with them in cafés and exchanged addresses. Our next trip was south to Ierapetra. We made the journey hitching rides with several people. One of them insisted he knew the very best place – right up in the mountains – for grilled keftedes (meatballs) – and insisted on treating us to a delicious meal with a stupendous view. It still seems to me that those grilled keftedes were the best I have ever tasted. . . We reached Ierapetra, where we were treated to more generosity by a café owner who discovered that Ian, like him, had lived in Egypt. It was the day we were due to leave town and he insisted that we should not pay the bill. Horrified that we were going to hitchhike, he insisted that he would walk with us, when he surreptitiously went to a periptero (kiosk) and borrowed money, which he tried to lend us to buy bus tickets, trusting completely that we would pay him back. We managed with great difficulty, to refuse, returned to Athens and then Oxford.

We had many more holidays in Greece, and even went to live there for three years later on. We explored a great number of islands and I came to love the country, its people, its history and its culture.

CHAPTER 6

People and Places

* * *

WE LIVED IN VARIOUS PLACES IN OXFORD. The first was a bedsit, where we painted the walls bright orange and the ceiling dark blue, covered with silver stars. The landlord didn't seem to mind. . . Later, before we found a flat, Ian went home for a while and Jules very kindly offered to put me up on his houseboat – the HB Vole – moored in Port Meadow – very convenient for my workplace in Binsey Lane. The so called houseboat was a small floating box with a tiny deck at the front approached by a gangplank, ie more a house than a boat – I am fairly sure it could not possibly have moved on water without toppling over. . . We had fun and took it in turns to cook delicious meals on the tiny cooker.

Ian and I then found a small flat, where, because it was not self-contained, we pretended to the landlady to be married. I bought a curtain ring from Woolworths and would slip this on my finger just before going through the front door of the house. Ian was retaking some exams and we continued to enjoy our lives in Oxford.

* * *

Anglesey

Jules' parents, Kitty and Reg, owned a small cottage in Anglesey, North Wales, and very generously encouraged Jules to go there for weekends and take friends, so we had many superb "*Withnail & I*" times. These trips (we would invariably go in a group) involved 5/6 hour drives on Friday evenings and a similar return trip on Sunday evenings, but the pay-off was always more than worth it.

It was a small stone cottage down a muddy lane, with stone flagged floors, and a well in the nearby field. It was cold, but for the fire. The spectacular view from the tiny window in the small main room, took in the whole range of Snowdonia and we were close to miles of stunning sandy beaches and dunes, where we went for long walks. It was wonderful. We got to know the local farmer who looked after the cottage and 'Eric the Coal', the neighbour. Shopping sometimes involved walking across fields to a bus stop and on one occasion, on my return, I was closely followed by some very large pigs which were extremely interested in the apples I had bought. I was terrified and arrived back at the cottage in tears. I was never allowed to forget it! There were trips to pubs, too, and some of us went shooting with locals using ancient shotguns. The outcome of this on one occasion, was us making an Elizabeth David recipe for lièvre à la royale – hare slow cooked all day in the side oven of the fire with copious quantities of red wine (topped up throughout the day), and vast numbers of garlic cloves and shallots. Memorable. On another occasion, there was a chase up in the loft and a very large foot and long leg suddenly appeared through the ceiling. Jules' parents were tolerant as well as generous.

* * *

Waterville

Max's parents were also very generous. They owned a bungalow on the west coast of Ireland at Waterville in County Kerry, and Max took several of us there on several occasions. We had the most glorious holidays. Waterville had a shop or two, pubs and a small hotel, mainly patronised by keen (often American) salmon fishermen. The group initially was made up of Max, Jules, David, Ian and me. A little later, Maggie joined us, as did Jenny, later again.

The bungalow which Max's parents lent us was on the cliff just outside town, looking over the sea – the big strand not far away, at the end of the cliff road. There was a lough on the other side of town, well-known for its salmon fishing – the local gillie and his boat could be hired to ensure a good catch. We went out in a boat on the lough a couple of times, but with rather less serious intentions. A lot of Guinness was consumed in the local pubs, vast meals were cooked and card games were played in the evenings. Our nearest neighbour was an old man called Edzie, who sat on his wall and exchanged a few words with us as we made our way back and forth to the village. His comment on the increase in the price of Guinness, was to complain that this was very bad news indeed: *"Guinness – tis food, you know"*, he would say.

The local strand was vast and sandy and Jackie Moran's riding stables provided horses which we hired to ride along it. Maggie was an experienced rider, but the rest of us had no experience. The horses very soon realised this and regularly took off down the beach in a group, at top speed, with us hanging on for dear life; Ian on one occasion sliding off on to the sands, in mid gallop. Nobody was hurt and we laughed a lot.

On 29th March 1969, Ian and I married. Having spent the first night of our honeymoon on the floor of Jules' brother's flat in Covent Garden, we set off to Ireland with the gang. The holiday, as usual, proved to be wonderful. Jules had taken his car and one evening, David, who had just passed his test, managed, in the gloaming, to take fright at a tractor ahead of us which had only one light blazing straight at us. It was impossible to see the width of the tractor on the small country road, and David drove us into the ditch. We all managed to climb out of the car to be faced with the farmer asking us *"are you all kilt then?"* Numerous trips to one of the pubs in Caherciveen were required to negotiate a settlement with the farmer – all done very amicably over several pints of Guinness.

Caherciveen was a slightly larger town not too far away, and we would go there to shop. The car was often besieged by local dogs, which would run barking at the car, risking getting run over. We found the answer was to shout the name of the town to which we were going out of the window, after which, they invariably gave up! Shopping for food in Ireland in those days was severely limited – the quality of vegetables was poor and on the whole, all that was available were soft and often mouldering potatoes, carrots and cabbages. Garlic was unheard of.

The town was renowned at that time, for having more pubs and bars than any other town in Ireland and it was certainly surprising to find bars at the back of a lot of shops – even the butcher had one. The butcher cut meat using a vast vertical electric saw called a 'Butcher Boy'. Whatever type of meat it was that you wanted, you received a great side of meat, including the most tender and the toughest. You could have this cut up or minced.

One of our favourite places to visit was the pub at Renard Point, the small port outside Caherciveen which was home to the ferry crossing to Valentia Island (there was no bridge then). The pub was at the end of the road with no other houses nearby, and was owned by Moira and Eamonn. Moira ran the pub and Eamonn was the Guinness agent for the area and also ran a mink farm. They were delightful people and great fun. It was their young daughter who asked Ian (bald head and beard) – as he nursed a glass of Guinness at the bar – "*why don't you cut off your beard and stick it on your head?*" Much appreciated by all.

Regular punters at the pub included the weather man from Valentia Island. We did go across to Valentia on a couple of occasions and unexpectedly discovered a small Burmese restaurant there – run by a Burmese woman and her Irish husband. We booked a table and made a special trip. The food and the atmosphere were great – it was somewhat unusual, to say the least, to find a Burmese restaurant off the West coast of Ireland in 1969.

The Spanish fishing trawlers came into Renard Point regularly and the fishermen would invariably arrive with gifts of fresh fish, particularly hake. This Moira would cook up with lots of garlic (the Spaniards must have brought that too), in an enormous heavy black frying pan in the kitchen behind the bar. Favoured drinkers were invited into the kitchen to share it. Delicious.

A regular feature of spending an evening there was that the pub did not, of course, close on time. It was the habit of the Gardai (police) to check up that the law was being kept after hours, so when the lights of their car were spotted coming down the road, all the pub lights were turned off and everyone crouched down and hid, some behind the bar. The Gardai would take a cursory look and then drive away; the pub lights went on again, and we would all leave in the early hours.

* * *

Arthur Nortje

Arthur also joined us a couple of times on our Irish jaunts. Arthur was a South African poet, officially classified by the apartheid South African government as "Coloured". He had won a scholarship to come to England and study at Jesus College. He greatly enlivened our holidays, despite spending huge amounts of time in the Lobster Bar, downing pints of Guinness. I seem to remember that one day he managed to drink 17 pints. He was not interested in the great outdoors but loved to socialise and generally lark around. He had a lively sense of humour and would write poems about everything and anything at the drop of a hat. He was a brilliant addition to our group.

Tragically, his drinking turned into a problem. When his studies at Oxford finished, he went to live and teach at a couple of universities in Canada, and drank very heavily. He used to write letters to us and to Maggie from which this became clear. After some time, he returned to Oxford to do a postgraduate degree and lived in digs on his own – all of us having left Oxford by then. Tragically, he was found dead one night in his room. Ian and I were living in Battersea, when the police knocked on the door to give us the news. Unsurprisingly, I remember it vividly. We immediately feared the worst – that he had killed himself – but the inquest declared an open verdict, since he had died inhaling his own vomit after taking (prescribed?) drugs and alcohol. We never did know the full circumstances. The desperately sad and shocking funeral took place at Jesus College. It was the first funeral I had ever attended. Arthur had been a good friend and we were very fond of him. He died on 11 December 1970 at the age of 27.

It was through Arthur that, when we went to live in Kentish Town, we very soon met some of our neighbours. Arthur had been taught at school by another South African poet, Dennis Brutus (an anti-apartheid activist who was imprisoned on Robben Island. On his release, he came to the UK, until in 1983, he won the right to stay in the USA as a political refugee). Cosmo, who was Dennis and Arthur's friend, lived with his family in the next street to us and we got to know the family well. In fact, it was Cosmo's wife Flo, who did almost all the cooking for our house-warming party, making a chicken biryani which took almost all day to prepare and cook (our house had no kitchen at that stage). I went round to help and remember sitting on Flo's kitchen floor with a mortar and pestle grinding up spice after spice. Cosmo and Flo had three daughters, the youngest girl very young then – I used to take her to Hampstead Heath for walks occasionally. It was shocking to discover that in South Africa, the two older daughters had been classified in different categories according to their skin colour. Accordingly, they had been sent to different schools. Both of them were badly affected by this. I remember them telling me, too, of how they had been interviewed on several occasions by representatives of the UK Home Office during the British passport application process. Insultingly, the family had been asked what food they ate.

Unfortunately, the relationship between Cosmo and Flo broke down and Cosmo followed Dennis Brutus to America, where he took up a university post. This left the family bereft. The eldest daughter threw herself out of a window and became permanently disabled thereafter; the mother became depressed; and the middle daughter suffered long-term psychiatric difficulties – from time to time being treated as a hospital in-patient. The youngest daughter was the least affected, as far as I knew. My brother, David, dated the middle daughter, for a while.

The family's saviour was the girls' uncle: Flo's brother Menzies (everyone called him Mingie), who held the family together, supported them, and was always there for them. He had another sister, Amy, a headteacher in South Africa, who would come over to London once a year, if she could. We got to know them all well and kept up with Mingie and Amy, for many years.

Posthumously, in 1973, Heinemann published some of Arthur's work in "Dead roots: poems". In addition, a number of collections of his poetry, essays and academic papers have been published on his work, mainly by the University of South Africa.

I was surprised recently, to find that Arthur has a Wikipedia entry. There is a lovely photo of him there.[119]

* * *

Loch Fyne

Richard and Trish invited us to join them on a holiday in Scotland where Trish's parents owned a remote cottage on the edge of Loch Fyne. The

---

119 https://en.wikipedia.org/wiki/Arthur_Nortje

long car journey involved stopping at what had become a famous café just the other side of the border, where Richard and Trish would traditionally order a Scottish breakfast. This place, in true Scottish style, still made many varieties of bread, baps, scones, tattie scones, bannocks, and other Scottish specialities. A huge fresh and warm selection of these would be served, set out on large four tiered cake stands. Impressive and very good indeed.

Aunt Ismini and Uncle Henryk had gone on holiday to Spain but had recently bought a Border Terrier puppy which they asked us to look after while they were away. He was very young, called Max, and gorgeous. I used to take him into work with me every day on the tube (my boss, Harold, was delighted) and he was admired by everyone. He went to Scotland with us.

Loch Fyne and the surrounding countryside were wild and beautiful and the cottage delightful – situated almost on the edge of the water. There was an outside loo, so we tried not to need that in the night. We took long walks over the heather covered hills which we all, including Max, loved. For Max, who was a very small puppy, a walk like this meant jumping over the heather rather than just running ahead and we reckoned that most of the time, he was probably using, relatively, double the amount of energy we were using. After one walk, we reached the lane leading back to the cottage, and Max simply gave up – he lay down on his tummy, in the middle of the lane, spread-eagled, legs akimbo, exhausted. He simply could not go any further and we carried him the rest of the way.

There was a rowing boat which belonged to the cottage which we would take out mackerel fishing. All that was needed was a line with lots of hooks on it which we would thow into the water and hey presto, after rowing about for a while, we would have a large catch of mackerel. The fish were so fresh and delicious (Max loved mackerel too) but we could not eat them all and had to give quantities of fish away to neighbours down the lane.

Ian and I set out in the boat one day to explore the loch. We got as far as the island in the middle when an unexpected storm blew up. To make things more exciting still, there was a colony of gannets there and they started dive bombing us. We tried to row back to the cottage, but the wind and the current were too much for us. We just could not row against them. It was alarming. One of the rollocks then broke and we were pushed by the wind to the other side of the loch. Luckily for us, two young English guys were camping there and looked after us while we waited for the storm to abate. They cooked up a meal for us, too, with hot tea.

Eventually, we were able to set off back to the cottage, which was a bit tricky with only one rollock, but we made it. It was a memorable holiday.

* * *

Gate-Crashing in Bristol

Bernard, a friend of Jules, was rebuilding a small house in the countryside outside Bristol and Jules and David at one point helped him with this project. Bernard invited a group of us to go and stay for a weekend. We slept high up on hay bales in a barn, worried about rats. Bernard knew some people who were having a party, so, naturally, he invited us all along, despite the fact that we had not been invited. It was a very suburban type of garden party, held in a large smart garden, and for some reason, I've no idea why, we decided that we would limit all discussion to the three phrases taught to some non-English speaking Portuguese in the 1947 film "Road to Rio" with Bob Hope, to make it look as if they spoke English: "This is murder"; "You're in the groove, Jackson" and "You're telling me!". Whenever one of us joined a group, we would come out with one of these lines and nothing else. We had a few drinks and thought we were hilarious – especially when we were trying not to laugh. However, we couldn't stop laughing hysterically and ended up playing croquet on the lawn and hitting the balls into the flower beds. I have no idea why we were not thrown out – perhaps we were. . .

When Ian, Alex, Kate and I went to live in Athens years later, we met Bernard again. He had decided to travel the world teaching English and was then working at the British Council in Athens. We discovered that they were putting on a dramatisation of "Captain Beaky" – a collection of songs extremely popular with all the children and particularly good for singing in the car on our way across Ireland – and Bernard was playing Captain Beaky!

* * *

Yugoslavia

Former Yugoslavia was as far as we got in our attempt to visit Turkey. Max and Flicky (not an item), Ian and I, set off for Turkey in a small ex-Post

Office van. The van did not have side windows at the back, and was fairly loaded up, with four of us plus our luggage. I drove us through Brussels – my first experience of driving on the right hand side of the road and I seem to remember that at that time, there was no such thing as a driving licence in Belgium. It was hair raising, especially going round the major roundabout in the city, but somehow, I managed.

Once we had driven across most of Germany, however, things went horribly wrong: I was driving again, when the van's steering failed. We were on an autobahn which, fortunately for us, was not crowded at the time. The van swerved across all three lanes and hit the central barrier just where there was a post. Flick's arm was out of the window and her elbow was crushed between the post and the van. We then swerved all the way back again before the van spun round under a bridge and came to a stop facing the wrong way, just as the back doors sprang open and Ian and Max fell out of the back. We were lucky there were no cars immediately behind us. Flick's arm was a mess and she was in agony. The rest of us were shaken, but uninjured. The emergency services arrived and Flick was taken to hospital in Freising, a medium sized town just northeast of Munich. We managed to get ourselves and all our gear – including tents etc., to an orchard just outside Freising, where we set up camp with the owner's permission. I have no recollection as to how we managed this. We stayed for a couple of days, visiting Flicky in hospital, until she was flown back to the UK. Fortunately, we were properly insured, so the costs of Flick's hospital treatment in Germany and of her getting back to the UK were covered, but not, of course, the after effects. She had some complicated surgery, which left her with a steel pin in her arm and an inability to straighten that arm, for the rest of her life. We abandoned the van and had it towed away.

Once Flick had returned to London, Max, Ian and I decided to continue our journey by hitchhiking, but to limit our trip to Yugoslavia rather than going on to Turkey. We tried hitch-hiking as a threesome, but that just did not work, so we split up. Max went into Munich where he had heard that hanging around in Munich station, there were nefarious people who made a living out of driving large second-hand German cars to Turkey and these people were looking for co-drivers. It took no time for Max to find such a person and to set out driving a large Mercedes to Turkey, on the basis that he would get a free ride. (With hindsight, it seems highly likely that he was uninsured.) He had a nightmare of a time – the man concerned was an appalling and dangerous driver; on one occasion, deliberately driving straight over a roundabout on the coast road. Ian and I were lucky and offered lifts without much difficulty. We had arranged a meeting place with Max – the main post-office in Split, twice a day – and so found each other again.

We found some rooms owned by a delightful middle-aged local woman with whom we could only communicate in very broken Italian. For breakfast, she gave us small glasses of neat Slivovitz containing roasted coffee beans. Horrible – impossible to down the coffee beans. She was very keen to feed us well and would urge us "mangiare, mangiare. . ."

We did manage to communicate to her that we planned to take a boat out to the island of Hvar for the day. She was slightly worried and kept making circles of her fingers and putting these up to her eyes as though she were looking through a pair of binoculars. We simply did not get it. However, we took the boat and as we arrived, we suddenly did get it. Around the jetty there were men with no clothes on but with their legs modestly crossed. The further we walked, the more nudists we came across. The island was a haven for nudists (mainly middle-aged German tourists) and all three of us laughed and laughed and laughed. When we reached the beach, a rather large older German man came up to me, standing very close, and asked me the time! I decided not to strip off and enjoyed a good day with my swimmers on. We also had a lobster lunch – making the mistake of ordering two lobsters between the three of us which was so much and so rich, that we only just got through it all.

We enjoyed the unexpected visit to Yugoslavia very much. The coast around Split was beautiful, the Mediterranean weather superb and the people very friendly. My impression at that time, was that the men seemed to be the most good looking in the world. Split, which is now in Croatia, was and probably still is, a beautiful town, with ancient city walls. One late afternoon, as we were walking under ancient arches, a group of perhaps ten young people walked towards us. Suddenly, they all burst into song – in harmony – all automatically taking their own parts. It sounded fantastic, echoing around the walls, and we stopped to listen. The other people I knew who could do this at the drop of a hat were Ian's mother and his two aunts, who were all good singers and sounded great when they sang in a threesome, automatically taking parts.

I do not remember how we returned to London, but we found Flick recovering.

Life continued in the Kentish Town House – Flick was doing her PhD in anthropology at the LSE, where she met Jeffrey, a Canadian postgraduate student, also doing a research degree. She introduced us to Jeffrey and he became a regular visitor and then a close friend. Initially, Flick used to hold gatherings of like-minded Marxist students in her room, once a week, for serious discussion on the state of the world. We used to joke that we might be raided. Otherwise, evenings would be spent sitting around smoking Gauloises or Disque Bleu cigarettes and listening to French music – particularly the late 60s records I had brought back from Paris. Jeffrey likes to remind me that one evening, I suggested there could be people sitting around in Paris nostalgically smoking Embassy cigarettes and listening to English pop music! Jeffrey met Elizabeth, also Canadian, someone who had been to just about every bit of the world on her own, but was currently living in London, and it was not long before we became a close-knit foursome. Flicky had to spend time in the field as part of her research and went to live in Madagascar for a year. My brother David then moved in upstairs.

* * *

Swiss Connections

Ian and his Oxford flatmate Pete had become friendly with a young Swiss woman, Brigitta, when she was visiting the UK. This later led to invitations to Ian and me from her mother, Ursula, to visit the family at their beautiful house just outside Zurich. It was also suggested that we take a short holiday in their chalet in the mountains. It was an offer we could not refuse. Brigitta was no longer living at home, but had joined Sotheby's Auction House and was on her way to becoming an international jewellery expert. She had a brother, Thomas, who was married and had a small child, and a younger sister, Zis. Ursula was very kind and generous to us. She treated us to a traditional cheese fondue one night and explained the process. She had visited an excellent favourite cheese shop and selected several cheeses in different quantities which were then grated into separate bags for her. The cheeses were then put into the fondue dish with white wine and slowly heated. We put small pieces of bread on special long forks with wooden handles and ate our fill. The key to a truly successful fondue was apparently to knock back a small glass of kirsch half way through. This is called the *"coup du milieu"*.

Ursula drove us up into the mountains outside Zurich – a journey of a couple of hours, or so, and dropped us at the most extraordinarily beautiful traditional timber chalet. It was idyllic and the views magnificent. In the middle of the main living area there was a traditional tall square stove, covered in decorated ceramic tiles. This kept the chalet warm. The duvets were unlike any I have ever slept under since – great clouds of lightweight warmth which buried you (this was our first experience of duvets, too – they had not yet arrived in England). We were not going to be there for long, and decided not to attempt skiing, but to walk everywhere. The chalet was on the sunny side of the valley, looking across to the north facing shady side, where the snow was at its thickest and where the skiing went on. We went down to the village by sliding down the steep slopes on our backsides. We also went across to the north side of the valley to take a look, and discovered the former premier Swiss bobsleigh run. It was a rather terrifying prospect – a very long icy slide with tall ice walls, but we were tempted by the fact that you could hire a toboggan for 10 francs and try out the run. Ian went first. I followed. It was horrendous. There were parts of the run where there were no walls, just a massive sheer drop down a cliff. At these points we both managed to get off our toboggans and walk. However, not too far from the bottom, Ian climbed on again and found himself shooting up one of the icy walls, managing to cling on as he came down again. When he got to the bottom he shouted up to me what I thought were encouraging words, so I climbed on to the toboggan, misjudged an icy corner wall completely and took off up into the air... He had actually shouted a warning... I was shaken but not injured, but have not been on a toboggan since.

Jules, at this time, was working for the Swiss Broadcasting Company based in Bern. We had fun tuning in to the radio, and listening to him broadcasting the news in English. We also visited Jules in Bern.

Later, Zis came to London to learn English and we asked Sarah's parents, Bunny and Andrew, whether they would take her as a lodger. They lived in a large house in Richmond with three dogs and regularly took in lodgers, so it was perfect – and Zis, who was still quite young – used to visit us in Battersea on weekends.

Later still, Ursula came to the UK to explore the north coast of Scotland and stayed with us in Kentish Town. Zis then married Marco, and they too came to stay with us in London. It was great to have the space to put people up and our house became something of a regular port of call for friends.

* * *

Bath and Around

We met Flicky's parents, who owned a thatched house in a small village outside Hungerford. They were also generous to the younger generation, and we were often invited to either stay with them or use the house when they were not there. The countryside was full of tiny lanes with tall hedges on either side; steep hills with huge views from the top; bluebell woods; ancient houses to visit; and thatched cottages.

Through Flicky we met Judy, when she was living in London with Flicky's sister, Corinna. The two of them moved out of London and bought a house together in Bath, where Flicky, Ian and I used to visit them for weekends, setting a model for years to come. We even took two of our Australian friends from Papua New Guinea, down to visit her once. We had memorable times exploring the most glorious unspoilt and surprisingly remote English countryside around Bath. Whenever we came across a ruined barn, we fantasised (and it was nothing more than a fantasy) about buying it and doing it up. In one of the idyllic hidden tiny valleys, we found a small place (not even in a village), where we could sit in an orchard next to a stream, eating cream tea.

After a while, Judy bought her own house in Bath and later moved to a small village outside the city where she created the most magical garden. I continued to visit her and later, took Alex and Kate with me for weekends, which they loved. Over the years, we had, and I continue to have, some wonderful times with Judy, usually going on country walks, always with a picnic, often with juicy chicken sandwiches and home-made elderflower champagne (Judy was a cook for many years). Judy's *modus operandi* is to hunt through the ordnance survey maps covering a significant area around Bath, drive somewhere new and interesting looking; and walk the footpaths. It works every time!

* * *

France

I visited France, a country I love, a great many times: on my own; with Ian; with family; and with friends; both "Earlier" and "Later". From living there as an au pair for six months, to camping with Alex when he was very small, we had many adventures.

* * *

Mystery Woman

On one of our first visits, Ian and I decided to hitchhike south and had an unsettling experience. On the first day, we were unlucky with lifts and ended up having to sleep in a field in the middle of nowhere south of Paris. There were straw bales in the field and with these, we built a large double bed in the middle of the field with a wall around it, and slept with all our clothes on since it was not very warm. In the middle of the night, I woke up being hit on the head with a straw bale, by Ian, who had half woken up, seen my head in the dark and taken it for a rat! I had been brutally awoken, but fortunately not hurt, and Ian was mortified! We laughed about it a lot once the sun came up.

In the morning (a bit desperate for something to drink and eat), we started hitching again and accepted a lift from a woman on her own. She behaved very strangely, driving erratically, changing her speed, slowing down and looking from left to right as if she were searching for something. She then picked up another hitch-hiker – a young man – and continued in much the same way. We were travelling through a large forest when she pulled up at the side of the road, got out and walked into the forest. We waited and waited and waited some more, but she did not return. She had left her car keys in the ignition and her handbag in the car. We got out and started looking for her, shouting through the trees, until we saw her shoes. . . The forest and the situation were sinister and we certainly did not want to go further into the forest for fear of what we might find. The car was parked at the top of a very long hill leading down to a couple of houses, so we decided to freewheel the car down the hill. We found a garage there and reported the problem. The gendarmes arrived quickly and set up a base at the top of the hill, with several vehicles. We were each interrogated individually, and were not allowed to leave. Our passports were confiscated. After some time, we were told we had to set off in a mini-bus with the gendarmes, driving on tracks into the forest. It was truly horrible, and very scary; we were expecting at any moment, to see a body. The first things found were her clothes, and some time later, we were allowed to go, but with no further information. Strangely, we never found out for sure whether they found the woman alive, but we assumed they must have done, otherwise we would surely have been contacted once we were back in the UK. We were given a ride in a lorry much further south and the driver started to recount the tale of the missing woman and the hitchhikers etc. . .

* * *

Normandy

We had an excellent holiday in Normandy with Jeffrey and Elizabeth. Jeffrey owned a white Triumph Herald with a fold-down top, so we explored in style! Jeffrey had a couple of student friends who lived in Rouen who put us all up for a couple of nights. Apart from visiting the city and the cathedral, we also went out into the country for a walk, during which we spent some time hurling hay at each other. On our return home, Jeffrey discovered that a tick had attached itself to him. He panicked, imagining, as in North America, that he was bound to get something horrible like Lyme's disease. The tick was removed and with gigantic amounts of showering and scrubbing and with gallons of water, he was reassured. After that we spent time pottering around the coast visiting places such as Honfleur and eating delicious and vast *plats de fruits de mer*.

* * *

Paris on the Cheap

There was also a trip to Paris with Ian, my brother David, and our friend Richard. We stayed in what must have been the cheapest hotel in central Paris and booked two very basic double rooms. We were all turning up at different times, so on the first night, we had only one double room booked, which Ian and Richard shared. On night two, Richard moved out of the room with Ian and I moved in, and he moved into a second double room with David! Management was unconcerned. . .! I remember arriving in

Paris very early in the morning having travelled overnight on the ferry, and drinking a glass of chilled Muscadet in a bar for breakfast – an excellent pick-me-up.

* * *

Au pair in Paris and Brittany

Once Ian had finished his studies in Oxford, he was due to do his clinical studies in London at University College Hospital Medical School (as it was called then).

Discussion took place as to where Ian and I should live and in Ian's view it would be impossible for us to live together in London because his parents would not accept that. I did not want us to live separately in the same city, so decided to apply to become an au-pair in Paris for a while, until matters became clearer. This was April 1968.

I went to what I thought must be a posh agency (it was located in Knightsbridge!) and explained that I was looking for an au pair position for six months, and importantly, wanted to live in the centre of Paris. They offered me a post and I duly arrived in France to find myself living with a very pleasant family a long way out in the Parisian suburbs. It turned out that the family, which had a very young child, had asked for someone to stay with them for a minimum of a year, so when we discussed matters, we came to a mutual agreement that we needed to contact the agency. The agency sorted out my problem, by offering me a position in the 17th arrondissement of Paris. Certainly central. I went for an interview which was held over lunch! The family lived in an enormous flat in a grand street (42 rue Ampère, off the Avenue de Wagram, which runs from the Arc de Triomphe) and they also lived in the grand style, with a cook, an all-day daily 'bonne', a once a week heavy duty cleaner and an au pair as well. Lunch was grand too – lots and lots of cutlery and crockery, a groaning sideboard, and delicious food. I heard Madame remark that my table manners were up to scratch and I was offered the job!

Monsieur was a lawyer and Madame was an obstetrician and gynaecologist, with Brigitte Bardot one of her patients. They had two sons who were nearly grown up and a younger daughter, Armelle, of nine years, who was to be looked after by me. I was taken to the girl's bedroom and told that one of my duties would be to keep her room clean and tidy. I would also be taking her to the nearby '*place*' regularly after school, to roller skate. My other duties included dusting and hoovering the large sitting room every day. Other than that, I would do the drying up after meals, buy the bread every day and go on other shopping trips, as and when. Buying the bread was not what you would call a chore: each day I would go to the baker and return with an armful of pains and baguettes. By the time I got back, I had torn off several pieces of fresh baguette and eaten them! In the kitchen, there was a drawer full of gruyère – used only for cooking (never for eating) – so as soon as I got back, bread and cheese became *de rigueur*. Wonderful. I would also be asked to order vegetables for delivery. On one occasion, I ordered the wrong type of green beans (so many varieties) and Madame was furious. Madame was also annoyed one day at lunch, declaring to Christianne, the 'bonne', that the plates could not have been rinsed properly because she could taste the washing-up liquid. I would be fed every day except on Sunday, when I had to fend for myself (I used to buy bread and cheese and kept a litre bottle of the cheapest Nicolas red wine on the top of my small cupboard). My allowance (pocket money) was 10 francs per week, which was fine – enough for travel, visits, and a little food.

As part of my introduction to the family flat, I was shown where the bathroom was, since I was told I would be living in one room upstairs but would be allowed to take baths in the flat. In most of the grand apartment blocks in that area of Paris, there is a front and a back staircase, each with its own door. The back staircase leads not only to the back doors of the apartments (for deliveries) but also up to the top floor where the servants live, an arrangement unchanged since the 19th century. My small room was on a long corridor on the 8th floor, at each end of which was a sink with a cold water tap and a lavatory. In some cases, whole families lived in one or two of the many rooms. Not everyone would have enjoyed this, but for me, I saw it as an advantage that I did not live in the flat with the family – I was independent.

I really enjoyed my time in Paris, particularly because the family employed a piano teacher for Armelle, called Nicole, who, as payment, was given rent free rooms on the same floor as me. Instead of one, however, she had two rooms, one of which was a tiny kitchen with a wonderful view of those famous Parisian rooftops. Not that she cooked too often, since she was invariably broke and would climb up the stairs in pain, clutching her stomach because she was so hungry. She did find other occasional work but it was limited, as was her income. Nicole came from Annecy in the Alps. She became a great companion and was one of the reasons my French improved. I arrived with very basic schoolgirl French, and whereas Madame did speak English, Nicole spoke none and provided me with the practice I needed.

I used to spend my Sundays exploring Paris and have vivid memories of all sorts of places: going for the first time to the Pont des Arts and eating the most delicious Charentais melon as I looked at the famous view; visiting well known sights and museums; going with Nicole to explore Pigalle, the red light district (quite an eye opener for me then) – with lots of cross-dressers around and two lesbians physically fighting in the street.

Nicole found a group of friends by chatting to a young man, Manuel, on the métro, about the music score she had with her. It turned out that he had a couple of friends who were music students – a young South African woman, Gerda, studying singing; a young Dutch(?) woman, Ann-Marie, also studying music; and a young American man, Steve, studying the organ with no less a person than Mme Nadine Boulanger. We got to know them all well and used to visit the two young women in their ground floor flat just off the rue Mouffetard (famous for its market), in the Quartier Latin. Gerda, who had contracted polio as a child, had callipers on her legs and generally managed brilliantly. However, when their loo refused to flush, things became a little more awkward. The loo was of the old fashioned variety and had a cast iron cistern high up on the wall with a long metal chain for flushing. Impetuously, I offered to help. I closed the lid of the loo and climbed on to it. All well so far, but when I lifted the lid of the water tank, the cover of the loo, unable to cope with the extra weight, broke. The loo itself (the porcelain bowl) shattered and I was left standing in the remains of the loo holding the cistern lid, surrounded by the contents of the loo all over the floor, and large, jagged dangerous spikes of ceramic sticking upwards. The laughter and hilarity that ensued went on for some time. It was very very funny, despite the fact that my calves could have been shaved off. It was, of course, a Sunday, so finding a plumber would be a problem and a repair would not be speedy. The difficulty was that Gerda would have to go somewhere nearby to use a loo and, with the callipers, she could not squat. Almost all loos in Paris at that time, however, were squat loos. My next task, therefore, was to visit all the local cafés to find one close enough to the flat, which had a sit down loo. It took some time and lots of strange looks, but eventually, I was successful.

My time in Paris was a great experience – my work was certainly not arduous and I learned and experienced a lot and enjoyed myself. It was May

1968, so the time of the student riots in Paris, around the University of the Sorbonne, in the Quartier Latin on the Left Bank. (These riots soon spread and turned into a massive general strike lasting for around two weeks and involving large numbers of people.)

Madame wanted to take a look for herself at what was going on and, surprisingly, asked me if I would like to go with her. Of course I was game, so we set off in her Mini to take a look. Obviously, we could not get very close in a car, but we saw enough to get a good idea of the situation.

It was then that Maggie came to visit me and one of the things we did very soon after she arrived, was to go and take a look at the riots. We were close enough to see students throwing cobble stones and tear gas being fired by the CRS (Compagnies Républicaines de Sécurité), the riot control forces of the French National Police. They were intimidating, helmeted, armed, wearing goggles, and carrying shields. It was a confused and violent situation with lots of students and others milling around, and Maggie and I became separated. . . I could not find her anywhere, and finally had to return home without her. Looking back on it, I am sure I should have reported her missing, but all I did was worry. I was unsure whether she even had a note of my address with her. However, all was well. She turned up the following day, having been looked after overnight by an American man who had apparently insisted on bathing her feet!

One of my new friends, Steve, had a ticket for a cheap return flight to London which he was not going to be able to use and he offered it to me, which was a bonus. I used a pen to rather unconvincingly change the Mr to Mrs – amusing to think that in those days you showed your ticket and your passport quite separately – so I got away with it.

Part of the family I was working for was soon to decamp to Brittany, where Monsieur's parents had a house. It is traditional in France for children to go on holiday with their grandparents so that the parents can take a break on their own, so it was decided that I should go to Brittany with the three children from our household plus Quentin, the child of Monsieur's brother. Very conveniently, this change of scene allowed me to make a week's visit to London using the free ticket. I wrote to Ian to let him know, and received a reply saying that even though his parents would be away on holiday, he was forbidden to allow me to stay in their house – basically for fear of what the neighbours would say! I was upset, obviously. However, undeterred, I sent a telegram setting out my arrival details and both Ian and Maggie were there to meet me. Initially, I stayed at Maggie's flat, but soon afterwards, went to Ian's parents' house in Wimbledon and enjoyed my week in London. Ian's parents, on their return, enquired as to what had happened and were hugely annoyed when they were told. When I returned to England at the end of my time in France, and visited them, I walked into the sitting room and Ian's father continued to read his newspaper without speaking to me. Ian's mother also refused to speak to me. This was too much for Ian, who, after I had gone, apparently told them he would never again accept behaviour like that from them. I was certainly amazed (and shocked) at how rude they had been (it seemed very out of character), but it never happened again.

Not long after my return to Paris, we set out for Brittany, where life turned out to be even less arduous for me and where we all had a fantastic holiday. The house was called Er Parc Braze, at Kerhostin, en Saint-Pierre-Quiberon, Brittany, a large house on the cliffs just above the sea. Saint-Pierre-Quiberon is a beautiful peninsula 9 miles long and 22 miles wide, also known for its Côte Sauvage. The beaches were stunning and we had good weather. I was allowed to use one of the family's bicycles and used to potter off on my own in my free time. I had a spacious room with its own small bathroom – no shower, nor bath, but basin and bidet – which, after all, is all one needs, especially if swimming a lot. Strip washes became the order of the holiday. I remember too, reading a lot and laughing out loud as I read Kingsley Amis' novel, "Lucky Jim".

Monsieur's father was also a lawyer (retired) and he and his wife lived in the rue du Faubourg St Honoré, in the 8th district of Paris, just behind and parallel with the Champs Elysée, with the house in Brittany their second home. They were both rather grand and formal, and I suspect, were dreadful snobs, but they were very pleasant while in their summer home. (I assumed this because I was told by their cook that if Monsieur saw her in the street in Paris, he would not acknowledge her(!) but in Brittany, he was friendly and quite normal. I once made the mistake (on a blackberry picking outing with her and the children) of addressing Madame using "*tu*" instead of "*vous*" and was very swiftly corrected.)

Monsieur loved fishing and he would go out in a small boat every evening with a local fisherman, the husband of the woman who cleaned and helped in the house, to put his nets out in the sea. They would then get up very early in the morning and go out again, to see what they had caught. He once invited me to go with them in the early morning, which was a treat. He would find all sorts of sea life in his nets and, when he got back home, everything he caught was laid out on the concrete apron in front of the garage, before being distributed. The catch could include enormous and hideous fish, the names of which escape me, other more normal fish, shellfish and crabs. The cook got used to finding large live crabs crawling around in the kitchen sink.

They employed a cook who not only lived with them in Paris but travelled with them to Brittany. She was a marvellous cook – from Normandy – and our meals were always superb. Her *soles à la normande* was quite brilliant – I still have her handwritten recipe for it. The main meal of the day was lunch. The first course was invariably seafood and just about anything that any of us, particularly Monsieur, brought in from the sea, found its way on to the lunch table. Wine was served but it was expected that you would water it down. They all seemed to take pleasure in the fact that, as they put it, I was a "*gourmande*" (NB: not a "*gourmet*"). One of the strange things we found in the sea was called "*pieds de l'elephants*" – slightly weird dark grey rubbery tubes, inside which was pale pink delicious flesh – a bit like prawn. I have no idea what these were – I cannot find any mention of such creatures on the internet, so assume that this was a very local name for these *fruits de mer*. Raw sea urchins would also turn up on the table along with all the small shellfish that the children used to bring in. Dessert was often a large bowl of fromage frais with some fruit. Fromage frais did not exist in England at that time, nor for a long time afterwards, and for me, it was quite a discovery.

Brittany, of course, is famous for its oysters, so we would eat those too, but when Monsieur's other son (a bit of an impoverished ne'er do well according to the staff! but apparently Madame's favourite) came to visit with his Vietnamese wife, special trips were made to the oyster sheds because he loved oysters so much. These wooden oyster sheds were fascinating – there were several different kinds of oyster, all laid out in wooden trays by type, quality, and size. There were so many oysters. . . They were expensive, but Madame bought lots and lots of oysters for her favourite son. When we got home, I was sent down to the beach to collect seaweed. The local Bretonne woman who helped in the house (wife of the fisherman) was a genius at opening the oysters at speed. They would then be laid out on large oval dishes decorated with the seaweed and quartered lemons. What a feast – they were superb. I remember the Vietnamese woman mainly because she was friendly but also because she showed me how she topped up her skin colour using tea. Their son Quentin, who was with us for the holiday, was a delightful boy and took great pleasure in regularly cooking very good plum clafoutis for us all. The atmosphere was very relaxed and I spent a lot of time in the sea and on the beach.

* * *

A barn in the Pyrenees?

Many years later, on our return from Australia, we thought we had saved enough money to buy a small barn in France which we could convert into a holiday cottage. We both loved France. After hunting around when we were on holiday, we found a beautifully located ruined barn in the foothills of the central French Pyrénées, in the Ariège, not far from St Girons. It was at the top of a narrow winding valley full of apple orchards and had magnificent open views across to snow capped mountains. We bought it. It had a spring nearby, but there was no well. Naively, we thought it would be quite easy to make the place habitable. We visited on a couple of occasions, getting quotations from local builders for the works necessary, but these turned out to be expensive – sadly, more than we could afford. It was a short-lived idea, and after not too long, we put the barn on the market again. It sold quickly and fortunately, we lost no money at all on our somewhat misguided pipe-dream.

* * *

Harold

In April 1969, just before I married, I found a permanent job – working for a small firm of Consulting Engineers called Richards & Bright at 21 Taviton Street in Bloomsbury (the building is now University College London's nursery). The firm was owned and run by Harold Bright (a descendant of John Bright, Quaker, Radical and Liberal MP).

Harold acted as an Expert Engineer in legal cases and regularly testified in court. He was quite a character – getting on in age when I joined – but with a full and vibrant work and social life. He was of medium height and weight but with a slightly pronounced belly – the result of thoroughly enjoying food and cooking – he typed out and gave me a recipe or two. He had a shiny bald pate which he frequently stroked, a ring of hair around the edges, and a trim beard. He wore thin gold framed spectacles when needed. He had inherited from his mother, a very large house in Connaught Square near Marble Arch and he ran his business from the ground and first floors of this fairly unkempt house in Bloomsbury, the upper floors of which he let to tenants. He had a work partner, a long suffering but kind man called Bill, whose job it was to design electrical and heating systems on large building projects, in liaison with firms of architects. There were a couple of draughtsmen, too, who worked with Bill on these projects. Bill was clearly competent, but deferred in all matters to Harold.

Harold also owned a house in the South of France, to which he would frequently invite groups of his friends, who all seemed to have a very good time together. He owned a medium sized black poodle called Topsy, which was always with us at work and which I regularly took for walks in Gordon Square. A dramatic situation arose on one occasion, when I took her to the Square when she was on heat, and a large dog managed to jump right over the very tall railings (the square was for key-holders only in those days) and made a bee-line for Topsy. I had to run round in circles with Topsy on the lead and then eventually pick her up and make our escape. When I told Harold, he immediately took her to the vet for a 'morning after' pill, not that anything had happened. He clipped Topsy himself and kept the soft hair, which he used to stuff cushions! He was quite eccentric but an attractive and unusual personality and life working in his office was certainly different.

At one stage, Harold had also been Mayor of Holborn – when there had been a Borough of Holborn, which by the time I began working for him in 1969, had been subsumed by the London Borough of Camden.

Harold had been married and his wife had become an alcoholic and lived in a clinic, not that I met her. He had also had a mistress who became an alcoholic. The difference between the two women was that Harold's ex-mistress, Peggy, lived in the basement flat of the building where we worked. The conditions in the flat were squalid and quite disgusting, and the situation bizarre. She was in a terrible state. Harold had not had a relationship with Peggy for many years, but clearly, he wanted to try and help her by providing her with safe and free accommodation. I became involved in checking up on her sometimes (not part of most job descriptions) and got used to her appearing occasionally in the hall looking quite normal; smart and made-up, going out shopping; and then returning wreathed in winning smiles, trying to hide the very obvious bottles in her bag. She ate very little and frequently became ill. It was very sad indeed. She told me she had been a regular drinker at the well-known 'French Pub' in Dean Street, where many writers and artists used to gather, and had known Dylan Thomas among others. A very sorry saga and a steep learning curve for me.

Things got so bad at one point that Harold had her admitted to St Pancras Hospital (which no longer exists) to dry out. While she was there she met a man who was also in hospital drying out – and they decided to get married. . . Her flat was so dreadful (it stank) that Harold told Peggy that she and her new husband could have one of the upstairs rooms. Chaos ensued almost as soon as they moved in – regular 'scenes' would take place in their room or on the stairs, usually at top volume, and they both had to go back to hospital fairly rapidly. Harold told me in a letter later, that eventually, Peggy, who had had a fall and become dependent on a wheelchair, was housed by Camden Council in one of the Brunswick Square flats. He wrote "Her husband, who appears to have a girlfriend, visits her daily and helps her to dress. She has made a lot of friends and has given up drinking. I feel that all of the trouble we all took in trying to help her has paid off after all."

There is not much doubt that Harold had always been something of a ladies' man, and continued to be one. He had a rather glamorous lady friend he would meet regularly for smart lunches in Soho and he had another very good lady friend who eventually moved into her own small house at the bottom of the garden in the house in France. His house was *'La Maison du Commandant'*, at St Maximin par Uzès, not far from Uzès in the Gard, and Harold showed me photos of it occasionally. When Maggie and I spent a holiday together in 2014, in the stunning small town of Uzès, one of the things we did was to visit this village to see if we could track down the house. Maggie was quite determined not to give up. Having wandered around with no luck, I asked an elderly couple we came across. They remembered almost immediately who Harold was, where the house was, and that a lady called Judy had lived there too, even though, as they pointedly said, they were not married! It was rather fantastic to find the handsome large early 19th century house and garden that I had heard so much about 45 years earlier. A complete refurbishment was just starting, so we were lucky to see it as it had been. We peered through the letterbox and saw all sorts of typical Harold gadgetry and paraphernalia.

Harold was a kind man and when Ian and I turned our thoughts to buying a house (despite Ian having no income as yet) Harold offered to act as our guarantor in a 100% mortgage application to the London Borough of Camden. He took a financial risk on our behalf and it was an offer which changed the course of our lives and allowed us to buy our first house. I do not think we could have done it without him – it would have been very difficult to find anyone else prepared to do this (our parents certainly would not have done so).

Harold decided to move from his house into a flat. In order to do so, he needed to either find a home for, or sell, various large items of furniture in his house. He very generously gave me an enormous and very handsome gilt-framed mirror – 6ft × 6ft – which we installed in the hall in our new house in Kentish Town, and later in the hall of our house in Muswell Hill. He also gave me a very large wooden Windsor-type chair with a high back.

I have six letters that Harold wrote to me from France. His letters were full of news, always including invitations for us to go and stay with him. He told me that his wife had died in 1979 and it was after this that he had decided to retire (Richards and Bright ceased to practice in 1980), and spend most of his time in France. While he was there, he had met the daughter-in-law (now widowed) of Madame Floris, the Hungarian lady who had set up the famous bakery in Brewer Street, Soho (the Queen's Royal appointed bakery) which then went on to make and sell chocolates and patisserie. They also decided to get married, Harold at the age of 80 and Kate, his wife, 25 years younger. They decided to live permanently in France and he sold his flat. He and his new wife had their honeymoon in the USA ("Kate's mother and sister live in Hollywood, a most frightful place")! But they had been all over America and made a second visit too, plus spending a short holiday in Denmark. In 1987 when he was 86, he wrote a 'testimonial' for me when I applied for a job at University College London. He wrote "Of course I will give you a testimonial, something like 'If you can persuade this lady to work for you, you will be very lucky' perhaps?"

When he was 90, Harold and Kate went round the world and he told me that, although they still lived in St Maximin, they had each sold their houses and lived in a rented house there. Later, he wrote "I am still in pretty good form although a bit doddery on my feet, but what can you expect at 92?"

They had also acquired a small apartment in a tiny hamlet in the Italian mountains north of San Remo, to which they would go when it got too hot or too full of tourists in the Gard. In the middle of a national park, there were only 102 inhabitants in the hamlet, including them, and he urged me to borrow it. I still regret never having taken him up on this offer. He also enclosed a photo of himself taken at his 93rd birthday party in which he looks very dapper and trim.

The last letter Harold sent me was dated Friday 18 November 1994, when he told me that he and his wife had taken a decision on the spur of the moment to visit London for a month, and said that he would like to take me out for lunch. He arranged that we should meet at the Danish Club, then at 62 Knightsbridge – a very smart venue. It was lovely to see Harold again (I had not seen him since the early 70s), but it seemed that his wife was oddly worried about me as a potential rival(!) – immediately asking where my husband was, at which point Harold had to shush her. There were tables and tables of smorgasbord and everything was appetising and looked beautiful. It was comfortable and we had lots of chats – Harold was in very good form. He was quite fragile, however, and as we went downstairs, he stumbled, and I caught him just in time to stop him falling. I did not see, nor hear from him again after that, and although I know that he had included me in his Will, leaving me £1000, which I found surprising and touching, there would have been reasons why he changed this later.

* * *

Love and Marriage

When the Brittany part of my au-pair contract came to an end, I returned to London. It was nearly the end of September 1968. Ian was still a student; not earning; and living in Wimbledon with his parents, so there was no question of us living together.

Maggie, as usual, was a brilliant friend, and asked her flat sharers whether I could camp on the sofa for a while until I found a place of my own. They all kindly agreed, and it did not take me long to find work as a temporary secretary working for an agency in central London (which is how I came to work for Harold), and also to find a bed-sit right in the centre of Hampstead village. The bed-sit was in a small flat lived in by one woman on the first floor above a bank. My room had a small two plate electric cooker with very limited equipment, and I had to wash up my dishes in the bathroom basin. The result was that I ate scrambled eggs on toast almost every evening, psyching myself up in advance as to how delicious my meal was going to be. What could have been cooler, though, than living on the first floor opposite the "Coffee Cup" on Hampstead High Street!

I used to see Ian regularly, but the situation was a bit bizarre and we decided that the answer would be to get married – that should put a stop to parental interference. When we announced this, we were told we could not possibly get married because we had no money. However, I was at this stage earning £20 a week which was quite good for those days; Ian had a little money; and we were sure we could survive.

Maggie's first boyfriend, Peter (the one who had visited her at school in a flashy sports car) had now qualified as a solicitor and was working at a firm of solicitors in Bloomsbury. He and Maggie were no longer an item, but kept in touch. Peter had bought a house in Eynsford in Kent from where he was going to commute. He suggested that Ian and I could live with him rent free, if we did the cooking, cleaning and gardening for him. We thought this could work out well and it certainly persuaded our parents that we would be able to afford to get married. What they did not take into account, however, was that although paying no rent, we had to pay for commuter rail fares, which, even then, were expensive, and more than made up for not paying rent.

Ian and I married on 29 March 1969 at the small church in Yateley, Surrey, where my parents had finally bought a house. To please my parents, it was a white wedding, in a church, with a traditional reception in a hotel nearby. We arranged a coach from London to take friends to the wedding and back again. David was Ian's best man and Jules played the organ for us. I'm fairly sure a good time was had by all. It was fun.

Our honeymoon plan was less traditional, however – we went to Ireland with our group of friends, as was usual at Easter. It was a terrific Irish holiday – as always.

When we returned to London, we joined Peter in his house in Kent. The arrangement did not last for long, because although it was lovely to arrive in a small village in Kent in a rural environment at the end of the day, the commuting was fairly awful. Not only was it expensive, but time consuming (we arrived home too late to really enjoy the rural environment), and the last train home was so early, that I remember having to leave a theatre before the end of a play, in order to catch it. We both disliked the commuting – I decided then that I would never commute again – and never have. We decided to look for somewhere to rent in London (parents had no influence, now!), and the friend we had met on our Cretan holiday, Flicky, found part of a house in Battersea which she suggested we share.

This worked out very well. The house was terraced and a very short distance from Albert Bridge Road at 55 Parkgate Road. We went to see it with Flick and were invited by the fairly hippy tenants to sit on the floor in a circle in the first floor front room, where we were treated to the sight of their small son running around with no nappy on, being followed by an anxious parent with a potty, which the little boy delightedly managed to avoid in order to defecate on the carpet in front of us all – the centre of attention – to a round of applause from his audience. . . We had never experienced anything like that before! Anyway, we took the place (without the carpet) and were pleased. Flick had a bedroom on the second floor, next to the son of the owners of the house and we had a bedroom on the first floor. We shared the first floor sitting room and kitchen with Flick. There was only one bathroom for the whole house, though, so we shared this with Flick's neighbour and also with the couple who lived downstairs. Our rent was £7 a week.

The couple downstairs were very pleasant. Janet was proud of being a cockney – the daughter of a London policeman – and she was married to Oscar, a painter/decorator from the Canary Islands. Whenever she shouted "Oscar!" it was a scream, at top volume, and she always called him more than once. Oscar himself could not stop painting the bathroom, which would frequently change colour completely, from top to bottom. They had a small garden at the back of the house, in which they kept a ferret, a rabbit, a duck and a cat. Surprisingly, the animals seemed to co-exist without too much difficulty. On one occasion, when Ian and I were eating our evening meal, Janet turned up with the ferret in her arms and asked Ian (a medical student, of course) to help her give the ferret some medication. She was quite a character – a hippy with long straight blonde hair down to her bottom. Whenever the 'totter' (the rag and bone man) came round the streets with his horse and cart, ringing his bell and collecting almost any unwanted items, she would run out into the road with a bucket and shovel, follow them around for a few blocks and collect any horse dung from the road, to put on her garden. She became pregnant and spent most of her pregnancy reading Tolkien's "Lord of the Rings", something which clearly influenced her in their choice of name when their child was born: he was named Frodo.

The kitchen was a good size and we used to entertain lots of friends. The bathroom, however, had a bit of a flaw – water was heated by a gas boiler which would take a while to ignite whenever the hot tap was turned on. . . ie there was a pause which you knew was too long, followed by a loud explosion. When Maggie and Jules stayed in our flat once while we were away, one of these explosions caused the mirror to shatter and fall off the wall! Maggie describes her stay in Battersea as being made up of regular walks along the King's Road with yet another mirror on her back. I am not sure how many mirrors broke!

We felt we had really made it when we bought an old black Ford Prefect, for £15. We were very pleased with it, but there was a difficulty: finding the money to buy petrol. I ran out of petrol on Albert Bridge, and in the middle of Trafalgar Square, among other places. In addition, the brakes failed (there were no MOTs in those days). I had them fixed and fortunately kept the receipt for the repair, because the following day, having just visited Kew Gardens, they failed again and I was unable to stop at a junction. I hit a small three wheeled vehicle (a Reliant Robin) but luckily no-one was hurt. However, I was summoned to appear at Richmond Magistrates Court for being in charge of a dangerous vehicle. I wrote out my plea in mitigation, showed it to my boss, Harold, read it out in Court, and also produced the garage's receipt from the day before. This put the Magistrate in a difficult position because he did not know how to proceed. Fortunately for me, there was a lawyer at the back of the Court, who stood up and said that h was prepared to act as an '*Amicus*' to the Court, and proposed that I should be found guilty but not punished. The Clerk of the Court seconded this and so although found guilty of being in possession of a dangerous vehicle, I was not fined and did not receive any points on my licence. The garage should probably have been prosecuted, of course. . .

* * *

Spain

Aunt Ismini and Uncle Henryk bought a flat in a small town south of Barcelona (later they bought a second in the same block) and they offered it to us for a holiday. Ian and I stayed there a couple of times, once on our own and once with his cousins Juliet and Margaret, which was somewhat crowded, but we managed. We hitchhiked through France to Spain and had a relaxing time – cooking wonderful paellas when we got there and spending time on the beach. Although it was a small town and you could buy superb locally grown vegetables (and snails – which we bought once and mistakenly let loose on the balcony!), there were unfortunately some ugly large tourist hotels right on the beach, and messages were broadcast to residents which could be heard by everyone on the beach. We soon discovered, however, that if you went a little bit further along the coast, you could escape, and enjoy the sea and the beach in peace. We were amused to see that at siesta time, young men on motorcycles would ride up and down the unmade road behind the beach, with binoculars at the ready, hoping to spy on any topless young women. It was the beginning of Spain's British tourist boom. We made a couple of daytrips into Barcelona by train. The view from the train (of almost uninterrupted flesh on the beaches) confirmed this. The city of Barcelona, however, was attractive, unspoilt, uncrowded, and a delight to visit.

* * *

Property Owners

We hunted around for a house we could afford and found a three storey terraced slum in Kentish Town for £5,250. We were just able to afford this by negotiating the price down from £5,750! The London Borough of Camden at that time was offering 100% mortgages (unimaginable in these days of vast deposits) and they also offered Discretionary Grants to enable owners to install hot water, heating, a bathroom, etc. where there were none. The house was at 21 Dunollie Road, Kentish Town, NW5, and this was when we were able to get a mortgage thanks to my boss Harold acting as a guarantor. It was in an appalling state (having been lived in by three families), with one functioning lavatory on the first floor and a non-functioning bathroom at the very back of the ground floor which had a broken gas geyser and an ancient bath used as a coal store. There was an outside lavatory as well, which did just function, but was in a terrible state. The house was damp, too, and the concrete garden at the back was covered in green slime. We applied for a Discretionary Grant to renovate it, and were awarded the maximum – £1,000.

When we were living with Peter in Eynsford, one of his solicitor colleagues joined us for a while. Later, he entered the property market – buying up places, refurbishing them and selling them on at a big profit. This was to prove a very slippery slope. . . It was through this work, however, that he had found a family of builders who were competent, reliable and not too expensive. He recommended them to us and the father and his sons did all the building work that was needed in our house. One of the sons was a builder, one a plumber, and one a carpenter. His nephew was an electrician. It was a big undertaking, but between them, they did all the major work. We did the decorating. The roof and guttering were repaired; they put concrete screed throughout the ground floor, installed new wiring, new plumbing, a new bathroom and two new kitchens. A new boiler and new radiators were installed too. We ended up with a large kitchen and dining area at the back of the house on the ground floor with lots of windows and a trendy blue brick floor, a large knocked through sitting room, two bedrooms on the first floor and a large bathroom at the back over the kitchen. There were also two rooms on the top floor, which we let to our friend Flicky, turning the smaller room facing the back, into a kitchen and the front room into a bed-sit. Ian and I smashed up all the concrete in the small back garden and built a brick garden with steps, a patio and raised beds. It became a fantastic home, where we invited lots of friends; became really quite good cooks; made home-made wines and beer; and stocked the larder with bottles of preserves and jams. There was a happy outgoing atmosphere.

We also introduced a kitten to the household, which we named Possum. Possum was a ginger and white delight! He seemed to think that he was a dog and loved to chase a squash ball down the long flight of stairs to the hall, fetch it and race back up the stairs again to whoever was doing the throwing. He would do this again and again. Sometimes, he would bring the ball to one of us and drop it at our feet, asking for a game! We took him on journeys – to my parents' house in Yateley, when we let him out of his basket on the train, much to other passengers' amazement, and up to Anglesey where he got his first (alarming) view from the window of a cow in close-up. Later, when Alex arrived on the scene, he became jealous, poor cat – making this quite plain by defecating in Alex's pram, parked in the hall. When we went abroad and let our house, we asked our tenants if they would look after him. They agreed, but we were never sure how well they had looked after him because on our return, we found, sadly, that he had become grumpy and neurotic.

We had got to know the builder's family well. They had regaled us with one amazing East End story after another – always with lots of laughs. After they had finished with our house, they went on to work for Maggie and Jules on their first house (which had a large crack all the way down the back wall) in Mildmay Grove, N1. They were not always easy – you had to take them as you found them – but we found them friendly and honest. The eldest son broke all the rules by having an affair (his first) with a hospital doctor (one of Ian's bosses), whose house he had been working on. His family was outraged because apparently she was using him solely as a toy boy and not taking him anywhere as her boyfriend.

It seems that Peter's (and our) friend overstretched himself financially. He once turned up at our front door, offering a ride in his Ferrari. . . He also became something of a womaniser and the result of all this was that later on, he became bankrupt and owed a lot of money to the builders, and to a local builders' merchant. He was taken to court and also worked in the builders' merchant's warehouse for nothing, to make an attempt to pay off some of his debts. Eventually he became a very affluent man once more, but did not work as a solicitor again, as far as I am aware. I am not sure whether the builders recouped all their lost money, either.

Before this, when Ian and I decided, in 1973, to live abroad and let our house while we were away, we asked this friend to act as our 'agent' and receive the rent for us. When we returned after nearly two years, we discovered that the rent was not in our account, but in one of his accounts. Unsurprisingly, we were shocked. Fortunately, we had arrived back before the worst had occurred and our 'friend' was able to pay our money back to us. In these days of internet banking, we would have been able to see that funds were not going into our account, but in those days, when we were living in Papua New Guinea and Australia, things were a little different.

* * *

Vera and Amsterdam

During the period we were in Battersea and in Kentish Town, we seem to have had a lot of holidays. We visited Amsterdam at least three times: with Flick, with Flick and Jules, and with Jeffrey and Elizabeth. We all became friends with Vera, a middle aged Dutch woman, who when we first met her, was the owner of the hotel in which we stayed, in a beautiful 17th century building on one of the canals. Vera was Jewish and during the war, had been put into a camp by the Germans where she was medically experimented upon. She had a number on her arm and a scar on her leg which, thanks to the experiment, never healed. It continually suppurated and had to be bandaged every day. She was a tall, statuesque, grand and very generous woman who wore very large hats, laughed a lot, and cut quite a figure. She had been married three times. On one of her visits to London we took her to Petticoat Lane market, where she certainly attracted a lot of attention. One of her favourite expressions was "*godverdomme*" which she pronounced frequently and with gusto.

We all loved the city of Amsterdam, which is beautiful, small and made for walking (or cycling, of course). We walked a lot, sat in cafés a lot, and visited art galleries and museums. We also visited Utrecht and a couple of other parts of Holland. It was a long time ago and I paid another visit to Amsterdam with Maggie and Jules in 2016, when we visited the Hieronymus Bosch exhibition in Hertogenbosch.

Vera took us to a well-known old Amsterdam café for breakfast one day (she wore a large hat for the occasion). The café was a beautiful period piece, with newspapers available on poles for customers to read. However, bacon with maple syrup (a Dutch, it turned out, not a Canadian invention) was not my favourite. There were foods in Amsterdam that were very good, however. The things that stick in my mind were chips which you could buy from self-service machines. These would emerge hot, wrapped in a cone of paper with mayonnaise on top. Also, street stalls sold tiny fillets of freshwater eels which were served on small squares of greaseproof paper. The customer was provided with toothpicks to eat them with, and very small pickled onions were offered alongside. They were very good. There was one occasion when we went to a street market where large live eels were being sold – you chose your eel and the female fishmonger, wearing a white apron covered in blood, chopped off the head of the eel and threw the body into a bucket where it continued to writhe. We did not buy any of those. . .

Vera was a magnificent woman and we became good friends. She was hugely likeable. Even my mother, who was living with us at one time, really liked Vera. She visited us in London a couple of times and even offered to take our cat, Possum, back to Amsterdam with her when we were going to live in Greece. I had Possum vaccinated, but it turned out that Vera suffered badly from sea sickness and could not travel on the ferry. The alternative – taking the cat by air – was very expensive, so, sadly, it did not work out.

Vera retired and moved out of the hotel into a flat, where she lived with her adopted adult son, whom she adored and spoiled. She also had a daughter who lived on a canal boat with her partner. She told us how her father had been affluent and left money for her in trust. However, knowing her well, her father had ensured that the terms of the trust should stipulate that she could not touch this money until she was 45 years old. Later she moved into another flat on an estate of smart modern blocks outside the city. We stayed with her at this flat too, arriving for the New Year. The weather was freezing, the winds blasting across the flat countryside, and the roads icy. We hitched a lift on a motorway in a VW beetle, and were terrified as the driver battled the wind which was trying to blow us across the ice. He was an excellent driver, fortunately, and kept us on course, despite the car having no weight at all at the front since the engine in those cars was in the boot. We celebrated New Year's Eve with Vera. The tradition in Holland then (a tradition adopted here much later), was that everyone let off fireworks on New Year's Eve, exactly on midnight. We ate home-made apple fritters (also traditional) standing on the balcony of Vera's flat, with a fine view of the fireworks across the city. Vera was invariably fun, warm and welcoming.

We gradually lost touch with Vera, however. We understood that she developed tinnitus; became anti-social; and did not want to see anybody. My mother tried to ring her once and was rebuffed. Sadly, we did not see Vera again.

* * *

Eyrephort, Connemara

In due course, Max's parents (sadly for us) sold their bungalow in Waterville, and we were keen to find somewhere else we could spend our annual Irish holidays. Ian was in Dublin taking some Membership exams (he stayed in a B&B where he was amused to be told that "a hot bag" had been put in his bed for him). After the exams, he took the opportunity to go almost as far west as he could go by train, to see what he could find. He found himself in Clifden, Co. Galway, where he met Ann Pryce. Ann was working in the pub where he was asking about possible accommodation, and it turned out that the Pryce family had a large bungalow with five bedrooms, which they were rather keen to let. That was the start of a very long and beautiful friendship, not only with the Pryce family, but with that part of Ireland.

The bungalow was off the Sky Road, with our lane running due west towards the setting sun. It was remote – surrounded by a few fields belonging to the Pryce family – and with dunes and sandy beaches in all directions. It could not have been more ideal, especially later, when we all had children. With the odd exception, Maggie, Jules, Ian and I went to the bungalow at Eyrephort every year at Easter for over thirty years. One year early on, we thought we needed somewhere larger because David and Sarah were coming too – which meant five small children, so we rented a vast house in Co. Cork. There were a couple of other exceptions for us, too: once when Ian and I were on the other side of the world, and once when I cancelled because Alex had suddenly become ill. Later, of course, I went with Maggie and Jules and Alex and Kate but without Ian. When Kate had measles, we still managed to get there, with poor little Kate flat out on the back seat, but soon recovering in the fresh Atlantic air.

Most of the trips there were made by car (a long journey) and we found a B&B en route where we made a habit of staying. It was owned and run by the Delaney sisters, one enormous woman and one tiny woman, but both equally hospitable in their own ways and very jolly. We would ring ahead and book, specially requesting that they cook their delicious fish pie for us for our evening meal. The children loved it and staying with the Delaney sisters became part of the adventure most years.

Singing in the car was standard too, both on the journey and when we were there – we all sang along loudly to Captain Beaky, Loudon Wainwright, Buddy Holly, the Beatles, and even, for some inexplicable reason, 'On the Road to Mandalay'.

On one memorable occasion, I was driving along the very narrow Sky Road with Kate and Alex, when the driver of a car coming in the opposite direction, rolled down his window and without further ado, asked "Am I on the right road?" I asked him where he was trying to get to and by some miracle, we all managed to keep our faces straight until he had gone by! Hopefully, he arrived wherever it was he wanted to get to.

When we finally arrived in Eyrephort, there was always the highly anticipated experience of getting out of the car and hearing absolutely nothing, except a lark . . . and possibly the sea. . .

The atmosphere at Eyrephort was magical and together with Maggie and Jules, and their children, Mia and Miranda, we became addicted to it. The first time we went there, Ann Pryce (the owner) had knitted Ian (whose name she always pronounced "iron"), a pair of knee length thick maroon woollen socks. On all other visits, there was always a large fruit cake laced with alcohol, which she had baked specially, and sometimes some soda bread. We used to reciprocate with bottles of duty-free whisky. We would visit Ann and Eddie's farm – up the next lane – where we would be given cups of tea and invited to visit the new lambs and calves. They had three children who we also got to know quite well – on one occasion John babysat for us while we went into Clifden one evening. He had a fairly terrible time – children running a bit wild and Maggie and Jules' dog going AWOL and then vomiting all over the kitchen floor. The youngest boy, Gerry, was to be seen at a very young age, on his own, confidently driving their tractor at speed up the lane.

We went on fantastic walks – up Errisbeg at Roundstone (which we often finished off with a cup of tea made on Jules' "Volcano"); along the Ballyconneely peninsula; up Tully Mountain; and round Killary Harbour. We rode bikes to Omey Island; rode horses over the hillsides on Errislannan; took the small packet boat from Cleggan to Inishboffin; cycled to Coral Beach where we had barbecued snags and dampers; and of course, made regular trips into Clifden to buy provisions and drink a Guinness or two. We all loved it and the four children had each other's company and could not have been happier. We cooked delicious meals, went on night-time walks around our local dunes which we dubbed 'the circuit', lying on our backs, gazing at the clear clear sky and the stars. We burned deliciously smelling peat in the sitting room in the evenings and fell asleep reading in front of the gently crackling fire in the dreamlike quiet. These were certainly among the best times of my life.

* * *

A Doctor in the House

In 1972, Ian qualified as a doctor, but before doctors were able to practise, they had to undertake two six-month pre-registration posts, one in Medicine and one in Surgery. The posts had to be in recognised and approved hospitals and the pre-registration doctors had to be supervised by recognised Consultants. As long as these criteria were met, the individual could choose where in the world to go. After that, s/he would be registered and able to practise independently.

Our friends Richard and Trish were both doctors and had arranged to do their pre-registration jobs in Papua New Guinea. They had set a precedent, and it seemed like a good idea to follow in their footsteps.

So, in the South Pacific, on the Papua New Guinean island of New Britain, just outside the small town of Rabaul, was Nonga Base Hospital, and it was there that we spent about sixteen superb months.

Anne Gaudie in Crete. 1966

Ian Macdonald in Crete. 1966

Ian Macdonald in Crete. 1966

ANNE MACDONALD

Anne Gaudie on holiday in Greece.

Ian Macdonald, in a Burmese Restaurant, Valentia Island, Eire. 1967

Ian and Anne. County Kerry, Eire. 1967

FROM THE ESK AND THE USK: OUT EAST AND BACK HOME

*Anne & Ian Macdonald – just married.
With Valerie & Glen Gaudie. 29 March 1969*

*Ian & Anne Macdonald – just married.
With Clio & Brian Macdonald. 29 March 1969*

CHAPTER 7

Across Asia

* * *

First Stop Delhi

WE TRAVELLED LIGHT. We made sure, though, that we had a very small number of our favourite music cassettes with us, although nothing to play them on! Very excitingly, we were going to live in the South Pacific and we liked the idea of a semi-overland journey to get there. We found flights from London to Delhi costing £62 each on Kuwaiti Airlines, and left London at midday on 10th October 1973. Due to the war in the Middle East, the plane did not take its usual route, but flew over Baghdad at night – quite a sight – all those lights twinkling along the River Tigris. A taste of exotic things to come.

Our arrival in Delhi was marked by a splendid reception – Indian officers and magnificent attendants in full regalia with gorgeous red and blue headdresses, along with striped marquees and flags flying. Unsurprisingly, this was not for us, but had been arranged for Mrs Gandhi, who was meeting the President of India. It made for a special arrival, though!

One of the first things we came across was the renowned Indian bureaucracy – a superabundance of paper – there were men all over the place, filling in forms, carrying forms, exchanging forms, stamping forms. Inside the Terminal building there was a barrier with enormous signs saying "Health", so we hauled out our innoculation cards, to find that, naturally, they were not wanted. By some miracle, our passports were stamped, non-addresses(!) checked, and we claimed our luggage.

We experienced the usual culture shock, which I think a lot of people experience, and although in 1973, there must have been much less development in India than there is today, I suspect the shock is not a lot different now. It certainly hit us hard. The trip from the airport into the city took us past miles of shanty town and the overwhelming initial impression for me, was the sheer number of people everywhere. We could be in no doubt that we were in a hugely populous country. The noise and the smells hit us – smoke, dung and dirt.

We stayed at the YMCA or the YWCA in most of the cities we visited – one or other in each city offered married accommodation. It was a brilliant idea to stay in these hostels – they were invariably inexpensive, clean, modestly comfortable and welcoming. In addition, they sometimes provided boiled water for drinking. Otherwise, we had to drink locally bottled Coca Cola (both of us disliked Coke). Of course, we drank lots of tea, especially when we were travelling by train – at stations, the 'chai wallahs' would walk along the length of the train, outside, selling sweetened milky tea in small clay cups, calling "chai, chai, char, char".

Not very sensibly, perhaps, and definitely naively, we threw ourselves into the experience at the deep end and ventured into the old city straight away – a maze of narrow streets packed with people, shoulder to shoulder, cycle rickshaws, shops and stalls on either side, and no other foreigners. There was a stall for everything under the sun, and everything was going on in the street – women ironing, men making sweets and cakes and white cows bumping into you. The smell of joss sticks was everywhere, often mixed with the smell of faeces and urine. It was colourful, but unsettling – and exhausting seeing beggar after cripple after beggar. Children constantly pestered us, grabbing our legs and grinning. People were making a living at anything – we saw a young man selling three glasses of water.

Most of the buildings in the old city were wooden and two-storeyed with dirty passageways and entrances with a strong smell of urine everywhere. The shops fronted on to the road which was eight to ten feet wide, the shops themselves varying between three feet and six feet wide and ten feet and twelve feet deep. Shop keepers were barefoot, squatting or sitting on their haunches. The food stalls were indescribably filthy and the cooks always male. Quantities of food were tiny, with little in the way of fresh food stuffs. We passed dramatic looking women in thick white cotton burkas which fell straight from their headdresses to the ground and others with black robes and full black veils. We also passed men lying in the streets, usually just in a loin cloth, with totally expressionless faces and eyes. Apart from the milling throng, the odd sacred cow pushed its way through, along with trucks, two seater tuk tuks, cars, tongas and bicycles. Soon, we were tense. Had we given it some thought, we might have realised we would be unwelcome. Just as we came to the bigger road back to the new city, something was thrown at me and landed on my sunglasses. We managed to get into a two-seater, finally escaping the clutches of a beggar girl, who would not leave us alone.

Having discovered two-seaters, tuk tuks (motor bikes with a little canopied chariot behind, which seats two comfortably), we became quite adventurous. You could go quite a long way for 2 rupees. The unwary could be fooled very easily by the non-metered variety, where the driver used the speedometer as a meter and charged whichever combination of digits he fancied. The four seaters were bigger bikes (Royal Enfield Bullets). To take one of these, it was vital to be a master of the art of bartering. We avoided them!

We booked our train tickets to Srinagar, Kashmir, for the following evening. This turned out to be a lengthy bureaucratic joke involving trips back and forth across the city. Initially, we had gone to a travel agent who told us that one needed to book ten to twenty days in advance. However, a rather nice Sikh man at the YMCA told us *(sotto voce)* "*If you want to go today, then there will be room today.*" We first went to the main station, queued, and then were directed to a different station, which we reached by taking a two-seater across the city. There, we filled in long forms, after which the clerk (immaculate hair and the thinnest moustache), telephoned the main station to find out which train we could go on(!); the forms were then stamped, and we were told we could have tickets from the tourists' quota if we returned to the reservation hall of the main station – where we had first started. If you travelled first class (which was not expensive) you automatically got a sleeper (*sotto voce again: "It is not like the Western Railways, sir"*).

After this Kafkaesque adventure, we visited the Red Fort – an enormous and impressive red sandstone fort with palace and gardens built by Shah Jehan in 1623. It was in need of some care and attention, but since part of it is now a UNESCO World Heritage site, I think it must have received some. The largest mosque in India, the 17th century Jama Masjid, was not too far away so we made the mistake of walking there. This, unbeknownst to us, meant going through an area of shanty town. It was squalid – appalling – we had expected poverty but simply had no way of knowing what it would really be like and, naive and inexperienced as we were, we were very shocked. It was a public holiday, and everyone was going to the mosque – even greater throngs of people. It was necessary to take one's shoes off to enter the mosque, but since the good Doc refused this option, we made our way back through the old city feeling very out of place. It was also shocking, but in a different way, to see a young western man begging on the street, and a young western woman uncaring of local culture, wearing a see through cotton top with no bra.

We saw another side of the city the following day, wandering around the newer (but not modern) areas. There were graceful women wearing brightly coloured sarees and trousers, and men wearing brilliant white cotton shirts and dhotis. We walked around the rather shabby Connaught Circus and saw a doctor's practice advertising the doctor as a "Specialist in Private Diseases"; plus quantities of years-old red marks on the walls made by men spitting red betel nut juice. We went to the Lakshmi Narayan temple, built in 1938, where people of all castes and religion are allowed within the temple grounds at Gandhi's stipulation. Ian managed to conquer his fear of ringworm, roundworm, hookworm, and whatever other worms he could think of, and took his shoes off to go inside.

We returned to a shop we had found earlier – one selling cottons and silks. Chaos reigned supreme inside. It was packed. Very many Indian ladies in their sarees, with hubbies in tow, were buying cotton shirts and trousers, shouting at assistants and holding items up for size. We eventually managed to reach the counter. The walls were lined, floor to ceiling, with drawer after drawer of every type, quality, texture and vivid colour of cotton garments. Everything was stunning and it was extremely difficult to restrict ourselves to buying one beautiful cotton shirt each. Up a couple of steps at the back of the shop were the silks. The walls of this area were lined with bolt after bolt of brilliant silk and several seated women were being treated to a display of them. A salesman was taking down one bolt of silk after another and throwing each one dramatically to the floor, displaying long lengths of gorgeously vibrant silk. It made for a fantastic show – we stood and watched for a while.

That evening we set off for Kashmir. Getting a two-seater was difficult because it was fairly late, but eventually we found a very young boy who took us to the wrong station! He got the message that we were panicking about time, and started to drive like a mad thing to Old Delhi station. It was Diwali – the Festival of Lights – when everyone puts a light in their windows and people carry lanterns around. We should have been enjoying it, but the journey was quite terrifying – although sometimes, we could hardly move because of the crowds. The combination of lights, people, smoke, smells and fantastic noise was extraordinary. However, by some miracle, we got there and then saw the station.

The station was enormous and crammed with people of every variety, either sleeping on the floor in a sort of first-come first-served arrangement, it seemed, or carrying three suitcases on their heads with vast bedding rolls under their arms. We had no idea where to go but just followed along: there was no notice indicating which platform for which train, so we walked along a bridge craning our necks and being jostled on every side trying to see where our train "The Kashmir Mail" went from. The noise, clamour and crowds were phenomenal, but we found our seats: by some fluke, after passing several platforms, we tried one which was right. There were no officials to ask, but we managed to find someone who showed us that on each carriage was pasted a typewritten list of passengers showing the compartment they had been allocated. It was reassuring when we found our names.

We were sharing with two men – one a delightful man wearing a white dhoti and shirt – as relaxed as could be – who sat cross-legged on the seat and immediately offered us cigarettes. The other man was wearing western clothes, wore glasses, had a black moustache and a whole briefcase of cosmetics. He put us all to shame by disappearing and then returning in very correct English style pyjamas, all ready for the night. They were both, as we found so often among the many Indians we met and chatted to, particularly charming and polite people.

Some of the most useful things we had with us were two sheet sleeping bags, each of which I had made by machining up the sides of two large cotton sheets. We used these frequently on our travels, especially when we were sleeping in trains. They allowed us to keep relatively cool, but maintain our modesty. This was particularly necessary, when we did not have sleeper compartments to ourselves. For obvious reasons, I took one of the upper bunks. We slept reasonably well and were woken for breakfast. I took great delight in watching, fascinated, as the man with the case of cosmetics did his toilette in the morning. The case was full of all his creams, potions, scissors, moustache dyes, waxes, etc., which he used with great care and precision. He sat on his bunk, making sure that his moustache received maximum attention and that he looked perfect from top to toe – unlike us!

We were at last able to see some of the country we were passing through. It was attractive despite the villages being poor and made up mainly of mud houses. There were people in turbans and sarees scattered around the landscape, plus a few bullocks. We saw the occasional person carrying an open black umbrella in the fields! It was flat and fairly dry but we crossed some beautiful wide almost dry river beds which looked lovely with tall grasses and trees growing along their banks. So we reached Jammu and found lots of buses waiting to take people up to Srinagar, the capital of Kashmir.

* * *

Kashmir

We bought tickets on an 'A' class bus – the difference being that instead of seats for three people each side of the gangway, there were two and these were padded and had headrests. Otherwise, the buses were in exactly the same battered condition as all the others. The army was very much in evidence and no sooner had we started than we had to stop at a police road block. A policeman climbed on to the top of the bus where the luggage was and we all had to get out. He asked everyone to open their suitcases except us. In one case, he discovered something that looked like a roll of electric flex and went berserk. The unfortunate owner was hauled off to a tent, accompanied by most of the other passengers all arguing the rights and wrongs of it all. After a wait of about an hour, we set off, plus man and suitcase!

The drive was stupendous – we rattled and flung our way round bend after bend and the countryside was magnificent. We kept climbing, looking down on stunning rivers and valleys with mountains all around us covered in pine woods. There was not a straight piece of road to be seen. The journey took twelve hours. We stopped quite frequently at small villages, which were just managing to hang on to the hillsides, and ate lots of delicious goodies and drank many, many, cups of tea. The small place where we had our supper was superb – hugely atmospheric – low ceilinged with a grassy roof of some kind, lit by small paraffin lamps and full of delicious smells. It was full of people, mainly Sikhs, many of whom were involved in intense and hushed discussions. There were several mud ovens about 3ft high, at the bottom of which a fire burned, each with a hole in the centre of the top (the equivalent of a hot plate). The cooks sat cross-legged or on their haunches, on top of the ovens, next to the holes, seemingly not minding the great heat, surrounded by their pots, pans and food. They occupied themselves by taking handfuls of dough, slapping them hard to flatten them, and smacking them on to the inside walls of the ovens. They had long tongs with which they retrieved the chapattis just as they were cooked and about to fall into the fire. They also had frying pans which they put on top of the hot chimneys, in which they cooked whatever was ordered. We ate delicious omelettes served on hot chapattis, which we ate with our hands. We were impressed by how charming the people were – extremely helpful – always smiling and chatting whenever the opportunity arose. We had a conversation with a Sikh who told us passionately that "the people are too poor and the fighting is too rich". He asked us whether there were many Indians in England and on hearing that there were, earnestly asked us whether they behaved themselves. When we said they did, he was delighted. Fine, he said, and then translated for the benefit of his friend, who looked equally pleased. He then warned us that in Kashmir, we must watch out for crooks and cheats.

On reaching Srinagar, we found that the bus terminus was in the Tourist Reception Centre which was where we intended to stay. The Kashmiri man in charge tried to get us to rent a houseboat and the night controller was quite obviously in on the houseboat racket too, and pretended at first that there was no room in the Reception Centre. However, we had brought with us a pamphlet on Kashmir, which listed accommodation and prices, so we insisted on staying at the Centre, which we finally did after the "*personal intervention, Sahib, of the night controller*". For a very small amount of money, we had a run-down old colonial 'suite' – sitting room, bedroom and bathroom. The suite had seen better days, despite its ornate walnut ceiling, as had the plumbing . . . but we were exhausted and slept soundly.

After so much travelling, we wanted to rest and walk for a couple of days, so we organised a trip into the mountains for the following day, choosing to go to Sonamarg (9,000 ft), just under 90km from Srinagar.

We wandered around exploring the old city. The buildings were two or three storeys high with ornate latticed balconies and sharply sloping roofs which were either covered in wooden tiles or corrugated iron. The houses are bigger upstairs than down, just as they had been in mediaeval England, the first floors jutting out above the streets. This was the first time I had seen so many Muslim women in burkas – in Srinagar the burkas were a beautiful shade of pale blue, and you could see nothing of the women at all, not even their eyes, which were covered by a matching fine blue cotton lattice.

We chatted to people as we went along, and politics was often the topic of discussion. People were either for independence or union with Pakistan – anything but remaining under the Indian yoke – hence the army encampments in Kashmir. However, most people could not see the faintest hope of independence.

We walked down to where the River Jhelum joins Dal Lake, thinking we would have a ride in a shikara and found one at the ghats. Shikaras are a little like punts with a higher prow than stern and are usually painted yellow and red. There is a little canopied area in the middle under which are long cushions with cushioned backrests. One glides along, lying down very close to the water. At first, our shikari punted us along the river. On the opposite bank from the ghat, there were long thin islands along which were the famed houseboats. I have photos of my mother with her mother and her brother on a houseboat on Lake Dal. Some of them are positively palatial in size and ornateness, with huge balconies covered in flowers, and very comfortable colonial style drawing rooms with shaded standard lamps. At the side of each was a kitchen boat with servants who waited on the occupants of the houseboat. On reaching Little Dal Lake, our shikari began to paddle rather than punt. It was glorious: peaceful, beautiful and quiet, with just the sound of the paddle gently hitting the water and the water rippling along the flat bottom of the boat. There were floating gardens and lines of poplars at the water's edge, with the mountains ranged around us in the distance. We were offered a water lily by a small girl in her plain wooden shikara. We stopped at a small island called Char Chinar where we had tea.

We arrived back in the river just as dusk was falling and the sun was disappearing behind the mountains. The water was like glass and mirrored in it were the tiny lights of the houseboats now all lit up. In the cool night air there was the scent of the wood fires and the spicy and appetising smell of food being cooked. We ate a tasty fish curry and went to bed with a nip of our Scotch.

The next day, we set off on our trip to Sonarmarg. Another mountain village, Gulmarg, is close to Srinagar at 8,500ft and I have a photo of my mother heading up there, but on horseback. That would have been around 1941.

Having paid our 42 rupees for two nights and bedding, we arrived at the bus station, choc a bloc with buses, at about 7am. The bus ride was magnificent, the scenery even more beautiful than we had expected. It was extremely rich and fertile with water everywhere and willow and plane trees in abundance. The countryside was terraced wherever possible – every tiny bit cultivated – each terrace with its small mud wall, most of them planted with rice. Walnuts were drying in the sun, too. To add to the views, the trees were in autumn mode – with every colour combination from lime green to bright gold to bronze, rust and even a plant that looked like red heather – all this offset against the deep green of the pines growing on the higher slopes. A lot of work had been done on irrigation channels and roads and we were told that a hydro-electric power station had already been built, with another one in progress. As we climbed higher, the peaks became more dramatic and stark and were covered in snow; the sky bright blue and the sun shining. We went through villages and saw several different types of people – some pale skinned with fine features; some with Tibetan features; and some very dark skinned. They were gentle and friendly.

Sonamarg is a flat green valley – not very large, surrounded by mountains of about 13,000 ft, with peaks covered in snow. There was evidence of the army, as there had been all the way up. The village itself was small and primitive, with a rest house with chairs and tables outside and a kitchen, all built in chalet bungalow style. We presented ourselves to the Tourist Officer, who allocated one of the tourist huts to us. We apparently had the whole bungalow to ourselves, but then surprised several workmen who were sleeping and living there. They were putting in drains – still open so that everything was on view outside. After a while, we were put into the next bungalow with the same drainage non-arrangements(!), and this one was slightly less depressing inside. We were given a sheet which had obviously been used by the whole season's tourists – it was hideously dirty. We took it back, asking for another, but were told there was no dhobi in the village. Our sheet sleeping bags saved us again. After some tea, we decided, despite ponies for hire, to walk up to the famous Thajwas glacier. To our surprise, some Indian tourists arrived, who had travelled to Sonamarg for the day by taxi, and they hired the ponies. The owners of the ponies were a great sight with their weather beaten mountain faces, wearing kaftans or blankets wrapped around themselves and making strange noises with their mouths to get the ponies to go faster. It was a lovely walk – about 5km, through a couple of beautiful valleys – but when we got there, the glacier turned out to be small, grimy and off-white. Despite this, some tourists from Calcutta climbed in their smart shoes and trousers up the last absolutely vertical section, to collect pieces of ice.

It had rained and it was now very cold, so we climbed back up to our bungalow through quantities of mud, and built a fire. The room filled with smoke but we needed some heat and managed to get a little sleep despite being kippered.

The next day we thought we would go for a long walk up the river. The weather was glorious, the scenery spectacular with its high, snow covered pointed mountain tops all around, and the river water in the valley bright blue and clear. At one point, we got a fright as two shepherds appeared out of the grass at the side of the road, one holding a vicious looking knife a bit like a scythe. They meant us no harm, but it was a scary moment. After about 4kms, we arrived at an army checkpoint at the Line of Control between India and Pakistan, where we were told we could go no further. Lieutenant Kumar told us that to get through we needed a pass from Delhi. We turned round and went back to the village and ate that evening in a tent with one candle in the now freezing cold.

Again we lit the fire in the bungalow, but the fireplace was hopeless – it gave out no heat and smoke poured, not up the chimney, but into the bedroom. We went to bed early, wearing every item of clothing we had including our anoraks, but could not get warm. We tried to read by candle-light, but our eyes streamed and we could hardly see round the room for smoke. It was autumn by then and we were in the Himalayas, and we had stupidly underestimated how cold it was likely to be at night. The Scotch again proved useful.

In the early hours, there were sudden noises at the window and we found that the 'chowdikar' (the nightwatchman) was trying to climb into our bedroom, his foot aiming at our heads. He had apparently forgotten we were there! A couple of loud 'heys' and he disappeared in shock. I laughed so much I could not get back to sleep. After breakfast, we watched the cook cleaning the brass cooking pots with earth – it was such an effective cleaning method that after rubbing hard and rinsing, the brass pots shone and gleamed in the sun.

Back in Srinagar, Ian was very keen to try the 'gushtaba' we had been told about –a traditional Kashmiri curry of smooth spicy lamb meatballs cooked in a curd sauce – and that evening, while we were shopping for dates and walnuts, a splendid looking moustachioed man spoke to us, and we asked him where we could find some. He took us to a stall where we found and ate gushtaba – it was delicious – and we were given the recipe, which Ian noted in our diary.[120]

Afterwards, we went with our newfound friend to a coffee house where we bought him a coffee. He turned out to be amusing and interesting. He dealt in anything and everything, particularly Kashmiri arts and crafts and was obviously a Srinagar personality since a lot of people knew him and shook his hand. He was an Anglophile, apparently, particularly liking the Scots, and we told him we were on our way to Australia. As we left the café, he said we should go home with him to eat whatever was there. We got into a three-wheeler cab with some of his mates and drove through the evening's milling streets towards the suburb where he lived, where there was no electricity. His house was in a tiny alley, quite dark, and we went up wooden stairs in the dim light to the main room where we took off our shoes and sat down on the carpet. He opened the shutters, which almost touched the house opposite and offered us wonderful Persian tea spiced with cinnamon and cardamom, which was served by his daughter. He also sent his servant Ahmed to buy half a bottle of malt whisky, which we all three finished that evening. Meanwhile, the hookah had been prepared by Ahmed using Tambako (tobacco and raw sugar apparently). This was not offered around. After bringing water and a silver dish in which we were invited to wash our hands, Ahmed brought up delicious food which was only for us – rice with mutton curry and spinach. We ate with our hands, after which we washed our hands again, and I was given a demonstration by the daughter as to how to put on a yashmak.

Looking back on it, we were naive to accept this invitation, since at the end of the meal, the conversation turned to our journey to Australia and then a number of items were brought into the room. Our host showed us some wooden articles he had made at his factory (90 workers)[121]. Included in these, there was a walnut coffee table with a hollow leg and secondly,

---

120 Take thin pieces of upper leg of lamb with no fat on them. Beat these pieces until they are almost flat and as thin as possible. Put a little butter on each piece and beat again, taking out any gristle or veins. Put on some salt, pepper, cinnamon and cardamom and with some more butter roll the pieces into balls. Make a sauce with ghee and curd milk and heat over the fire, making sure it is smooth (up to boiling). Put the balls into the sauce and cook together.

121 Ian omitted the next part of the story from the diary, and I have omitted our host's name!

there was a suitcase with a false bottom. It did not take us long to get the hang of what was going on! We made it quite clear that we were not going to smuggle drugs into Australia, and as politely as possible made our getaway. Neither Ian nor I would have involved ourselves in such a scheme, but pity the poor traveller who was tempted and then caught by the Australian authorities – the penalties were fiendish. A cab came to collect us and our friend kissed Ian on the eye and told me to "look after his brother". There seemed to be no hard feelings – win some, lose some, I suppose.

We flew from Srinagar to Delhi via Amritsar – the views were stupendous – 16,000-20,000 ft peaks jutting above the clouds.

* * *

Off to Nepal

Wandering around and sightseeing was our occupation over the next couple of days in Delhi. We were becoming quite well acquainted with how to get around the city and also became expert at finding vegetarian restaurants serving delicious food at very low prices. A chicken restaurant in the old quarter was recommended, so we went there by rickshaw one evening, and found a beautiful walled garden, with droves of waiters and lots of fairly posh clients – obviously the place to go. It was good but not outstanding. Vegetarian restaurants were clearly the best option.

The next stage of our journey was to take the 9pm train to Lucknow. This time, we took a cab and entered the station from the front, with a porter who took us to the right train. We had a two-berth compartment. The conductor was drunk and very merry. He came in later with some pieces of tandoori chicken and gave them to us while he told us his life story amidst much hilarity. We slept quite well, arriving at Lucknow at about 8am. However, we had to wait on the platform for nearly five hours for the connection, which gave us plenty of time to observe all the weird and wonderful people. There were many sadhus (men who had given up the world and lived on donations). They were painted with white markings on their heads and arms – one man was covered all over in ash. There were also many cripples and beggars, one wearing just a loin cloth who we had to steer clear of because he smelt so bad, and, of course, plenty of monkeys climbing and jumping all over the station roofs.

By a fluke, Ian happened to wake up 15 minutes before our arrival at Muzzafapur at 6.30am the next morning, and we caught our connecting train by a hair's breadth. This time, 1st class was rather different (ie worse) – we had a compartment for two with a loo off it and there was no corridor. We were startled, however, when, just as the train was setting off, a blind old beggar climbed in with a small boy, a lad selling betel, and two very aggressive men. We told them the compartment was reserved and they said it was free for all. At the next stop, Ian got out and spoke to the guard who told the two men (the others had got out) that they must get out too, which fortunately, they did. The guard said we must keep the door locked because people know they should not be getting in, but do so on purpose. It was a horrible thing to do and we felt bad about it, but decided, for various reasons, to do as he said.

The countryside we passed through was flat. There had been flooding, which we were told had spoiled a good many crops as well as houses. The plain was clearly fertile with irrigation canals here and there, and lots of rice and sugar cane growing, but the villages were very poor. After some changes of train, a crowded bus ride, a tonga ride, and having passed through small informal immigration and customs posts, we had a stroke of luck and found a bus just about to set off for Kathmandu. We left the Nepalese border town of Birgunj for an eight hour journey.

* * *

Kathmandu and around

We went through the most stunning countryside – extremely lush, terraced right up to the tops of the hills, with winding roads and sheer drops down to sharp deep valleys below and a beautiful river. The road continued up and up and the views became more and more astounding. After some time, we stopped at a remote rest stop, quite high up, for something to eat. I was served with a plate of thick white stuck-together rice (with no sauce), which, when I had eaten a couple of mouthfuls, proved to contain a dead fly. . .

While we passengers were sitting down, we noticed that our driver was engaged in an earnest conversation with the driver of a large tanker lorry. Once we started our journey again, it became obvious that they had taken a bet with each other as to whether the bus could overtake the tanker lorry on the mountain road. . .

We were lucky to survive the next part of our journey. Our driver got more and more excited as he tried again and again, to overtake the tanker lorry. It was a mountain road, narrow and twisting, full of bends, and with long sheer drops down the mountain from the edge of the road. Our driver, a small, thin, wiry Sikh, kept getting the bus very close to the back of the lorry, pulling out and sounding his horn non-stop. He kept not quite making it, and then, becoming extremely worked up, grabbed his turban from his head and hurled it to the floor, grabbing the steering wheel furiously as he tried harder and harder to get past. It was nerve wracking. There was not much conversation among the passengers! Eventually, and luckily for us, he made it and we continued more normally. We were amused to see notices at the side of the road, especially at bends, with exhortations to drivers (in English), such as "No Hurry, No Worry" and "Always Alert, Accident Avert".

It was dark as we came over the top of the mountain to reach the beginning of the last downhill to Kathmandu. Our driver suddenly shouted "Kathmandu" pointing to the twinkling lights of the city in the flat valley below us. It was midnight and quite a moment.

There were some small boys hanging around at the bus station, who led us, carrying a bag between them, to the 'International Lodge' which Tricia and Richard had told us about. This must have been one of the cheapest places to stay in Kathmandu and was fairly sordid, but we did sleep. We woke up not too early and discovered the bathroom – a room with a large tin barrel with a tap on it which was meant to be a shower, which did not work at all – and squat variety loos which stank. However, on learning that the charge was 6 rupees for both of us (25p), we decided that we could put up with this. Our room was covered in drawings of heads with syringes pointing at them; pictures of mushrooms; and remarks about airing your ego on acid!

We made our first foray into the city and found a place to hire bikes. Cycling through and around the town was wonderful – it was not a big place and the biking was on the flat valley floor, so it was a great way to get around. The weather was perfect – with sun, blue skies and crystal clear air – and all around us in the distance, picture perfect, were the snow covered Himalayas. It was beautiful.

We were delighted with the city – after Delhi, something of a paradise. The great thing about it was that, unlike many others – where an ordinary more modern city often surrounds an old centre – the whole place was old, traditional and attractive. There were many temples and picturesque houses with several storeys, carved balconies and rooms with ceilings covered in enormous beams.[122] The people were charming, friendly and polite and took 'no' for an answer if you did not want to buy something (in stark contrast to the situation we had found in India). The people ranged from very Indian looking to Tibetan. The Indian, Tibetan and Chinese influences were all strong – noticeable in the food, clothes and religions. The market was fantastic and full of many temptations (wool, cotton, brass, pottery) and all very cheap, but with no money and no space, we held back.

We needed to arrange our on-going travel and rode our bikes some distance to the Burmese Embassy where there was a clerk (an original version of "computer says No") who said we could not get our visas to Burma until the following Monday. We tried various ploys to persuade him, including Ian telling him that we simply would not be able to go to Burma at all and they would lose foreign currency(!). We had no luck, however, and Ian walked off. However, I walked into another office and spoke to someone in authority, who immediately told the clerk to get on with it and have the visas ready for us by 3pm!

I then managed to shear off the entire pedal and pin from my bike. However, the bike was replaced, and we went to the Tiger Tops office to enquire about Sagar Rana[123], one of the Directors. Ian had made friends at Oxford with Sagar, a Nepali prince, who had encouraged Ian to visit him if he ever went to Kathmandu. The only clue Ian had was that, among other things, he owned a tour company, which took people riding on elephants, to see tigers in the jungle. Having tried several likely looking tour offices, we eventually found the right one but were told that Sagar was on holiday in Delhi. We decided to try again later.

We booked our flights from Calcutta to Bangkok with a stopover in Rangoon, at a cost of £67 for both of us, after which, we succumbed (in a small way) to the shopping urge. In a Tibetan shop in the market, we found

---

122 I am keenly aware of how lucky we were to have seen the temples and old buildings then, since I am writing this one year on exactly from the April 2015 earthquake in Nepal, which killed nearly 9000 people and destroyed so many of the temples and buildings.
123 Sagar Rana is to be found on YouTube being interviewed by the Nepali Times about his book "Singha Durbar: Rise and Fall of the Rana Regime of Nepal": https://www.youtube.com/watch?v=-0masX9G7ok

some great local products – wrap-over shirts; wrap-over dress; brightly coloured jacket made of fabrics from Bhutan; a Nepalese hat; brightly coloured little bag; etc. It was still Diwali – the Festival of Lights – and the streets in the evenings sparkled – with candles in windows and doorways, and children letting off fireworks.

In the next couple of days we visited Bhadgaon where we saw the largest and most magnificent pagoda in Nepal; the renowned Golden Gate; and the Pashupati temple covered in erotic carvings. We also went to Patan. Ian's diary entry says *"The buses here only go short distances but each time they stop, they do so for a long, long time, as everyone who wants to get on, does so, no matter how full the bus."*

We discovered that Sagar had returned to Kathmandu. He insisted that we go over immediately to his place to have dinner with him. He already had another friend from Oxford there who had just arrived. We took a taxi to his house, which was a new large two storey stone villa in a secluded and hilly position. It was magnificently furnished and there were maybe a dozen servants. They lived in some style – hands were clapped at the table when anything was needed, when a bevy of servants would appear. Sagar's main line of work since he had given up practising law, was Nepali arts and crafts, as well as being a Director of Tiger Tops. His wife, Brinda, was delightful, a northern Indian who, like her husband, spoke excellent English. They insisted that we should stay for another day, so that we could go up into the hills with them, taking a picnic, and having a Tibetan meal in the evening. We were excited at this prospect and postponed our bus trip by a day.

The following morning we rang Sagar who told us to meet him at the Tiger Tops office, which we did, and found Anthony – the other visitor. We chatted to Sagar's partner, an Englishman, who gave us a lift to Sagar's handicrafts factory in the firm's Range Rover. Sagar and Brinda met us and gave us an interesting guided tour of the place. We watched as workers made metal figurines of goddesses, using the lost wax method. The finished objects were well done but quite touristy in type. He also made items to order for international buyers.

We had a coffee and then all climbed into a robust Land Rover and started out on our trip. We soon found ourselves on dirt tracks with huge holes and ruts and after taking the wrong road a couple of times and overcoming worries about running out of petrol, we collected a guide from a village and reached our destination. We passed though beautiful countryside with sharp hills and valleys, all very fertile, covered in picture-book terraced fields. Rice was growing everywhere, along with mustard – creating dramatic colour contrasts. We had the most wonderful walk through attractive, remote and unpopulated countryside. We could see ahead of us a steep little hill with a golden temple roof on the top of it, glinting in the sun. It was a romantic scene. The floor of the valley we were in was large and flat and surrounded by hills with no apparent exit, adding to the feeling of remoteness. The weather was glorious again – hot, sunny and with a slight breeze. We stopped for the picnic lunch our friends had brought for us all, and as we chatted, they told us that they had had an arranged marriage and were very happy indeed. It was the custom then, so were told, for Nepalese men to marry Indian women, since Nepalese society was very small. We then visited the temple which, sadly, was in a state of mild ruin inside, with priceless stone carvings lying around. It was remote, peaceful and calm. Our hosts pointed out that places like that were unfortunately becoming prey to treasure hunters, since such sites were completely unprotected.

As a bonus, just before sunset, the clouds over the peaks cleared, and we had a superb view of the high snow covered mountains to the north of the valley. Sagar, Brinda and Anthony were great company and it was a memorable day.

We returned to our hostel (we certainly did not mention to Sagar and Brinda where we were staying!) to wash, and then went to their house (quite a contrast) for a drink, prior to going out with them for a meal. We were taken to the "Yak and Yeti" restaurant – the smoothest place in town opened by Boris, a White Russian. It was sophisticated, with fairly good food, and Sagar said that taking into account the food and the atmosphere, there was nowhere remotely similar in Nepal or India. It was a fun evening and our hosts were very hospitable, absolutely refusing to allow us to pay. We exchanged addresses before parting company.

* * *

Heading East – Back into India

It was time to move on. Rather than going south back to northern India, we were going to head south east from Kathmandu, crossing Nepal all the way to the eastern border with India and on to Siliguri – the same Siliguri where my father had been driven to his office from my parents' house in the tea gardens, when I was a child. This was quite an unusual route to take. The journey would be about 500km and would take us along the eastern length of the southern part of Nepal. It would take at least 15 hours by bus and we would stop for the night.

We started by travelling some distance back up the road we had taken from India. This was a real bonus, since it had been dark when we did this part of the journey on the way into Kathmandu, and now, not only could we see staggering views in all directions, but we stopped at Daman (about 80km from Kathmandu at an altitude of nearly 8,000ft), which was and is famous for its panoramic views of the Himalayas, including Everest. The view was clear and breathtaking – the sheer scale of the mountains something quite new – making everything else look tiny. In the near distance, the foothills; further on, mountains and then: towering above everything else, the snow covered Himalayas – the whole arc almost, from Annapurna on the left to Everest itself on the right. I was aware of adjusting my viewing angle – lifting my chin, to look high, high, up in the sky at the 29,000ft snowy mountains. It was superb.

After the mountains, we reached the plain where the road ran straight, through jungly forest. We reached Janakhpur – a small dusty settlement in the middle of nowhere, where there was one extremely basic hotel. We were given a room and even huge mosquito nets, but the place was filthy and the floor of our room busy with cockroaches, plus every other kind of beetle and insect.

We made it to the next morning – I suppose because at least the cockroaches could not climb up into the bed! We were up at 4.45am to catch the 5.30am bus. As before, we were the only non-locals on the bus, which continued eastwards until after about half an hour, we arrived at a large river bed and ploughed across the sand until we reached the edge of the water. There was no bridge! and we had to get out of the bus and wade. It was an enormous river bed, mainly dry, but with several fairly wide (45m) bands of water running through it. These were quite fast flowing and for me, the water was quite high – almost crotch level. Fortunately there were plenty of porters who carried most of the luggage over to another bus (astonishingly) waiting for us on the other side. We carried one suitcase and various bags. Ian and I rolled our trousers up and took off our shoes but got completely soaked anyway – not that it mattered at all. It was a stunning scene – the very wide sandy river bed, palm trees on the other side silhouetted against the rising sun, and the passengers like little dots in this huge river bed all wading, either with their lungis or their sarees raised high.

We continued through very flat country and then came within sight of the mountains again, where the country changed: the jungle had been cleared in many areas, and rice was growing for miles. Houses tended to be on stilts and reminded me of old films about Malaya. The colours were dazzling – lime green paddy in the foreground, dark green trees on the mountains, all slightly hazy with a bright blue sky. We soon came to another river with no bridge! This time the river was deep and fast moving but very narrow. The answer was to take it in turns to get ourselves, a few passengers at a time, plus our luggage, into a small boat, which was pushed sideways by two men standing in the water! We sat in the boat for about a minute and then had to get out and wade several more small rivers. The Nepali and Indian men pulled up their lungis and carried their luggage on their heads. This time, Ian too decided to expose his thighs to the world, so we were treated to a rather Livingstone type figure striding across a river bed about a quarter of a mile wide with a porter carrying his "pant" and shoes and case! I got soaked again since I could hardly remove my trousers. Again, amazingly, there was another bus waiting for us on the other side. We assumed that this journey could only be done in the dry season – in the wet season the rivers would have been in full spate and getting across them would surely have been impossible. Presumably, bridges have been built by now.

We had bought tickets all the way to the border and had been assured time and again that we could reach Siliguri in two days, but when we arrived at a place in the middle of nowhere, the bus stopped and we were told that it did not go to Siliguri; that the other bus did not go for another three hours; and that since one could not cross the river in the dark, one could not get there that evening! We created a fuss and demanded our money back, which we got and then, by the skin of our teeth, we managed to catch a bus going in the right direction. At one stop we had an extremely funny experience: we got out of the bus to have some tea and when we went back to the bus, found that everyone else had got there first and that there were even more passengers – the bus was rammed with people cheek by jowl and it was impossible for us to get on. We were staggered, however, to see that our seats (with a couple of our bags) had been saved for us and were free – ready and waiting, if only we could get on the bus! The bus was high and very straight sided and the windows quite small, so we were taken aback at the conductor's suggestion that we should climb in through a window!

However, we managed it: I climbed in first with Ian helping me up and people pulling me from inside, and then it was Ian's turn and he managed too, with some help from the driver and from me doing some pulling. The whole bus load of people was laughing and enjoying the situation – all incredibly good-humoured, and so we continued on our way.

There was a wonderful sunset and at about 6.30pm the bus stopped and we were told we had to get out and stay where we were for the night and that we could cross the border and the river the next morning. We said we had to get to Siliguri that evening and after a huge discussion, it turned out that the bus was going to the border anyway! We got back into the bus and reached the border about five minutes later!

As soon as we got off the bus, we were surrounded by people, some trying to bargain over a jeep, others telling us it was impossible to go over the border that evening etc. One particular guy was really flash – looked like a London East End spiv, but we were, fortunately, able to shake him off. The customs and passport office was a small hut and the so called officials were terrified of letting us through at 8pm, but after a lot of cajoling and mumbling and grumbling, we got a stamp.

We had arranged for a jeep to take us for 25 Indian rupees and we jumped in with the young boy who spoke two words of English but had undertaken to look after us. We were scared – my mother's descriptions of 'dacoits' ie bandits, seemed to have stuck in my mind – but Ian was nervous too. It was a dangerous situation. We thought we would probably be safe if we went in a jeep with just one driver, but it soon became apparent that this was out of the question. We were about to leave, when three other men climbed in. We objected strongly, but they refused to get out, one of them saying he was the owner of the jeep. This particular character had nearly driven us mad already, interfering the whole time at the passport office and also, as customs went through all our bags, asking us why we were carrying certain things. Ian had told him to mind his own business. It was very daunting – we did not want to be in a jeep full of men – we were scared of being robbed or worse. We would be travelling through jungle and it was dark. We said that we had paid for the whole jeep and asked why others should cadge a lift etc., and the reply was "to help the driver". At that point, the main man said we just could not go and Ian went mad. Meanwhile the young boy had been slapped on the face by a group of men and sent home in disgrace. Ian tried everything, from yelling, to handing round cigarettes, all to no avail.

We were saved, however, by a very nice man who spoke good English. He had chatted to me earlier, saying that if the worst came to the worst, we could cross the river on foot (over the bridge) with porters, and get a jeep on the Indian side – this would take half an hour – in the pitch black! He disappeared, and came back with a mate who had a jeep and they said they would take us. This was great because we were able to tell the others to go to hell. We got going and no more than one minute later, had to go through a police check point! Unbelievable, but true – they went through all our baggage again, this time taking everything out until Ian (extremely sensitive about his immaculate packing) told them that he would handle his stuff, not them. More problems were brought up: robbers on the road; we might not be able to get into India – we did not have the right visas, etc. etc. By this time, we were exasperated but climbed once more into the jeep with the expectation that there would be more of the same on the Indian side. The journey was quite an experience, very daunting, travelling for 30km in an open jeep with two men we did not know, bouncing through thick jungle, on an unmade road seemingly in the middle of nowhere, in the pitch dark. All turned out well, however, and we were lucky to arrive safely.

By some miracle, everything was shut at the Indian border post – no passport control, no customs – and we arrived in Siliguri at about 9pm. The hotel where they dropped us off was great – clean beds and sheets with a clean bathroom attached, with a shower that worked. We had a very good meal, washed properly (marvellous), and collapsed in a heap. Darjeeling was twinkling up on the hill.

* * *

On to Calcutta

It was the first day of November and we planned a relaxing day not doing very much except getting our laundry done. However, we had all the usual problems with getting tickets and had to go 15km to New Jalpaiguri in a cycle rickshaw. The bank finally opened at 10.00, and although they were able to cash travellers' cheques (involving innumerable forms and signatures), they were unable to change our Nepalese money, despite being right next to the Nepalese border. We were told that the money could only be changed at the Reserve Bank of India in Calcutta – some 350 miles away!

Asking to see the manager made no difference at all – a benign smile and a shrug of the shoulders.

The whole of the next day was spent on the train – the slow train – finally leaving, after an hour's delay, at about 10.30, chugging its way tortuously south and stopping at every hut and village on the way. As usual, we kept ourselves going with delicious little Indian goodies. We should have arrived in Calcutta at 05.45am but at 08.00 we were shunted into a siding where we waited for an hour. Nobody complained – it must have been quite normal. Ian saw several people leave the train and catch a local train, so we thought we would do likewise -- get off, cross the tracks and catch the next local train. We were helped across by a little elderly Indian man who spoke fair English and we got into a third class carriage with him. After a while we got some seats and he told us (laughing, amazingly) about the terrible shortages – rice had gone up by about 15-20 rupees and kerosene and petrol prices had also risen. He told us about the corruption and the black market and how most of them were given too little rice from the government as a weekly ration and therefore had to go and buy at three to four times the price on the black market. The passive fatalism of people in India in the face of such difficulties, which we had come across before, was evident, as our fellow passengers said several times "but what can we do?".

We also heard an interesting view of the Naxalites (a revolutionary Marxist group which functioned in West Bengal): two people in the compartment said that the Naxalites were a paid group egged on by the Congress Party to bring disrepute on the Communist and other opposition parties. They could not see a democratically elected Communist government on the state level (ie West Bengal) because the Congress Party would keep them out of governing.

As we approached Calcutta the train became a commuter train with more and more people climbing in, heading for their work in the city. Forget the crowds you have seen at London mainline stations or in the underground, or anywhere else for that matter, these are as nothing compared to the vast crushing sea of people we saw in Calcutta station. Hundreds and hundreds of people made their way from trains through the station into the city. We saw a woman(?) who appeared to be dying of dysentery, covered by a filthy rag and lying on the station floor. People ignored this and simply stepped over her/him, hurrying on. It was desperate.

We were on our way to Kolkata airport and needed to get to the airline offices in the old city. Unfortunately, there was a strike in the city of all taxi drivers (due to the increase in the price of petrol), including not only cars, but, in solidarity, the black gharries pulled by horses (which it would have been interesting to travel in) and the tongas. Hundreds of people were waiting on the station concourse for some kind of transport. We were at a loss as to what to do, when we were approached by a young man on his cycle rickshaw, who wanted to take us. This meant that both of us and our luggage were to be pulled along by one man on a bicycle. The journey involved crossing the bridge (with its steep gradient), over the wide Hooghly River. I remember this as one of the worst experiences I had in India. Our "rickshaw wallah" was cheerful, tall, sinewy and obviously strong, but to see him just in front of us, skinny and pouring with sweat as he hauled us along for about 25 minutes, was terrible, and I felt ashamed. There really was no other way for us to reach our destination in time, though, especially in the full sun, with our luggage, so at least we paid him decently.

We passed through shockingly deprived areas of the city, populated by people living in primitive conditions. Right next to us at one point, a small child was defecating in the road, surrounded by basic shanty houses and stalls. To us, there was a big difference between Delhi and Calcutta at that time. We were told there was a better side to Calcutta, however, and we only passed through one area, so our impression was limited, but still. . .

It was a huge relief to reach the airline offices, from where we were given a lift to Calcutta's Dum Dum airport for our flight to Rangoon. The plane had about twenty passengers on board and of those as Ian put it *"most of them could have been characters in a Graham Greene novel. There was a Bishop Neill; a freelance journalist; two members of the Burmese politburo; three missionaries (two men who were wearing identical sun hat trilbys in off-white); a mad Australian salesman with long Beatle-like hair brushed forward in a fringe and he must have been 40 – I also remember he wore white socks and black shoes – rather worn – and lastly, two smooth Americans"*. Tourist visas at that time were only valid for seven days, so maybe there were other categories of visa too. . .

As we left India, our view was of the mighty Ganges delta.

* * *

Rangoon

We were hit by a wall of heat and humidity as we left the plane in Rangoon. There were rigorous formalities, particularly about money, and we were given a lousy rate of exchange (half the rate in Singapore) on top of which 15% commission was charged. Ian had a few choice words to say about so-called Democratic Socialist Republics and impoverished young capitalists!

We stayed at the YMCA which was fairly dirty and decidedly seedy, but at least had clean sheets. The Australian attached himself to us and that evening suggested we eat out together. We walked about the unlit and smelly streets slightly haphazardly. There was no drainage system and the whole beleaguered city centre stank of the open drains. We started talking to an elderly Indian man called David, who had lived in Burma for years. He took us to an Indian restaurant, which unfortunately turned out to be indescribably filthy. I ate nothing, but Ian ate a little – which was to be his undoing in due course – particularly since he smoked a Burmese cigar into the bargain. David then took us to see a street troupe performing traditional Burmese dances and mime. The children in the street were very friendly and the people pleasant enough, given their evident poverty and our relative wealth. Very few foreigners were visiting Burma at that time.

The next day we woke up full of enthusiasm to book our tickets to Pagan. At the station, however, we found that the following day's express train was fully booked. It was suggested that we take that afternoon's train which would travel overnight. However, as we could only afford third class tickets with no berths, we would need to return later to buy the tickets. We returned to the YMCA, where we saw a number of notices on the board, written by others, mostly students, who had travelled by train third class, and been robbed. The robbers' usual method, they said, particularly at night, was to board trains as they slowed down to climb hills.

By this time, we had discovered that it was almost impossible to find anything drinkable; water, of course, being out of the question. Our stand-by – Coke (even locally produced Coke) – was unavailable anywhere in the country and the bottled synthetic drinks made in Burma at that time were horrible. We went to a small place where we had had a sugar cane drink the night before (delicious but dodgy – all going through an ancient fly ridden metal mangle affair) and asked for beer. However, the only beer available, we were told, was at the very expensive hotels, spirits only being available. We ordered ginger beer but the bottles arrived full of black bits. The young man who served us was very embarrassed, saying that the bottles arrived from the factory like that, so we settled for some scented lemonade.

We had found a city where people, despite being friendly, were unable to speak freely due to the military dictatorship in power at the time. The young Burmese man who served us, was delightful. He started to speak to us in English and told us his tragic story: he had been a student, but because he had been one of the leaders of a student demonstration, he had been banned from studying, and his passport had been confiscated. He seemed pleased to be able to talk to outsiders about the situation in his country. He told us about the people's poverty: serious shortages, from rice to building bricks to fabrics; about price rises of between 200% to 300% with one wage increase of 15%, and how people could afford very little. It was particularly striking to hear of rice shortages in Burma, which before the war had been one of the largest rice-producing countries in the world. He had been arrested and jailed for two years and when released, had been refused his passport; told he could not leave the country, and was not allowed to attend the university again. He told us that the Burmese could be cunning, and that if you were wearing a new lungi, someone was likely to report you to the police. He said that it would be possible to get out of the country illegally over the border and that he wanted to get to West Germany where he had friends and could get a grant (this in 1973!). He confidently predicted a revolution within about five years.

We headed to the Holy Trinity Cathedral to look at the register recording my mother's baptism there on 19 June 1921 and my own on 8 February 1947. We were depressed by our experiences of the country so far, and wandered rather listlessly towards the Cathedral, discussing the thought that we should perhaps leave straight away, although sad at the prospect of missing Pagan. We reached the Cathedral and were taken to the vicarage where we met the Vicar. He told us that at the outbreak of the war the Vicar then, whose name was Higginbottom, had fled north with all the records; been clubbed with a gun, and died of double pneumonia. All the records had been lost or destroyed. He was a nice man, telling us that we had missed a wonderful "feet" the day before when Bishop Neill had been there. Bishop Neill had apparently been in Ceylon for many years, spoke Tamil like a local and had declined the Bishopric of Rangoon. Having retired, he had come to visit.

We wandered along the deserted streets. Rangoon was rather reminiscent of a ghost town then – huge wide boulevards (no cars) and many large colonial style buildings, most of which were decaying and/or falling down, nothing having been done to maintain them since the war – the economic situation in the country disastrous.

Almost without discussing it, we realised, after a couple more visits, that we were not enjoying being in Rangoon, so we re-confirmed our tickets for the next day. In the evening, we went to the Strand Hotel for a beer – hugely expensive but a delicious boost. The hotel was vast, depressing and gloomy although by the time of my visit in 2015, it had been entirely refurbished and returned to its original 'grand' state. Back at the 'Y' we gave the receptionist some money to post some Shan pants ("Bombies": the kind my father always wore in bed) to us in Papua New Guinea, once there was sufficient fabric available to make them. He underlined that nothing is available unless you pay very inflated prices on the black market and said that he just did not know how people were managing to live. Sadly, but not surprisingly, we did not receive the Shan pants.

* * *

Bangkok and on to Singapore

The YMCA in Bangkok was sheer luxury – I wrote in our diary: "for 30 bob a head we got a super air conditioned double room with a bathroom attached, all modern and spotlessly clean and actually with a bath! – first one since England." It was brand new and decorated throughout in a sort of Swedish sauna style with pine everywhere. It was the seventies after all!

We had not planned to stay for long. We took very cheap local buses through what seemed to us more like a modern American city after the extremely quiet and run-down city of Rangoon. I was trying to relate what I was seeing to my experience of living in Bangkok as a child from 1951 to 1953, but I found little I recognised, until we visited some of the tourist sites. I had no idea which area of Bangkok we had lived in, and I suspected that if we had found the area (a nearly impossible task with no address), the house itself would probably have been demolished by then. However, when we visited the two main Wats (temples): Wat Phra Kaew – temple of the emerald Buddha – and Wat Pho – temple of the reclining Buddha – I remembered ciné films my mother had made. Both temples were impressive – the reclining Buddha itself being huge – about 40ft high and 150ft long. We were unable to visit the Royal Palace because Ian was not wearing a coat and tie. Unfortunately, Ian was feeling unwell with bouts of nausea and had to keep resting. We went back to the 'Y' in a three wheeler and almost choked on the exhaust fumes. The traffic was appalling – just as it is now in Yangon.

The following day, during most of which Ian continued to feel unwell, we went to see the floating market, which we had had to book as a package deal. We were collected at 06.00 for this, but when we arrived at the jetty there were already hundreds of tourists all getting into boats. It was chaotic, with men using loud hailers trying to organise us. Fortunately, our group was very small (only nine people) and we set off up the large and muddy Chao Phraya River. We turned into one of the klongs and immediately joined a long queue of river craft all jammed with tourists. It was very disappointing and quite unlike how it had been when I was a young child there.

We saw only three or four local boats, selling almost no fruit except bananas and were soon taken to a large shop full of tourist style Thai arts and crafts. There was a sad baby elephant tied to a post and covered in ribbons, which looked decidedly frightened as tourists took pictures of each other 'with an elephant'. It was all a bit grim. After this we returned to the main river and visited Wat Arun (Temple of Dawn) which was impressive, and then to a shop where we bought two pieces of Thai silk, fortunately just before our wallet was stolen. Luckily, the wallet only contained about £6 worth of Thai Bahts.

We left Bangkok the next afternoon by train, which was clean (hoorah!), with vast seating areas. After passing through countryside made up mainly of flat paddy fields, a man turned up to pull down our upper bunk and make our beds. These were classic – curtained off – almost exactly as in the film 'Some Like it Hot'!

The countryside started to become more jungly the following day. At the Thailand/Malaysia border we all had to get out of the train, fill in forms, declare how much money we had and how long we intended to stay in the country. This took an hour or so, after which we re-boarded the train which continued on to Penang. We thought we would try visiting Penang for a day, so crossed the Straits of Penang, by ferry, seeing lots of ships in the harbour and in the 'roads'. However, after being cycled through a few picturesque parts of Penang in a rickshaw, we found that the YMCA would not take females and the YWCA was full. We decided not to stay, and returned to the train to carry on to Kuala Lumpur and Singapore.

Back over the water and at the station, we found that there were no second class berths on the train, these having been booked for weeks. For all those who had travelled from Bangkok, unbelievably, there were no berths! We did get some seats, though, and were hugely entertained by an Englishman who recounted the incredibly eventful story of his mishap-filled journey from England to Nepal by bus. However, one second class bunk became available and Ian selflessly booked this for me. However, he began to feel very unwell again, and later on joined me in the single bunk.

We arrived in Kuala Lumpur early in the morning and had to change trains for the last part of our 1,233 mile train journey down the Thai and Malaysian peninsula. The countryside now became as we had imagined it might be. There were huge rubber plantations – mostly owned by Dunlop – all very organised with bright red/orange sand roads, and little clearings every so often with paddy fields and small patches of vegetables and a few houses on stilts. Behind these it was very hilly with thick jungle – beautiful lush tropical rainforest with innumerable flowering trees. As we approached Johore and Singapore Island, there were large plantations of newly sown pineapple trees. The irrigation schemes were the most advanced we had seen so far, with bricked canals and efficient sluice-gates.

When we arrived in Singapore, we had another brush with Customs. We were both tired and had forgotten to declare our Burmese cigars(!) – naturally, these were the first things the Customs officer found . . . Ian wrote: ". . . he tried to get stroppy but didn't reckon with Anne who got even stroppier and the issue was finally settled with just a few feathers out of place".

We got a cab to the YWCA, the driver initially pretending he did not know where it was. . . The rooms were expensive, but we luxuriated in the warm bath.

The next morning, we went into town by bus and collected our post from the Poste Restante which we read over breakfast in a slightly sleazy place on Clifford Pier. We collected our £200 from the European Asian Bank – a vast ice-cold palace with potted plants everywhere. Money was being sent to us by our friend and solicitor, David, who was acting as our agent in the letting of our house.

We had not planned to stay in Singapore for long, but had hoped to be able to go to Port Moresby by sea. We visited the Harbour Master's office to enquire about boats to Papua, but they knew next to nothing and told us that '*The Straits Times*' was as good a source of information as any other. We also visited various shipping agents, but to no avail. However, we discovered eventually that a boat was expected on approximately 26th November. We considered this option but worked out that staying in Singapore for the extra time would, with the boat fare, add up to about the same amount as flying to Port Moresby. Offices were closing for the weekend, so we could do no more research, and instead, walked around lots of shops in huge air conditioned shopping malls, trying to find the best price for a radio/cassette. We found the experience annoying but amusing, with prices varying ridiculously from place to place. At least we were cool. . .

Singapore at that time was not too big – very modern mostly, mainly made up of vast shopping complexes, all refrigerated and very cold. Major building works were going on everywhere and people seemed to be doing very nicely. The port was magnificent with the best view from the centre: there were hundreds and hundreds of ships of every shape and size. It was frustrating for us, knowing that out there somewhere, there was quite possibly a small boat setting off soon for Port Moresby. The city itself struck us as slightly soulless – western attitudes and ideas having taken over to a large extent. Most people were wearing western style clothes with young women in mini-skirts, and even Chinese food was giving way to fried chicken and steaks. No advantage had been taken of the city's location either – there was not one café or restaurant on the sea front – and little seemed to be going on. I suspect that it is different now. However, the collection of orchids and butterflies at the Botanical Gardens, was marvellous. The heat everywhere was phenomenal and humidity high.

We found ads in the paper for charter flights to Australia, and soon realised that we did not have enough money to go by air! We cabled David, asking him to send £150 urgently. Since we had had our quota already, we hoped that this would be possible. There was only one flight per week to Port Moresby – if the money did not come before this, we would have to wait another week . . . and pay more hotel bills.

We moved to a cheaper room, and to our relief, our money arrived just in time. We packed, checked out, sent a cable to our contact in Port Moresby, collected our money and paid for two tickets on that evening's Qantas flight via Darwin. The airport was far too small for the enormous number of people going through it, with virtually nowhere to sit except for a noisy barn-like drinking hall. It had not yet been developed and was a very far cry indeed from today's vast, sophisticated and comfortable airport with its innumerable entertainments.

After India and Nepal, we had visited three such very different South East Asian cities in a short space of time. It had given us a quick lesson in the journey such cities make as they develop. From Rangoon: deserted and decaying, poverty stricken and economically depressed, with almost no tourists; the people and the country in the grip of a repressive military junta; to Bangkok: bustling, becoming prosperous, but with unimaginative new buildings and roads choked with traffic and fumes; tourism already flourishing; to Singapore: a small already organised island city state with a somewhat soulless atmosphere; a frenzy of building; huge cold shopping malls and a newly affluent first world culture.

Such a brilliant, adventure-filled and eye-opening journey it had been, moving on slowly from one extraordinary place and experience to the next.

We were nearing our journey's end and looking forward to the adventures ahead.

CHAPTER 8

The South Pacific

* * *

Arrival

THERE WAS SOMETHING WRONG – something was missing – there was no green in the landscape – anywhere! Despite the sparkling blue green sea, with its coral reefs just under the surface, and the small islands with brilliant white sand beaches, the landscape was dry and unrelentingly brown as we flew over and then landed in Port Moresby. How could we have travelled half way round the world to the tropics, only to find this distinctly uninviting, untropical and unlovely looking place? We were told that it becomes very dry in Moresby in the dry season, unlike some other areas of the country, and that New Britain was completely different.

We were driven by truck to an expensive German hotel and slept straight away, terrified at the thought of how much the hotel would cost us[124]. Later, Ian went to see our contact, and was told that we were booked on a flight to Rabaul, our destination, early the following morning. We wandered around the town and sat under some coconut palms, gazing at the Coral Sea, hoping against hope. . .

Our evening meal turned out to be bizarre – there were six ways of having oysters – and that was just for starters! Ian had to comply with

---

124 We had no reason to worry – the bill was paid for us.

the notices stipulating that men must wear trousers and ties at dinner and thongs (flip-flops) were banned at lunch time, when the dress code was shorts and long socks. We ordered steaks – first we had huge paper bibs tied round our necks and then two enormous sizzling steaks were served. They were so big we were unable to finish them. A small band struck up, with an electric organ, and dancing started. We had a good giggle as lots of white middle aged couples jostled for space on their Friday night out. We seemed to be in some sort of colonial time warp – and hoped we would soon emerge into a more normal present day.

The next morning, Saturday 17th November 1973, five weeks after we had set out, we took a taxi at 06.00 to Port Moresby airport, where we boarded a small Fokker Friendship plane and flew to Rabaul, just south of the Equator, on the Gazelle Peninsula of the island of New Britain. We had travelled around ten thousand miles.

* * *

Rabaul – Papua New Guinea

We flew over a smoking volcano, part of a nearly complete ring of volcanoes around the huge, dramatic, stunning, bright blue Simpson Harbour. All the volcanoes and surrounding countryside were clothed in lush, dense green forest – completely unspoiled. It had to have been one of the most spectacular harbours on earth at that time and we were so excited. We had arrived!

As we landed and taxied towards the airport building, the first things we saw from the aircraft windows were the hats of the young men working on the runway. They were bright green and yellow and bore just two words "South Pacific". How brilliant!

We were met by one of the senior Australian doctors from Nonga Base Hospital, who drove us the five miles or so to Nonga. He was extremely welcoming. We drove out of town along Frangipani Avenue, lined with frangipani trees. We were soon passing hibiscus, bougainvillea, coconut palms, cocoa trees, banana palms, pawpaw (papaya) trees and small villages along the road, most of the houses with their own vegetable gardens.

We turned left off the road into a smaller one, leading down to the sea. There were about a dozen bungalow style houses on stilts in this road, some larger than others, and we were taken to one of them – our new home. This was one of the larger bungalows, with three bedrooms, a good wooden floor throughout and a fridge and washing machine. There was even a good sized garden with banana palms in it. The only downside, which we discovered rather quickly, was that there were quite a few cockroaches, so we hastily invested in quantities of spray to use under the kitchen sink.

We were taken up the road to the hospital (*haus sick*) and introduced to staff, including Ian's new boss. After that, we bought a few provisions at the local trade store; unpacked; and potted up a couple of plants from the garden which we took inside.

And then, it was time for a swim! Bliss! The sea was about 500 yards away down the road and across an open field of grass – very beautiful and the water very warm. It was so warm that you almost felt in need of a cool current. This was the Bismarck Sea. The sand was very fine and almost black since the region is volcanic, and the trees went down almost to the water's edge. The colours were superb and it looked exactly as a tropical beach should: idyllic.

The next day was a Sunday so we went for quite a long walk along the beach and had another swim. We met various neighbours and went to the sisters' mess for supper. Afterwards, we were taken into town by some neighbours who drove us up to the top of the hill overlooking Rabaul harbour after dark – the small town twinkling below us and the sky and the stars magnificent.

The next few days were spent with Ian working very hard with long hours. He usually returned home exhausted after 8pm. Meanwhile, I had it a lot easier – meeting neighbours, shopping and swimming. . . I did my first bit of snorkelling (during which I got very burnt) and was astounded – there were fish of every shape, size and colour: luminous blues, bright yellows with black stripes, some with red patches, others orange. . . It was stunning and unlike anything I had ever seen before. Likewise, the market: this was superb and sold just about every kind of fruit and vegetable you could imagine. It was exciting and full of very friendly Tolai people. You could buy a pineapple for 5cents, 10cents or 20cents – the 20cent ones were enormous.

One morning a man arrived at the house to mow the grass and asked if he could have a coconut from our tree. I watched him as he shinned up the tree and then skinned a couple of coconuts for me. The inside of the coconuts was almost like yoghurt – so fresh – and the coconut water, sweet and delicious.

One of our first tasks was to try to arrange a loan from the bank. Ian and I went to the bank together and told the very surprised bank manager that we had arrived with no money at all after our travels. Fortunately, since Ian had a contract of employment, he soon agreed a loan, and we were able to buy some clothes appropriate for the great heat and humidity (average high temperature for November 31°C, with average morning humidity for November 93%)[125]. Importantly too, we needed a car, which we bought very soon – a battered but robust pale blue Datsun saloon, which lasted our time in Rabaul.

After a couple of days, we were moved to another house on higher stilts on the other side of the road. This suited us much better since it was smaller and a little newer. We parked the car underneath the house. Next to the staircase at one end of the house, was a pawpaw tree, the fruit of which were gorged on at night by flying foxes. The volcanic soil was extremely fertile – a broken off branch of, say, a croton shrub, stuck into the ground, would very soon start to grow. There was roughly mown grass around the house but beyond that there were tropical shrubs, trees and banana palms. Although in theory, there was a wet and a dry season in New Britain, the two seasons varied only slightly, so everything was permanently lush and green.

Very soon we received a letter from Ian's parents which told an amazing story: Ian's father, Brian, wrote that he had been driving through Covent Garden in London when he realised he had a puncture. He stopped and was having a look at the tyre (he was not the most practical of people) when a young couple, John and Dierdre, offered to help. As they kindly changed the tyre, Brian chatted to them. He commented on their Australian accents and they said that they were indeed from Australia but were on holiday in London. However, they explained that they did not live in Australia, but in Papua New Guinea! It is not difficult to imagine Brian's surprise at being told this, so he went on to tell them that Ian and I were on our way there right then. John explained that he had been brought up in PNG, and had been one of the first Australians to attend the University of Papua New Guinea in Port Moresby. He said that he was now a malaria control officer but was based in New Britain, where Dierdre also worked – as a nurse. Curiouser and curiouser. . . It emerged that not only did Deirdre and

---

125 Weatherbase.com: *http://www.weatherbase.com/weather/weather.php3?s=58049*

John live and work just outside the town of Rabaul, but Dierdre worked at Nonga Base Hospital! Even more amazingly, it turned out that they lived in the house almost immediately opposite ours! Ian father's comment to us was, of course, that he had met our neighbours before we had. Probably one of the better coincidence stories. . .

Ian and I knew next to nothing about PNG when we arrived, but after a while, not only did we enjoy it more and more, but also learned a little about it as well.

"In the nineteenth century, Germany ruled the northern half of the country as a colony for some decades, beginning in 1884, as German New Guinea. The southern half was colonised in the same year by the United Kingdom as British New Guinea. With the Papua Act 1905 it transferred this territory to the newly formed Commonwealth of Australia, which took on its administration. Additionally, from 1905, British New Guinea was renamed the Territory of Papua.

Early in World War I, German New Guinea was captured by Australian forces in a small military campaign, and after the war was given to Australia to administer as a League of Nations Mandate. Papua, by contrast, was deemed to be an External Territory of the Australian Commonwealth, though as a matter of law it remained a British possession. This was significant for the country's post-independence legal system. The difference in legal status meant that until 1949 Papua and New Guinea had entirely separate administrations, both controlled by Australia.

During World War II, the New Guinea campaign (1942–1945) was one of the major military campaigns. Approximately 216,000 Japanese, Australian, and US servicemen died. After World War II, the two territories were combined into the Territory of Papua and New Guinea, which later was simply referred to as "Papua New Guinea"."[126]

In 1942 Rabaul was captured by the Japanese and due, no doubt, to its huge harbour, they turned it into the main base of Japanese military and naval activity in the South Pacific. There were relics and remains of this period in the countryside around Rabaul – fighter planes which had crashed into the jungle, and many underground tunnels dug by the Japanese to defend themselves from bombardment. The Japanese managed to remain there, despite a severe shortage of supplies latterly, until the Japanese surrender of 1945.

---

126 https://en.wikipedia.org/wiki/Papua_New_Guinea

FROM THE ESK AND THE USK: OUT EAST AND BACK HOME

> *"Papua New Guinea is one of the most <u>culturally diverse</u> countries in the world; 852 <u>languages</u> are listed for the country. . ."*[127]

We were often told that there were hundreds of languages across the country – particularly in areas of the Highlands where isolated villages were often built on the tops of ridges for defensive reasons, and where hostility between these villages and their neighbours, was common. (Headhunting had only relatively recently been eliminated.) The lingua franca in PNG, however, was "Tok Pisin" ie Pidgin, which incorporated various German and Australian words and expressions; a well-known example being "*I bagarap*" to describe something broken. Ian and I learned a little Pidgin; enough to just get by. Ian learned more than I did, because it was more useful in his work than mine, but sadly, we did not master the language.

The other piece of information frequently passed around, was that PNG had more Christian missionaries in the country, for its size, than anywhere else in the world.

"The 2011 census found that 95.6% of citizens identified themselves as members of a Christian church. . . Many citizens combine their Christian faith with some traditional indigenous religious practices."[128]

It was certainly difficult not to notice the influence of western religion where we were: what with religious processions winding through the countryside with people carrying crucifixes aloft and singing; with Christian chapels on remote islands; and stories of a complete dearth of local artefacts from New Ireland because Christian missionaries had made sure such things were either removed or destroyed. . .

Despite this, however, old beliefs and traditions persisted. There was a secret society among the Tolai, which believed in spirits and held 'secret' ceremonies. This was called the Duk-Duk where males (the duk-duk men) donned special large conical masks made of painted cane and fibre; with a cape of leaves covering the rest of their bodies except for their legs. They danced at these ceremonies to invoke both male (duk-duk) and female (tubuan) spirits. Duk-duk men traditionally appeared only at the full moon, and women and children were forbidden to look at them. Strangers, too, had been unwelcome in earlier times, but times had changed and Ian and

---

127 https://en.wikipedia.org/wiki/Papua_New_Guinea
128 https://en.wikipedia.org/wiki/Papua_New_Guinea

I did manage to go to one of these ceremonies. It was quite an experience; duk duk men gathering on the beach at dawn. The dancers looked impressive in their costumes and despite it not being a formal ceremony (it was slightly chaotic), it was still being taken seriously, and we were careful to show respect. Boats were involved in the proceedings, as well. I see that this tradition has, inevitably, become a significant tourist attraction.

A difficult part of the PNG culture was the 'pay-back' system. This was used by an individual, a family or a tribe to take revenge on anyone who hurt a relative, friend, or possession, in any way. We were warned of this danger in case we were ever to be involved in a road accident. Had that happened, we were told, we would probably have had to leave the country immediately. Fortunately, nothing at all like that did happen while we were there.

The administration of PNG at that time was Australian. Government workers, doctors, teachers, business people, were almost entirely Australian, assisted by local people. The next largest population of foreigners was the Chinese, who ran the majority of the trade stores, selling everything from groceries to fabrics.

The plantations were in the main owned by Australian companies, which employed workers either from the Highlands or from the Sepik River areas on the mainland. As a result, there developed an undesirable but standard colonial set-up: significant numbers of male workers were living on the plantations, far from home and without their families. They lived in male-only barrack-like accommodation and soon 'discovered' beer and spirits. Drunkenness, violence and even very occasionally, worse, were the result. In Rabaul, behaviour of this kind was rare but in the PNG capital, Australians had already started to build high walls around their properties.

We found the Tolai people, the indigenous people of the Gazelle Peninsula of East New Britain and the Duke of York's Islands, very friendly. They looked quite distinct from people we encountered from other areas. Their skin was brown in colour (in contrast to the Bukans – the people of Bougainville – who were very dark skinned) and they sometimes bleached their hair blonde. Their village houses were built on stilts and the villagers grew vegetables in their gardens. The majority of the women wore cotton short sleeved tops with puffed sleeves called in Tok Pisin *"meri blouses"* (*"meri"* as in the name Mary – was the word for a woman) and cotton wrap-around skirts called lap-laps. Almost all the women used bilum bags which were hand-made of multi-coloured string, with one long knotted-in handle. These bilums hung down women's backs, with the string handles across their foreheads, and were used to carry everything, including babies. The men generally wore cotton shorts and short-sleeved shirts. Ian and I did not want to subscribe to the usual practice of employing local people as servants, so since we were both young and fit, we did our own housework.

One of the habits of the local people (as with others in PNG) was to chew "buai", the local name for betel nut, a mild stimulant which grows in the Pacific. It was common to see people chewing it (with the usual bright red teeth), and sometimes, to drive behind a small truck being driven fairly erratically and to understand the reason why! Ian was very busy at work, where people were being treated for many things, including some particularly local problems: enlarged spleens (often due to malaria), and serious injuries from falling coconuts and from wild pig attacks (on one occasion, a crocodile attack). Later on, he did a couple of 'flying doctor' trips, flying to remote areas in a single-engined plane. This made me nervous, because there had been a couple of relatively recent crashes of single-engined planes over jungle areas. As for our own health, we took chloroquin tablets a couple of times a week to protect against malaria.

I soon began to look for work and I do not remember how, but very quickly became secretary to the managing director of the only supermarket in town, owned by the Steamships Trading Company – which had a long history in PNG. However, I had almost nothing to do apart from sit on a towel-covered chair at my desk all day (it was so hot that to have sweating legs was normal) and I quickly became very bored. The supermarket was not large, and was notable for having a very old fashioned cooling arrangement. Across the width of the ceiling were long poles, attached to which were large flaps of canvas which were all moved slowly backwards and forwards. My mother would have called these punkahs (the word for fans in Hindustani), but at least it was electricity that moved the whole system, rather than a person pulling a rope. I guess that these canvas flaps may originally have been dampened. I very soon gave up that job.

The next work I took involved two part-time jobs. The first was working as secretary to the managing director of Coconut Products Ltd, a company which registered in Rabaul in 1930. It owned coconut plantations which were underplanted with cocoa, and a copra oil mill. The copra oil (oil pressed from the dried flesh of coconuts) and other coconut products, were collected from the docks in Rabaul by large tanker ships for export. It was interesting to see the business side of Rabaul and the people who worked there. They were very different indeed from the people I mostly came into contact with. On one occasion, I was taken to the PNG Club (which sounds much grander than it was) by two of my male colleagues, and immediately saw in action, the racism of the members and the club. I never went there again. The most remarkable thing about the company, however, was that it had two tea 'boys' who would bring tea to the office staff. Their names were Penis 1 and Penis 2 (pronounced, however, in the same way as pen)!

My second part-time job was at the Malaguna Technical College, teaching typing. It was mentioned to me by a friend who worked there, that the College could do with an extra typing teacher. I had to formally register as a teacher (I had the typing qualifications but had never taught) and was then offered a job – which turned out to be very unusual, interesting, satisfying and fun. The students were all male and from the Highlands of the mainland; none of them knew how old they were and it was clear that there was quite a range of ages. It was anticipated that they would find jobs with the new skills they were learning. The young men did not know what to make of me, especially since I encouraged them to progress at their own rate, something they were not at all used to and which at first they did not like. When they got the point of it, though, it became popular and we all got on very well indeed.

Years later, I told this story to the well-known female director (at the time) of a highly prestigious UK national scientific funding institution. She left the room after a while, saying that she would be back soon, and returned with a smile, having popped out to Dillons (as it was then) and bought me a copy of Alexander McCall Smith's delightful book "The Kalahari Typing School for Men"! How thoughtful, and how amusing and appropriate. I certainly enjoyed reading it.

I used to drive home for my two hour lunch break between jobs. There I had a boiling hot siesta – spread-eagled on the bed, unable to get cool. Unfortunately the bedroom was on the sunny side of the house at that time of day. Our house did not have hot water, but a cool shower was just the thing.

Every evening, almost without fail, we would make our way down to the sea at the bottom of the road and across the field, for a wonderful swim in that warm soft placid sea. The sea would turn pink and then mauve as the sun set.

Life in Rabaul was good to us. We made several friends, some with children, some of whom we met up with when we got to Melbourne and others who came to visit us in London. This group of friends was made up of doctors (the Australian health service used to send young doctors at Registrar level to PNG for six monthly stints as part of their contracts, so we met several of around our age), including an Indian surgeon from Goa and his family; nurses; a pharmacist; teachers; an agronomist; a young New Zealander working in plantation management and, of course, the malaria control officer. We enjoyed good times.

There were no poisonous snakes on the island of New Britain but many poisonous and dangerous things in the sea. Apart from sharks, which very rarely came up on to a reef, but were, of course, the most terrifying; there were stone fish; scorpion fish; poisonous cone shells; sea snakes, etc., almost all of which could prove extremely dangerous and some lethal. There were several rules which we adopted immediately, to cope with this. It was vital to wear shoes in the sea and generally, to only swim above a reef if you were any distance from the beach. It was also important to wear a T shirt when snorkelling, to avoid sunburn. We kept strictly to the rules.

The sea was invariably beautiful and snorkelling over a reef was usually spectacular. We used to visit various beaches with friends on weekends. One that we visited early on, stands out: it was right up at the top of the Gazelle Peninsula, at Tavui Point, on the edge of a plantation. There was nothing else there and it was known as Submarine Base. This was because, quite close to the beach, the reef fell away, sheer, into the deepest scariest blue blue depths. (It was said that it had got its name because Japanese submarines had been able to hide very close to the shore, at depth.)

This reef itself was hardly ever visited and was covered in thousands and thousands of fish of all types and myriad vivid colours. To see this reef was an amazing, wonderful and unique experience. When I reached the edge of the reef, however, I found I could just about manage to swim along immediately above the edge, but was far too terrified of the depths below to go even a tiny distance out beyond the edge. I just could not bring myself do it! At one point, someone thought they saw a shark and called out. I realised very quickly, that despite my very best efforts, I was a very slow swimmer. Fortunately, the shark did not materialise.

We bought a small dingy, sharing it with another couple, Adrian and Suzanne. It was a GP14 and its name was 007 (how embarrassing). Neither Ian nor I had sailed before but our friends had, and gave us a few basic lessons. We were hopeless and at one point went straight into the rocks on the shore and had to lead the boat back to the small yacht club on a rope, having holed the hull. We had it repaired and eventually started to get the hang of it and even entered club races in the harbour – although we almost invariably came last. Amusingly, we even joined the flotilla of boats (our friend was at the helm, not us!) that welcomed HMS Britannia to Simpson Harbour in February 1974 when the Queen visited PNG. Otherwise, it was fantastic to be out in the middle of the harbour, hanging out over the side of the boat as we sailed at speed over the blue water (once I fell overboard, but fortunately still had hold of the rope. . .).

Suzanne's brother, Greg, visited Rabaul for a few months. He owned a good-sized yacht and was an expert sailor. We were lucky enough to be invited to join him and others on sailing trips, sometimes for the day and sometimes for a whole weekend. It was wonderful. One of our favourite destinations was the spectacular Duke of York's Islands. There were very few people living on these islands – which, picture postcard-like – had white, fine, powdery sand with palm trees growing down to the beach and a few local people on the sea in their outrigger canoes. We would sleep on the boat, moored in a small inlet surrounded by mangrove trees, and first thing in the morning, dive overboard into the clearest turquoise water you could ever see.

Our social lives were busy. Ian played squash, at which he was excellent, having learned the game from his father (amateur squash champion in Egypt in the '40s). There was also another excellent player living in Rabaul at that time; he had been Western Australian champion. There were several young Australian men who also played well, so the standard generally was high. A couple of top Pakistani squash players were on a world tour playing and demonstrating squash and, incredibly, came to Rabaul. Even more incredibly, Ian got the chance to play one of them and although he did not win, he did very well, and there was a good crowd. I had not played squash before, but gave it a go. I simply found it far far too hot. I found it necessary to re-tie my laces (to have a surreptitious breather) a little too often! Chasing round a squash court in that heat, sweating profusely and becoming exhausted, was not my idea of fun, so I did not regret giving it up fairly soon.

Ron, the hospital pharmacist, who lived almost opposite us with his wife Marg and two children, was a keen scuba diver. He would tell us tales of scary encounters he had had under water. One story was not about him, but about the local GP, a Chinese man, who had gone fishing on a reef with a harpoon, with his boat moored alongside the reef. He was walking over the shallow reef, trailing a line of fish he had caught, when in front of him he saw a shark heading straight for him. He almost froze with fear; however, he thought fast about how sharks are attracted to the smell of blood; dropped the line of fish for the shark; and made it back to the boat. Just before we arrived, someone had tragically died while scuba diving in Rabaul. This put the frighteners on us and neither of us had the courage to try it. We were content to hear stories second-hand, though, over a freezing cold beer. Whenever we saw our neighbour heading towards our house, we had to run to the fridge to check that there were bottles of beer, not in the fridge, but in the freezer. He would almost not drink beer unless it had been in the freezer. The 'South Pacific' beer came in two types – in green bottles or brown bottles – known as greenies or brownies, and was an excellent drink on a hot day.

Ian (in Australian sporting mode) also decided to try his hand at golf. He would get up at the crack of dawn and play before work. There were a couple of golf courses – basic, but fine. A couple of times, I went with him to get a flavour of it. One early morning we drove to Kokopo, where there was a small golf course scenically positioned right next to the sea. It was the rainy season and there were large areas which had flooded – including parts of this golf course. The result of the flooding was a mass invasion of frogs. On the course, there were so many, it was almost impossible to walk across the grass. I had flip flops on my feet and was trying hard not to scream as I tried to find gaps between the frogs, so that I could avoid stepping on one. It was horrible! Frogs would also congregate under our house when it was very wet, so returning home by car after dark became fairly horrible too. Getting out of the car, in the dark, wearing flip-flops . . . ughh. . .

There was another much smaller golf course (where Ian did not play) some distance along the North Coast Road near the agricultural research station. One day, our agronomist friend took us round the experimental growing areas of the research station, where we saw all sorts of spices growing: vanilla, cinnamon, nutmeg, etc. It was fascinating and rather beautiful – vanilla, for example, is an orchid. Afterwards, we went to the golf course area, which we had been told was ringed by enormous avocado trees. Years later, holidaying on the island of Madeira with Kate, there were a couple of avocado trees in our small garden, which were laden with fruit, and a huge treat, but here, there were simply masses of trees. Their branches are low, and it took no time to almost fill the car boot. When in season, avocados were part of our lunch almost every day.

There was a small cinema in Rabaul which we visited very occasionally. A notice outside banned the wearing of thongs (as in footwear!), which was clearly an attempt to deter local people (who almost always wore thongs) from entering. Yours truly invariably wore thongs as a matter of principle, but, unsurprisingly, was never turned away. . .

Every weekend, I took enormous pleasure from visiting the wonderful, large and picturesque Rabaul market. I would stock up with every kind of fruit and vegetable. It was not only tropical produce that was on offer. Almost everything was available (often in several sizes), with very few exceptions. I had acquired a very large cane basket, which I took to the market with me. I would fill it up, empty it into the boot of the car, and go back for a second load. I had had a few simple sleeveless cotton dresses made up for me at the Chinese trade stores (where they sold a huge variety of fabrics) and I had never been at the market long before whichever dress I was wearing, would be dark with sweat. It was really hot. Towels on the seats of everyone's cars were the norm – the plastic seat covers becoming sizzling hot and impossible to sit on.

On the odd occasion, we were invited to a party given by Tolai hospital staff and would eat food cooked using the local method. This involved heating large stones in a fire and digging a pit in the ground. Meat and vegetables (including *kaukau* – a type of sweet potato), would be wrapped in banana palm leaves, put into the pit with the hot stones and then covered over with earth and left. Once the food was cooked, the parcels were taken out and the food handed round. It was good.

There were a couple of small restaurants to which we would go occasionally, too. One of these, in Rabaul town, served sushi as a starter, followed by steak. The menu was unusual: it warned customers that in the event of an earthquake, we should immediately put our heads down between our knees. We felt earthquakes from time to time – they were never strong, but enough to make the glasses tinkle against each other at home.

The other restaurant was called the Kulau Lodge; a car drive along the coast. (A kulau is a young green coconut and here, they cut them in half and served alcoholic drinks in them.) The main grass covered building was on its own, right next to the beach, and there was a good space for dancing as well as eating. Sitting outside next to the calm warm sea and looking up at the enormous moon and its reflection on the sea, was superb, especially after energetic dancing.

We spent a weekend in New Ireland once. This is a group of islands north of New Britain. Ian had met the one doctor who lived there – a Filipino man, who invited us to visit him. We flew to the small main town of Kavieng. There were reefs along the sandy coast of the main island, which formed beautiful turquoise lagoons and here the sand was white. Our new friend's house was not in town, but on the edge of one of these lagoons – the swimming was glorious. He was hospitable and fun and suggested that he might take us out that night to hunt for crabs. There was no-one else around as we walked along the tropical beach with an enormous black and twinkling sky above us, carrying torches and looking for crabs. They were there for the taking, so we picked up several big ones and put them into our esky to take back with us the following day. It was not a clever move and we regretted what we had done. We took a tell-tale smell with us into the small plane and found when we got back home, that a couple of the crabs had died.

We had a memorable Christmas in 1974. One of our friends lived in a beautiful rented ex-plantation owner's house not far away and he invited us to join him. The house was situated at the top of a low rise above a small bay, with roughly mown grass leading down to the beach. We celebrated Christmas Day on a sharply bright and clear day, sitting on the verandah and eating our meal looking down at the brilliant blue sea with its constant curl of small white waves breaking on the reef not far off-shore. It was idyllic. I even cooked a very alcoholic Christmas pudding.

There was sometimes a party in Sal and Dave's house on weekends and several of us were mad keen dancers. The music we danced to included "American Pie" and "Sailing", both popular in the 70s. We also held a party ourselves, with a barbecue in the garden, to which we invited quite a number of people. It went on very late and some of us decided that we would climb Mt Kombui, the volcano known as 'The Mother' just the other side of Rabaul, the idea being to get to the top in time to see the dawn. Mt Kombui is about 700m above sea level (the highest mountain in East New Britain). Somehow, we found a Tolai guide, who hardly raised a sweat getting to the top. However, we had all had a few drinks . . . and climbing a volcano involves climbing at an unrelieved 45 degree angle all the way up. The volcano was largely covered in kunai grass[129], which can grow up to10ft

---

129 Kunai grass: a tough long bladed grass: the leaves are about 2 cm wide near the base of the plant and narrow to a sharp point at the top. It grows from 2ft to 10ft tall.

and was certainly taller than me. I was following others and getting tired, so decided to sit down, wondering whether I could carry on. It did not take me long to remember the wild pigs, so I quickly got going again, joined the others, and made it to the top. Our reward was a superb panoramic view as the sun rose. We were very glad indeed to have made the climb. Going down was almost worse. It was so steep, our legs turned to jelly.

Tragically, in 1994, nineteen years after we left Rabaul, there was a massive volcanic eruption when more than one volcano erupted simultaneously, almost entirely destroying the town. There had been a planned evacuation of the town before the eruption but I have read that five people were killed. Rabaul was covered in ash and the town had to be abandoned and re-located. I was unaware of this until years later, when I was working at UCL and picked up a UCL magazine, where I was surprised to find an illustrated article about the dramatic eruption. Later, I saw a television programme showing the extent of the devastation caused by the lava and ash. I understand that the volcanoes continue to emit ash clouds and are scheduled to erupt again.

* * *

Leaving Papua New Guinea

We left Rabaul after 16 months, on Tuesday 4th March 1975. We had packed up, sent the majority of our belongings to London, and were heading for Melbourne, Australia, where we planned to stay for a while before returning to the UK. First, however, we had planned to have a couple of weeks' holiday in PNG, before we left the country. We were driven to the airport by Dave – he of the Christmas Day celebration – where a small group saw us off. Ian asked John to take a couple of presents to nurses Immaculata and Kauiop for him.

We flew to Lae, where we drank milk; quantities of it – we had not had fresh milk for 16 months. We bought some unusual and interesting artefacts from a specialist shop, which we sent directly back to the UK – most of which I still have. We also visited the botanical gardens where there was a good collection of orchids.

Ian kept a diary for the first four days. One of the stories he recorded is particularly good:

> *"Had dinner at the Buablung which was very ordinary but at least we were surrounded by young local people working or studying in Lae...*
>
> *"... Sat next to an American missionary from Penn at dinner – young chap with a massive beard. He had come from the Southern Highlands, south of Mendi, to buy cattle for the people in his area, for whom the mission was starting a form of cooperative ranch. He's the kind of practical no nonsense missionary this country needs – not the proselytisers. He was the one who told us the story about the man who walked into Mt. Hagen hospital with an arrow through his heart and sticking out of his back. The story goes that he sat down and waited to be seen and the doctor just pulled the thing out and hoped for the best. He's still alive."*

The next day we set off at midday on the MV Totol, travelling in first class(!) accommodation (pairs of bunks in the open at the back of the top deck with plastic roofing and canvas sides). The coastline was impressive with rolling hills of kunai grass interspersed with areas of forest, and with fairly high mountains in the background also covered in forest. We had a reasonable night's sleep in our sheet sleeping bags. During the night the sea became quite rough so Ian confined himself to his bunk. As the weather worsened, so poor Ian felt more and more seasick. He survived, however, and 18 hours later we reached Madang, where we stayed at the CWA (Country Women's Association) where you could stay very inexpensively in a cottage with a bedroom, kitchen and bathroom.

Madang was very attractive, with a great many islands just offshore from the town, most of them with golden sandy beaches and a number of inlets and lagoons fingering their way into the town. It was while walking along beside one of these inlets that on a small beach very close to a changing hut, we saw a notice tacked to a tree, which read *"Lukaut long puk puk"* meaning beware, crocodiles! We could not believe our eyes! Anyone going for a swim where there are crocodiles of any kind, let alone saltwater crocodiles (the largest reptiles on earth), has to be more than a little mad!

We hired a car and set off the next morning on the next stage of our journey – we were heading to the Highlands. Unfortunately, we did not have a four-wheel drive car and the unmade road (optimistically named the Highlands Highway), which twisted and turned up the mountains, was badly rutted on most of the sharp corners, and these ruts were covered in very fine sandy earth. This problem had been caused by rain washing silt down from the hillsides above. It made driving difficult and dangerous – it was very slippery and almost like driving on ice.

Our first stop was Goroka – a small township with a good market. The place we stayed in overnight offered us tree tomatoes – something we had not eaten before. They were a reddish purple fruit; egg-shaped, about the size of a good tomato, and when cut in half, purple. They were tamarillos we discovered later, and delicious. We saw the strange and impressive Goroka Mud Men before travelling on to Mount Hagen. We gave a lift to a local tribesman at one stage. The smell in the car was strong and distinctive, and must have been typical of generations of tribespeople – a mixture of unwashed body and smoke.

Mount Hagen market was filled with local tribesmen, many wearing traditional clothes: the men with a bunch of grass at the back, tucked into a belt at the waist, to vaguely cover the buttocks (generally called 'arse grass'); and sometimes bark cloth at the front or a grass skirt. Some of them wore a head covering. Some wore cotton shorts. The women in the town were less flamboyant, usually wearing necklaces, and bracelets as ornaments and a piece of fabric worn on the head and hanging down like a shawl, although many women wore the same cotton short sleeved tops and skirts as they had in Rabaul. Traditionally, however, they would have worn nothing on their upper bodies and grass or bark cloth worn as a skirt.

While we were in Mount Hagan, we went to see some tribesmen wearing their warrior costumes. They looked fantastic: with huge feather headdresses; pieces of fur and grasses as decoration; pig tusks or bone pierced through their nostrils; and large kina shell necklaces. Their outfits varied, according to the tribe they were from. They were impressive. Gatherings of tribes and other festivals were generally known as "*sing-sings*".

We also went to see some birds of paradise, but this was somewhat underwhelming since it was not the right time of year for them to be in their full finery.

Certain shells were used as currency in PNG. Shells or tiny discs of shell were threaded on to a string of some kind – this was called tabu – and was typical of the Gazelle Peninsula. Large flat kina shells were valuable and used for trade in the Highlands, the kina shells often worn by men around their necks. I had bought a kina shell necklace and some strings of tabu when we were in Lae, along with other artefacts. Once the country became independent, the official currency of PNG was named the kina.

The next stage of our trip around the country was to visit the Sepik River. Having urged Ian not to take single-engined planes if he could help it, when we reached the airfield, we saw that the plane in which we were due to fly was very small indeed – a four-seater single-engined Cessna – and did not look particularly new. Ian insisted that I should sit next to the pilot and he sat behind us with no-one next to him. It was an extraordinary and very special experience. The views were fantastic – impenetrable forest in all directions with the odd settlement here and there. It almost felt as though we could touch the trees below us. When a mountain appeared in front of us, there was no question of going over it – we turned to one side and went around it, flying along valleys. After a while, we left the mountains behind and could see the Sepik River below us – huge meandering loops across flat country (the longest river in PNG) – flowing towards the northern coast of the mainland.

We reached our first main destination, the village of Angoram on the Sepik River. It was a beautiful traditional village with lush green vegetation and houses on stilts and a large *haus tambaran* – a traditional spirit house – used as a meeting house and for rituals. These buildings are also on stilts and the front, with the entrance in the centre, is a tall, highly decorated triangular shaped wall. In the 70s, the villagers had started to allow visitors to enter the *haus tambaran* as long as they were respectful, but previously, the *haus tambaran* had been for the men of the village only. The inside of the building was full of carved, coloured, and highly decorated masks, hooks and large and small carvings – a treasure trove of wonderful cultural objects and artefacts.

The next day we took a boat up the Sepik to visit another village and saw something of the crocodile skin trade. The boat was very basic; quite small, with an outboard and a tarpaulin held up on poles at each corner for shade. The river was wide and brown with villages appearing now and then. A local boatman took us upstream for a couple of hours – we were the only passengers. When we arrived, we explored another beautiful traditional village and then went to visit a shed, right on the edge of the river, where a white man was trading in crocodile skins. The local people would catch crocodiles – a highly dangerous activity – and take them to him in exchange for money. He would then skin the animals and salt the skins, which he put into large wooden crates for export to various places around the world, including, he told us, Hong Kong. It was a very primitive set-up, but presumably a great deal of money was being made – not, of course, by the locals.

After the wonderful time we had spent living and working in Rabaul and our exotic and remarkable adventures in PNG, it was time for us to leave. We returned to Port Moresby to take our flights to Australia.

After we left PNG, which we did in March 1975, the country became independent.

"The natives of Papua appealed to the United Nations for oversight and independence. The nation established independence from Australia on 16 September 1975, and maintains close ties. . . Papua New Guinea was admitted to membership in the United Nations on 10 October 1975."[130]

* * *

Oz

We flew to Brisbane, Queensland, where we hired a camper van for our journey down the southern half of the Eastern seaboard of Australia. Our idea was to see some of Australia but also to work and save some money for our flights home. We had decided to live and work in Melbourne, mainly because we had made friends in PNG who lived there.

We were strongly advised not to park the van for the night just anywhere we fancied, on the basis that it was dangerous and that we were likely to be robbed. We followed this advice and stayed in camp sites in unspoilt places – for example just behind sand dunes right next to the sea, a site we reached in time to see a dramatic sunset.

We passed from tropical countryside to orange groves to vineyards. We saw those wonderful blue hazy dry landscapes dotted with gum trees and with far reaching views to blue hills in the distance. We began to get an understanding of the immensity and beauty of the country. We were surprised when we reached the state border between New South Wales and Victoria, to find that we had to remove and throw away all fruit and vegetables from the van before we were allowed to continue our journey.

On arrival, we soon found a cheap modern flat to rent in North Melbourne. I found temporary work as a secretary, working for a decent salary for some very nice people in a small design company, which I enjoyed.

---

130 https://en.wikipedia.org/wiki/Papua_New_Guinea

Ian registered with an agency which provided 24 hour on-call medical care. He worked mostly at night, was provided with a car and a driver, and waited for the calls to come in. This was not an Accident & Emergency service, more of a GP service. He visited a huge variety of patients and dealt with a huge variety of problems. All doctors in Australia were paid very well at that time, and he was no exception, especially since he was providing a night-time service.

We looked up our doctor friends Sal and Dave, who had bought an attractive Victorian house which they were doing up. We had plenty of fun with them and they took us south of Melbourne for a weekend in Lorne, where the coast and the countryside are lovely and Sal's family had a house. Melbourne had many attractions for us: it was surprisingly cosmopolitan, with a large Greek population and with the fabulous fruit and vegetable market full of Chinese. We liked the city with its tree lined streets and green trams and we enjoyed the art gallery, the concert hall, and the friendly Australians. We did not come across the stereotypical supposed attitude of Australians towards the 'Poms'. I remember seeing lacrosse being played in a park in North Melbourne – all the players were wearing strong face guards – very different to how it had been in my UK boarding school!

We visited some of the 'sights' – a restored gold-rush town inland from Melbourne; the fairy penguins coming onshore at night on Phillip Island; koala bears; and we ate out occasionally too. We had good times.

We had a memorable visit to Lou and Rob, who had returned to Australia and were living on Lou's family's enormous ranch-like farm in the outback. They took us out in one of their trucks; Ian and I standing up in the open back of the pick-up. There were a couple of sheep dogs riding along with Lou and Rob in the cab and hanging on hooks in the cab were small leather bootees which were put on the dogs' feet to protect them as they raced across miles and miles of hard, dry ground. There were no roads but it was their land and they knew where they were going. We were miles from anywhere when suddenly, there was a group of kangaroos rocking along right in front of us. They looked to me like little old ladies doing their knitting in rocking chairs. A taste of the real outback.

However, we were both beginning to feel the need to go home. I left first and Ian followed me a few weeks later. My flight to London was the longest flight I have ever made – 23 hours. I travelled with Thai Airways and, charmingly, every passenger was presented with a beautiful exotic orchid.

CHAPTER 9

London and Athens

* * *

Home Again

LATE SUMMER IN LONDON marked our return to our house in Kentish Town. The tenants moved out and we moved in. The house needed some fairly drastic cleaning, but otherwise, it was more than fine. It was great to be back.

Ian was now a registered medical practitioner and started work at a hospital in east London as a junior doctor. We bought a small motorbike – a Honda 90 – which Ian used to commute to and from work, and which we also used to go shopping at the markets in Kentish Town and Camden Town. Wobbling home on the bike carrying bags and bags of fruit and vegetables, became the norm.

Ian's on-call rota was one-in-two (ie he was on-call every other night, when he had to live in the hospital). The weekend on-call rota was also one-in-two, so sometimes he would go to work on Friday morning and not return until Monday evening, after which he would be at work again on Tuesday morning. This was punishing. It was in 1975 that for the first time, British doctors officially went on strike over hours and pay, and this led to one-in-two on-call arrangements eventually disappearing. It was around this time, also, that London became 'dark' – various strikes meant that electricity supplies were cut. It was hugely atmospheric (a trip back in time) to walk home through streets where the only light came from the candles inside other people's houses.

I was interviewed for and registered at the North East London Polytechnic to study economics. I had wanted to study sociology, but the course was full, and I was told that I could probably transfer to the sociology course later on. However, I found that I enjoyed the economics, found it interesting, and did fine – even doing well in maths. I used to run at top speed every morning to catch the Kentish Town overground train to Barking, and wrote essays in the evenings.

Ian's next job was at the Whittington Hospital, working as Casualty Officer in Accident & Emergency. This job was much closer to home, but involved three separate shifts which changed every week: early morning to early afternoon; early afternoon to evening; and overnight. It was demanding and not good for Ian's body clock, nor his health.

After a different kind of wobble – this time, in our marriage – we put things together again, and after a while, our son, Alexander James, was born on 15 September 1977 – a beautiful dark-haired baby we both adored. In those days, mothers of first babies stayed in hospital for eight days(!) and were taught how to change a nappy, give a baby a bath, etc. Also, on the night before you were due to be discharged, the hospital offered to look after your baby, encouraging you to go out for a meal with your other half. Quite extraordinary to think of this now.

A lot of the time, I was looking after Alex on my own because of Ian's on-call commitments, and that was challenging, but also rewarding – I had always wanted to be a full-time mother while my children were young.

We liked the idea of living in a greener and quieter neighbourhood, so we sold our house and moved to 4 Cecil Road, Muswell Hill, N10, in 1978, when Alex was about six months old. A lot of work was needed on the house, but nothing like the total transformation we had had to carry out on the previous one. We soon settled into what became a very comfortable home, got to know our neighbours, and enjoyed our new life.

Junior doctors' posts were usually based on six month contracts, so Ian changed his job once more and took a post at the Royal Northern Hospital (associated with the Whittington), firstly as a Junior Registrar in Anaesthetics and then as a Locum Senior Registrar in Anaesthetics. He also provided anaesthetics on-call cover for St Ann's Hospital, which meant he could be on call at night from home. I remember him going out to a case, returning, climbing into bed and the phone ringing again almost immediately. Epidural injections seemed to be much in demand by women in labour at St Ann's, and he was kept very busy.

I joined a newly forming group of young women who all lived locally and had small babies – a crèche group. There were about six of us and we would take it in turns to meet each week, with our babies, at one or other of our houses. It was an excellent arrangement. After a while, my new friend from the group, Sally, and I began to take it in turns to look after each other's babies for half a day. Alex and her son, Tim, got on well, and in due course they went to the same primary school. My friendship with Sally continues to this day.

When Alex was exactly one year old, we visited Elizabeth and Jeffrey in Montreal, which we liked a lot – a vibrant, attractive and multi-cultural city. After a few days, we all drove down to visit New York together. As we approached the city, Elizabeth instructed us that we should lock our car doors and close all the windows – we were a little apprehensive. We stayed in an inexpensive but centrally located and comfortable hotel where we had large old-fashioned suites. It was hard not to notice the numbers of distressed and intimidating people out and about on the streets and also in the subway, where we ventured only once, since the atmosphere made us feel decidedly uneasy. Nonetheless, people would stop to admire baby Alex, saying how unusual it was to see families with babies and children on the streets of Manhattan. We had a great time. Trips included visits to galleries and also to Greenwich Village (before it was gentrified) – where we ate frozen yoghurt ice-cream, years and years before it had even been heard of in the UK.

Unfortunately, back home, Alex developed a thyroglossal cyst on his neck – he had to wear a dressing on his neck at all times – and surgery seemed to be the only answer. However, in the event, several operations had to be carried out, because every unwanted cell had to be removed and this, we understood, was difficult. Having had a couple of operations at the Royal Northern Hospital, he was referred to the Middlesex for a third. I was in the Middlesex with him for this and saw him being wheeled out of theatre after the operation, with his teddy next to him, also wearing a dressing on his neck(!). I was overcome with relief and immediately went into premature labour. I called Ian, who called his mother, who rather brilliantly, packed an overnight bag and came to the hospital immediately to be with Alex, so that Ian could be with me at University College Hospital for the birth. I remember jumping the taxi queue, rather dramatically saying that I was in labour and had to be quick. . .

On 21 May 1980 our daughter was born and Ian made it to the hospital in time for her birth. We named this very small and beautiful baby Katriona

Anne Calliope and, of course, fell in love with her too. I had always wanted a daughter named Kate, and the Scottish version of Katherine seemed just right.

Before Alex was born, we had decided we would like to give our children international names, so both the children's names can be found (in one version or another) in many parts of the world: in Scotland, Alexander and Katriona; in Greece, Alexandros and Katerina; in Russia and Armenia, Aleksandr and Ekaterina.

That third operation on Alex's neck also did not do the trick. However, some time later, Alex was kicking a small football around in the school playground when the ball hit his neck in exactly the area of the cyst. Incredibly, this finally did do the trick – the cyst disappeared and he was cured!

Kate was born prematurely by about one month. She and I had an ABO blood incompatibility which resulted in Kate becoming jaundiced and having to spend some time in an incubator. To protect her eyes from the phototherapy light treatment, she was fitted with little mini-goggle affairs which made her look very cute – as if she were about to go skiing. She also had a small breathing problem initially. I was alarmed, when I found she was not with me. However, we were re-united after not too long, and made our way home, where Alex was doing fine after his operation. Ian's life over the last few days had been somewhat hectic, rushing back and forth between the two hospitals, which, fortunately, were not far from each other.

I thoroughly enjoyed being with the children at home. There was never a dull moment and I did not get bored. I kept us in home-made bread, amongst other things, which was delicious, but it was wholemeal, and both Alex and Kate preferred my neighbour's homemade bread, which was white!

At the age of about three, Alex joined the 345 Playgroup in the Grove, in Alexandra Park. Leaving him there initially was heart wrenching – he hated being left (and I hated leaving him), but he soon settled in. He was asked one day if he knew a song he could sing, so standing up in the 'circle', he sang "Whisky you're the devil, you're leading me astray. . ." which raised a few smiles – it was a song we used to sing in the car on the way to our holidays in Ireland. He also started to learn the violin, using the Suzuki method. This involved a short practice every day and a trip to the Suzuki group in Highgate once a week. The sessions were a delight, as were the trips to the man in Camden Lock market who sold every size of violin, including the very smallest.

It was in the late 70s that my mother finally managed to sell her house in Yateley, Hampshire. However, she did not manage to do this at the same time as finding somewhere to buy. She had made a significant loss on her house because of a major damp problem there, and was constrained, therefore, as to what she could afford. However, taking action and making decisions had always been big problems for her, so we realised it was unlikely that she would make a purchase quickly. We suggested, therefore, that she should move in with us while she searched, and so she put her furniture into storage and moved in. It would have been for the best had my mother decided to find somewhere to live in north London, even if small, but nothing she looked at had sufficient room for her furniture, which had become a defining factor (despite most of it having by now become redundant). She would not be persuaded. She was very slow and her property viewings were few and far between. In the end, she stayed with us for eight months, which was difficult and too long. We had to ask her to hurry up, which resulted in her finding a flat fairly soon afterwards, in Sanderstead, near Croydon, Surrey. It had been difficult having my mother around – she was not good at helping and, for example, did not offer to baby-sit. Once or twice I asked her to babysit, and was met with resentment. Fortunately, however, her move went smoothly, and she seemed pleased with her new home. However, for us to visit her from north London became quite an undertaking, especially as she grew older and I visited her every two weeks. . .

* * *

Difficulties

Sal, our doctor friend from Australia (who we had met in PNG), came to stay with us for a while (when Kate was about nine months). It was during her stay, that I phoned Ian one evening when he was supposed to be on-call, to discover that he was not on-call at all. It was so good to have Sal there while I went through the horrible and painful process of discovering that Ian was having an affair with a nurse and of throwing him out of the house – Sal was a great support and very good company.

Ian then moved out and lived in Bounds Green with his girlfriend. At around the same time, he decided that anaesthetics was too stressful and that he should leave the profession to avoid having another heart attack (he had had a minor heart attack while he was at work, sometime before). He had no job, a mortgage and rent to pay, and at one point, he started cleaning windows to try to make a buck. . . After a while, however, he went back to working as a doctor – working through an agency as a locum GP. For quite some time, Ian's visits to us were few and far between.

However, life rolled on.

Maggie and Jules invited us to go on holiday with them to Italy with their daughter Mia (who is almost the same age as Kate). They rented a flat in a country house south of Naples, which even had a swimming pool we could use, in an olive grove. We made day trips to Pompeii and Paestum, both of which were fantastic places to visit with young children and we had very good times. We were near the coast and spent time at the beach, where Kate excelled herself by crawling determinedly down the beach towards the waves again and again and again. . .

We had inherited a small red tricycle (called Chippy) from our next-door neighbour. First Alex and then Kate, loved riding this little bike and later, we took it to Athens with us for Kate. I spent time with Alex in Durnsford Park, teaching him to ride his new two-wheeler. When he finally got going, I realised I had forgotten to tell him how to stop, so he cycled straight into the hedge! In Athens, we would go down to the local plateia for bike rides. These were the first stages in Alex's on-going passion for bikes and bike riding.

It was in 1983 that Ian's Uncle Henryk rang to tell me that he had seen the perfect job for Ian in a pharmaceutical industry magazine. The job was based in Athens and the post was Medical Director for the Middle East for a well-known German pharmaceutical company. It looked as if the job had been written for him. The company required an English doctor who could also speak Greek. The Director in Athens was Greek and Ian was interviewed by him and offered the job. It was a great stroke of luck and timing. Ian proposed that we should 'try again' and all go to live in Athens for his initial two year contract. He admitted that the boss was a family man and wanted whoever took the post to live in Athens with his/her family. Despite this, I thought it over and agreed to the idea.

* * *

ANNE MACDONALD

Athens, Greece and the Islands

By now Alex was at Rhodes Avenue Primary School and Kate was at the 345 playgroup, both in Muswell Hill. It was at the playgroup that I met Janette and her youngest daughter Daphne (the same age as Kate and also at the playgroup) and her elder daughter Lisa, the same age as Alex and also at Rhodes Avenue. They lived very close to us and our relationships turned into long-term friendships. Janette, an Australian, and her husband, Thanos, a Greek, had been living and working in London for 16 years and were planning to move to Greece soon. Having told them that we were going to live in Athens, it was a mere six weeks later that Thanos was also offered a post there, which he accepted. This was a great stroke of luck, cemented our friendships, and led to many memorable weekends and holidays in Greece.

Before we went to live in Athens, however, we had visited Greece and its islands many times and knew something of the country already. And loved it.

The central Plaka area of Athens, with its narrow streets and picturesque cafés had been a regular haunt in the early days, when we would meet Auntie Olga for a meal with Ian's parents: once at the smart Lycabettus restaurant high up on the hill; occasionally in an old-fashioned restaurant to eat bacalau (dried and salted cod), but usually in a taverna. There were often musicians playing in these traditional tavernas, and singing would invariably break out, with the customers singing along to all the old tunes. The atmosphere was full of nostalgia, but it was fun to try singing along too. Not once during my times in Greece, did I see anyone hurling plates to the floor in a taverna, but there was one particular place where, while the music played, a waiter would dance around the room carrying one of the tables between his teeth!

Apart from our wonderful six week holiday in Crete in 1966, we had had holidays on Limnos and Lesbos with Ian's parents. Immediately Ian returned from Australia, we flew to Athens, where Brian and Clio were just beginning their holiday and were very surprised and pleased to find us knocking at their hotel bedroom door one morning. We all set off to Limnos together a couple of days later, the others staying in the hotel they had booked and us finding local rooms. We swam, and we walked up on the dry herb-scented hills. Our visit to Lesbos, also with Ian's parents, took place when I was eight months pregnant with Alex. I would swim in the pool of their hotel, watched by concerned Greek ladies, worried that I would "drown the baby".

Alex must have been about two when we went to Samos with Elizabeth and Jeffrey, who had flown over from Canada. We went to the town of Pythagorion, with its picturesque long arc of a harbour. It was a lazy holiday, introducing Alex to the joys of the sea, reading in the shade on the beach, taking siestas, and eating in tavernas overlooking the sea in the evenings.

We also went to Pythagorion with David and Sarah, who took their first child, Ed, a little younger than Alex. Judy came with us too. In her intrepid way, and knowing Greece very well, she hired a scooter and set off up into the mountains on her own. One day, however, she skidded around a corner on the way down and came off the scooter. Luckily, she managed to get back to us – late, battered, bruised and cold but fortunately, fine. A little distance from the town by car, the land fell steeply down to the sea. There was a wonderful small village with shutters of every colour, tumbling down the hill, but not much else apart from olive groves. There were hippies living in tents in these olive groves (which, sadly, they were not looking after) but below them was the most beautiful rocky coast. There were spectacular pools between the rocks, lined with huge pure white stones and white sand. Every detail of the floor of the pools through the turquoise water, was sharp and crystal clear.

Later, when Kate was four months old, we had a holiday in Cephallonia with Ian's parents and sister, Patty. The place we stayed in had been recommended by a young couple living in Athens – Macdonald family friends from Egypt. It was very basic (we showered in an old outhouse) but delightful. The lady of the house prepared a meal for our arrival – a casserole with huge amounts of garlic and beans. I was breastfeeding and the effect of this meal on poor Kate was that she screamed for most of the night; the lady of the house mystified as to what could be wrong! Days on the beach were hot and we had to keep Kate carefully in the shade. In the evenings at the taverna, her pram was pushed gently back and forth as we ate.

However, now that we were going to live in Athens, Ian had the task of finding us somewhere to live. I said that I would prefer to have a garden, but this proved well nigh impossible, since almost all the accommodation available was in flats. However, Ian managed to find us a really superb flat. It was on the first floor of a low-rise three-flat block, surrounded by modest lawns with a large fig tree at the back, and an underground garage. It was in Paleo Psychiko, an upmarket, attractive, quiet and green area not far from the centre of the city. The flat was large, with three bedrooms and a vast living area. The best things of all, however, were the balconies. The main balcony was huge, on which we had a table and chairs for our meals; comfortable chairs for sitting and reading, with good lights in the ceiling; and I bought and planted lots of terracotta pots – I even had a small bergamot tree. Once the children were in bed, evenings for me often meant taking off my shoes to water the plants, and then sitting outside, reading in the balmy, jasmine-scented evening air. What could be better?

We bought a car – fairly elderly and a little battered – a dirty orange VW Passat estate. This allowed us to explore many islands and other areas of Greece, without having to worry about the quality of the roads – we followed unmade roads wherever they led.

Both Alex and Kate were enrolled at an English language school founded and run by Jack Meyer (of Millfield School fame) – Kate at three years, in a small nursery group led by a young Swedish woman who played the guitar, and Alex at six years, in a small class for his age group led by an English woman married to a Greek. He surprised them by playing Beethoven's Minuet in G on his violin. The majority of the pupils had an English/American/Australian parent and a Greek one, but there were English speaking children from elsewhere too, for example, from Bulgaria and Iran. Both children enjoyed it, settled in well, and made friends. The atmosphere in the school seemed to be strongly influenced by the kind and caring attitude of the Greeks towards children. There was no bullying and children of all ages looked out for each other – if a child fell over in the playground, other children would rush to help. This was very different to the culture we would experience later in English schools. The school music teacher produced a children's play in which Alex, dressed as a cricket, played his violin. The teacher's name, however, caused some confusion: Mr Themistocleos, according to Alex, was The Mister Cleos!

Alex and Kate would regularly invite friends over to play. It was important (for the sake of the neighbours) to keep the children quiet during siesta time and this was quite difficult. Even drivers are not supposed to sound their horns during siesta hours, which in Greece, is really saying something. One of the children's favourite activities when friends came over, was to turn on the hose on the second biggest balcony; strip off down to their underpants; lie on their stomachs on the marble balcony floor and push off on the by now extremely slippery wet marble. We had our own water slide! We held birthday parties at home, which usually involved a number of friends; dressing up; taking part in races in the garden; and guzzling delicious cakes. Throughout their younger years, in London and in Athens, Daphne and Kate only had to see each other to rush off and dress up. We have photos of them with their underpants on their heads!

We found a well thought of musical family living very near us, in which both sons played and taught the violin. Alex had regular lessons from the younger son, Stamos, who provided him with an excellent and lively role model. The household was one of hushed, almost reverential, cultured middle-class, but with a very friendly welcome.

Later on, there was a split at the school and St Lawrence College was founded, which both children joined. This hardly affected them, since they still had all the same friends and most of the same teachers. We were some of the parents actively involved in setting up the new school. One evening, a meeting of all those parents interested in supporting this new school, met at our flat. This was in the aftermath of two newspaper publishers being assassinated in Athens. On the evening of the meeting, we were surprised to see a couple of large black cars with darkened windows outside our flat, along with security guards and chauffeurs. As the meeting ended and I showed one of the fathers out, I was shocked to see a gun fall out of his jacket and bounce down the marble staircase.

Janette and Thanos lived slightly further away from the city centre and Lisa and Daphne went to different schools.

Our life in Athens was a huge pleasure. Everyday life was hot but never humid and the sun shone in a blue sky a lot of the time. In summer, vegetables left on the back shelf of the car would cook, but once at least, winter brought snow to our balcony railings. In winter there was efficient central heating and in summer all the many sliding doors were kept wide open, with the shutters closed.

There was, of course, the 'nefos' problem in the 1980s – the pollution cloud which would form over the city on hot days, surrounded as it is by mountains. I used to see the cloud's progress from our flat, as it enveloped more and more of the city. Fortunately, we were outside its range. A law was brought in which allowed cars into the city on alternate days, depending on their car registration numbers, but the police had a significant problem trying to enforce this.

In August, Athens became uncomfortably hot and large numbers of people left the city and went to the islands, including us. Household preparations for the summer (not ours) included lifting carpets from the marble floors. All over Athens, small open backed vans filled with rolled up carpets could be seen – they were carting carpets to the cleaners and then to storage, until the beginning of winter, when they would all be driven back again and returned to their owners.

As we settled into Athens, we tended to visit more of the wider city and surrounding areas than we had previously. We made visits to ancient sites both in the city and in the countryside round about; to museums (one of my favourites being the Cycladic Museum) and to the odd concert in the Herod Atticus ancient theatre just below the Acropolis. Occasionally, we went for walks up on Mount Hymettus (which we could see from our kitchen window), and fly kites with Janette, Lisa and Daphne on 'Clean Monday' in the surprisingly large and natural Sygrou park – which in spring is awash with hundreds of species of wildflower.

On weekends, we would often make a trip to the sea – usually at Marathon – or sometimes, like the Greeks, eat Sunday lunch in a packed taverna. Our trips out of Athens invariably involved stopping on our return journey to buy terracotta bowls full of freshly made sheep's milk yoghurt with a thick skin on top. This was superb. Wherever we were, sitting outside on a sunny day, eating thin crisp slices of deep fried courgettes and aubergines was great.

Other trips around the mainland included visits to the ancient site of Delphi and to Mount Pelion, above Volos. At every turn of the road up Mount Pelion, locally grown apples and flowering gardenia plants were for sale, displayed by the side of the road. There was a dramatic forest fire high up on the southern flank of the mountain while we were there, and we watched the fire-fighting planes flying down to sea level on the huge bay at Volos, collecting sea water and flying straight towards us as they gained height, before heading up the mountain to dump the water on the fire.

We made a trip to the Peleponnese, which included visits to the fortified Byzantine town of Mystras; to the ancient city of Mycenae; the ancient theatre of Epidauros; and also to the central peninsula of the Mani with its tower villages and beaches in the south. We all loved exploring.

My life was enjoyable and interesting. I made friends from among the school parents; attended classes in Greek near the city centre; bought an old loom; and attended fascinating courses with Janette on weaving, and also dyeing, using plants and other natural dyes. We also attended a course run by the British Council, on Teaching English as a Foreign Language.

There was plenty of good food to be bought, too. I found myself a large shopping basket on wheels and would visit the local produce market, the *"laiki"*, every Friday. Conveniently, it was a short distance from the flat and I would return home with quantities of fresh fruits and vegetables. The oranges were some of the best I have ever eaten – sadly, they are not imported into the UK. Then there were the glorious tomatoes, peaches, and quince. I would peel and lightly stew the quince, making sure there was always a bowl of them in the fridge, ready to be eaten with yoghurt. On the main road, not too far from us, there were two large supermarkets, where just about everything was available. As far as I was concerned, the best thing of all was the feta cheese, the best available from the less smart shop, where it was kept in barrels of brine. It came in various ages, and you had to ask for what you wanted. My favourite was the really young very soft feta, which was delicious. The word in Greek for soft is *'malako'*, not under any circumstances to be confused with the word *'malaka'!*

Aunt Olga, who had lived and worked in Athens since she left Egypt, had retired, and would visit us from time to time, always bringing boxes of cakes, baklava, biscuits and sweets and running around after Alex and Kate, worrying that they were barefoot on the marble and might catch cold. "Where are your slippers? where are your slippers?" was the repeated cry in Greek. Olga became known for a couple of expressions which she used frequently. Her habitual response when answering the phone and being asked how she was, would be to say "I'm still alive", but as an inveterate fatalist, she became even more well known for her frequent use of a typical Greek expression, said in a particularly resigned and entirely hopeless way: *"ti na kanoume?"* – "what can we do?"

We would often go to one of the islands for a weekend. A drive to Piraeus and a ferry ride with the car, would take us somewhere idyllic not too far away – Aegina, Poros, or Spetses, for example. Over the years, both before we went to live in Greece, while we were there, and afterwards, we made innumerable trips to many many different islands, often with friends. Each island is pretty much unique; almost invariably very beautiful in its own way. On almost all, however, there are hills or mountains covered in sweet smelling wild thyme, oregano, and other herbs, and in spring a profusion of wildflowers; brilliant blue skies; glorious clear seas; and on many of the islands, ancient classical monuments and archaeological sites. Add to all this the welcoming and friendly Greeks; the relaxed atmosphere of tavernas open all hours; still warm but cooler evenings; the scent of jasmine on the air; and of course, lamb grilling on charcoal; and it is not difficult to see why I grew to love Greece so much.

The nearest island, Aegina, was a destination for us on at least three occasions: once just us four; once I went with Janette and our four children; and once with David and Sarah (who went there directly from England) plus our friend from Athens, Diana, and her two sons. My 40th birthday fell during this latter trip and I told no-one until the evening (not wanting to think about my increasing age) and went snorkelling, looking for octopuses. However, we did celebrate over our evening meal in the taverna. The small main town, even then, was a tourist trap to be completely avoided, and we never stayed there. The first time we went to Aegina, therefore, we were very pleased to find real old-fashioned estiatoria (restaurants) on the other side of the island, offering ranges of delicious slow-cooked dishes (including rabbit stew) – rather than the grilled meat generally on offer in tavernas.

We had never booked accommodation prior to setting off on an island trip, because the convention was that as you came off the ferry, local people would approach you, offering rooms for rent. There was never a problem. However, we went to Kea at least twice and on the first of these occasions, when all four of us went, we had our come-uppance. We had not thought about the fact that the weekend we chose was a local religious holiday, so when we arrived, there was simply no accommodation available – anywhere. We went to the police for help thinking we would have to sleep in the cells(!), but one of the local hotels finally came to our rescue and allowed us to sleep in the corridor. Fortunately, this was only necessary for one night. Kea is in the Cyclades and the channel of sea between the island and the mainland port of Lavrion can be very windy and rough. The small ferry rocked and rolled through the bumpy sea emitting clouds of filthy black smoke from its funnel, making it necessary to go inside. The saloon was old, damp and battered – the seat coverings mouldy and ripped and the walls grimy. I spotted a brass plaque on the wall which announced that the ferry we were in had once been a Mersey ferry! Admittedly, Kea is not too far from the mainland, but the ferry had been designed to cope with Liverpool's calm River Mersey, not the waters of the Aegean Sea when it was rough. On another visit there, when only Alex, Kate and I went, we managed to stay in probably one of the most unusual hotels in Greece. It was at the very top of the old town of Ioulis with a terrace overlooking spectacular views. It was very run down[131] and there was only one other person staying there. This was an English academic – a specialist in ancient teeth(!), who had been attending a conference and was visiting the island for the weekend. He was very interesting and relaxed, and we all went for a long walk together along a remote valley to the coast (we saw only one other person on the way – an elderly woman, who offered us figs as we passed by). Kea in the summer is brown and very dry. Fortunately, we had a very large water container with us and some huge juicy peaches. We reached the remains of an ancient ruined city on a hill, below which was a beach, where there was nobody and where we swam. It was a memorable experience – Greece totally beautiful, unspoiled, empty and unexploited. Later, this kind man (whose name I do not remember) sent Kate and Alex, individually addressed to each of them, a copy of a children's story he had written.

Judy visited us while we were living in Athens and we took the ferry from the port of Rafina, to the Cycladic island of Andros. We found rooms in the most delightful house. These surrounded a small courtyard with steps, leading up to a small garden with lemon trees; and the lady of the house, Angeliki, was sweetness itself. We went for walks along the typical walled donkey trails which wind all over Andros and gathered capers whenever we saw them, which our hostess showed us how to salt or pickle. We also spent time on the beach, and it was here that Kate learned to swim. We explored the island by car: at one stage, there was a huge gale, which lasted for three days (a fairly common occurrence on Andros). Driving on the coast road in the gale, I had to stay in first gear for most of the way. On one adventure, we scrambled down a trackless steep hillside through prickly trees and shrubs to reach a remote beach, and were amazed and delighted when we got to the bottom, to come across a small farm where outhouses had been built using ancient classical marble columns.

---

131 *"There is also an old hotel on the rock with a restaurant and amazing views but it has been closed for years and who knows if it will ever re-open. The story is that it was owned by an old couple who rarely answered their phones or took reservations and finally left owing the town millions of drachma in back rent. If you are planning to stay in Ioulis this would be the place to be and hopefully one day it will be a hotel again. Like any high point in the village the views are spectacular whether you are looking across the island to the mainland or at the rest of the village on the adjoining hillside. . . Strangely enough some of the most popular guidebooks still list this hotel though it has been closed for at least 15 years!"* https://www.greektravel.com/greekislands/kea/ioulis.html

Trips to the mainland included a visit to Corinth and the north of the Peleponnese for a holiday with Maggie, who visited with Mia and Miranda. We drove there with our children and had a very good time until Miranda became worryingly sick. Ian, having been with us at the start of the trip, was no longer with us to help. Fortunately, however, she recovered after a couple of days and all was well. I had my most terrifying Greek driving experience on this trip: on the main road from Athens to Corinth, a lorry came pounding towards us on the wrong side of the dual-carriageway.

Our London neighbours, Margaret and her daughter Melanie, also visited us and we went to Evia together, where I tried (unsuccessfully) to teach Margaret to swim and we hired paddle boards to look at lots and lots of the biggest jellyfish I have ever seen – huge floating fried eggs on the surface of the water.

There was a raffle at the school which I won (I have never before, nor since, won anything). The prize was presented by Olympic Airways two free return tickets to Rhodes. We had not been to Rhodes, so we were pleased. However, it emerged that the free tickets were not standard tickets at all, but stand-by tickets. The flight we chose turned out to be fully booked and we were therefore unable to get on the plane, despite my best efforts (including Greek-style tantrum and suggesting we should sit on the 'jump' seats). Some prize! After waiting around for ages, we decided we should just pay for our flights ourselves and enjoy our long weekend regardless. It was very good to be in Rhodes in the off-season, even though the skies were grey. The old mediaeval town of Rhodes is surrounded by huge fortified and castellated walls and towers. We explored the town with its old narrow streets and hired a car to explore some of the island too, including Lindos. We went for a walk in butterfly valley, where, at that time of year, there were very few butterflies, but no tourists either.

We had two invitations to the island of Ithaka. One was from the school's headmaster, whose mother lived there in a very small house, and the other was from the sister of Kate's nursery teacher, whose son had become one of Kate's friends. I took the headmaster's two daughters with us and Janette, Lisa and Daphne also joined us. To start with, Alex, Kate and I stayed in the tiny house with the headmaster's two children and their grandmother. There was strict water rationing on the island and only a couple of hours when water was available, at which point, every conceivable vessel had to be filled[132]. Because it was such a tiny house, Janette and the girls stayed in rooms in the town. On our expeditions to the beach or anywhere else, we were two women and six children – three and three in terms of their ages . . . quite a gaggle, but nobody seemed to think twice about it. I had taken our car with us, and we set out on an adventure to the end of the island, a remote area, where there was an ancient well. When we arrived, we were told there were large snakes near this well with red heads. Janette fearlessly (despite my misgivings) led us through the scrub, but fortunately, the snakes had gone by the time we got there. As we were leaving, I managed to drive one wheel of the car into a deep hole. Luckily for us, someone turned up in a camper van, to draw water from the well, and they pulled us out. After our spell in the tiny village house, we moved for a couple of days into a rather larger house – this was a grand house, belonging to a ship owner's family, in the town overlooking the bay. It belonged to the family of Kate's class teacher (whose sister had joined us with her son) and although it was no longer permanently lived in, was still in good condition – with sheets and pillowcases bearing the embroidered initials of the family(!). It was a good holiday and Alex took enormous pleasure in finding sea cucumbers on the seabed and at every available opportunity, throwing them at the girls!

Skyros was an island we visited more than once. One of those visits was with Maggie and Jules and our children. The visit had its downside, because one night Maggie became seriously ill. We were staying in rooms on the hot dry plain below Skyros town, which was up on the hill. We discovered later, that Maggie had over-heated – a dangerous condition. With basic Greek, I managed to wake up the lady of the house, who rang for a taxi to take us to a doctor. Jules stayed with all the children and I went (terrified) with Maggie, who was in a state of near collapse, lying across my knees in the taxi. The taxi driver took us up and up the hill and through winding streets to the very top of the town, where we reached the small cottage hospital. The doctor was not to be found at first, but did appear, fortunately, and was able to help. Later on, we were able to return to Jules, who, unsurprisingly, had been very worried, but all was well. In contrast, an amusing story from that holiday was the one about Kate, who when she was in the sea with me (still quite small) pointed at an extremely hairy man, also in the sea, and said very loudly, in English, which he certainly understood, that there was

---

132 I believe there is now a de-salination plant.

a gorilla in the sea! It was just a little embarrassing. . . We had lots of fun on that holiday with plenty of time spent on beaches. On one of these we celebrated Mia's birthday with a party on the beach. This involved a cake, with candles on it, floating on the sea, much to the children's delight. We also went to Skopelos on that holiday, where we rented a small house in an olive grove, and were surrounded at close quarters, by hundreds of the loudest cicadas I have ever heard anywhere. It was from Skopelos that we took a rather small ferry on a very rough sea (which turned Jules green), and which made most of the local Greek passengers cling, white-knuckled, to the boat's railings, muttering prayers.

Janette and Thanos have a small house on the island of Hydra, which I have visited with them and with Kate, on several occasions. The island is preserved as a national monument, so to keep things in character, the island rules on development, are very strict. As a result, the town and the island remain very unspoilt. There are no cars, which are banned – mules being the only form of transport. The port town of Hydra is extremely picturesque, the town built amphitheatrically around the harbour. To get anywhere – in particular to their house – very large numbers of steep steps must be climbed – interesting after an evening out! The island is rocky with only a few small beaches, but the water is beautiful.

When Kate and Daphne were teenagers, Janette and I stayed on Hydra while the girls visited Santorini with a girlfriend of Daphne's, where they stayed in a converted cave. The girls then joined us in Hydra and the five of us took the 'Flying Dolphin' (the hydrofoil) to Monemvasia – a mediaeval fortress town on its own small island on the easternmost finger of the Peleponnese, linked to the mainland by a causeway. We stayed with Janette's friend, the mother of the third girl, in a large ancient castle-like house with hugely thick walls, just above the sea. It was a dramatic place and the sea clear and pristine. I remember floating above an octopus for ages, with my goggles on, watching it watching me.

In 2016, Alex, Kate, Anne, Paul and I went to Hydra for Daphne and Gareth's wedding, which was in every way, a truly fabulous occasion.

After we had left Greece, Kate and I returned to have a holiday with Janette and Thanos. They came up with the suggestion that we should all go to the island of Naxos. Janette drove us all in their car and we arrived, after a long ferry journey, full of anticipation. However, this was another of those religious holiday weeks, and no matter how hard we searched, there was simply no accommodation available in town and it was too late in the day to search elsewhere. The answer was to sleep on the beach! The seats were taken out of the car and put on the beach to make beds for Daphne and Kate, and we unpacked as many clothes and towels as we had, because it was distinctly chilly. We all laughed a lot – Janette and I on the outside and three children, sardine-like between us. It was difficult to get much sleep: it was cold, uncomfortable and noisy (there was a nightclub somewhere in town that was pumping out music late into the night) but also, there was a decidedly strange man lying on the beach not far from us whose cigarette ends glowed red almost continuously in the dark. The next day, we extended our search to the rest of the island and found somewhere all on its own, in the middle of nowhere. The facilities were basic but it was a short walk to a beach where the sea was the cleanest and clearest you could ever find. The snorkelling was fantastic. Thanos joined us for the weekend when we managed to find somewhere to stay with more space and cooking facilities. We made many trips across the island, including a visit to the ancient marble quarry, where we picked up a couple of small rocks covered in orange earth and cracked them hard to make them split. The marble exposed was (and remains – I still have some small pieces of it) the purest and most startling white and was used in ancient times for sculpture. Janette and I visited the Archaeological Museum in Naxos town before we left.

Later still, soon after Kate had left Scotland and returned to London, the two of us went to the island of Lefkas for a holiday. There were quite a few Brits on the island – keen sailors, who kept to particular harbours, and tourists who all seemed to stay in one very unattractive and busy small coastal town. We were based in a very quiet place, and drove all over the island exploring. The bright white cliffs and sand beaches of the western coast, reached via long and extremely steep roads, with one double bend after another, were beautiful and unspoilt, and there were almost no visitors. As usual, Greece worked its magic.

* * *

Complications

It was after Ian's mother, Clio, died, during our first year in Athens, that Ian's father, Brian, came to stay with us for about six weeks, which was lovely for all of us. The children loved their "Gramps". He had not been with us long, however, when I arrived home one day, to find that Ian was in the bedroom, on the phone to London. Brian knew who Ian was calling, and so did I, but we did not discuss it. As time went by, more and more often, Ian's trips abroad for work, which were numerous, went via London.

It was in the summer of our second year, by which time we had decided to stay on in Greece for one more year, that I went with the children to the island of Chios for our summer holiday. Chios is a fascinating island, split into three main areas. The northern part of the island is dry and bleak, rather like a moonscape. The central band of the island is green and fertile, full of estates surrounded by high walls enclosing large houses and citrus orchards. Some of these estates have grand, rectangular cisterns full of water, and in a few of them, large water wheels still survive. These were used in the past to carry water from the cisterns into irrigation channels for the citrus orchards. The high walls created a mysterious atmosphere, since it was impossible to see inside most of the gardens. The southern part of the island is completely different – with fortified villages called the Mastikachoria – mastic cultivating villages. The flat-roofed houses are highly decorated, covered all over with dramatic black and white geometric patterns with strings of bright red tomatoes and peppers hanging high up on the walls to dry. The mastic was highly prized and even now, its production in Chios is granted EU protected designation of origin.

Ian had joined us at the start of the Chios holiday, but had to leave fairly soon. Later, he flew back, to give me the news that his girlfriend was pregnant. He knew where we were staying, and joined us at the beach. The children were playing on the sand below us and we were sitting in the taverna just above them. He flew out again very early the next morning. I am sure Ian expected me to leave him and Greece immediately, but I thought matters over carefully, and decided that would be the wrong course of action.

Since we had already made plans to stay on in Greece for another year, we had not only extended the rental agreement on our house in Muswell Hill, but also, had been in touch with Highgate School (where Alex had been offered a place), to defer his arrival by a year. I decided that we would continue to live in Athens as happily married Dr and Mrs Macdonald and that the children and I would leave Athens at the end of the following summer. Friends were unaware of the situation but I did tell Maggie over the phone in due course. Ian was away a lot of the time, and Kate, Alex and I continued to enjoy our time in Greece. It turned out to be an extremely good decision.

Ian with Alexander James in Kentish Town, London. 1977

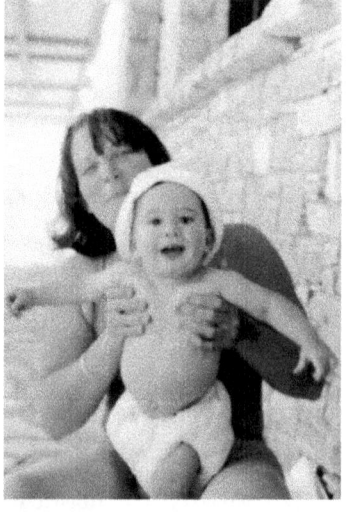

Anne & Alex on holiday in Greece. 1978

Anne and Ian Macdonald on holiday in Cephallonia, Greece. 1980

Ian Macdonald on holiday in Cephallonia, Greece. 1980

Katriona and Alexander on holiday in Cephallonia, Greece. 1980

Anne Macdonald with Katriona Anne Calliope on country walk with Judy outside Bath. 1980/81.

Grandma Clio with Kate. Wimbledon, London. 1980/81

Grandpa Brian (Gramps) with Alex. On holiday in Cephallonia, Greece. 1980

Ian with Alex at Aunt Ismini's house in Surbiton, London.

Anne with Kate. 1980/81

Alex and Kate in Muswell Hill, London. 1981ish

Kate in Muswell Hill, London, 1982?

Kate and Alex – ready for school (Kate's first day). Athens. 1983

Anne with Alex & Kate on holiday with Judy in Andros, Greece. 1984?

Alex in Durnsford Park, Muswell Hill, London. 1983

Kate in Durnsford Park, Muswell Hill, London. 1983

Turkey

Before returning to the UK, Ian and I decided to take one more holiday together with the children, to visit Turkey. It seemed too good an opportunity to miss. We flew to Samos, where Ian had arranged with an agent in Athens for us to take a boat from Pythagorion to Kusadasi on the Turkish coast. We took a taxi across the island, arriving to discover our potential landlord sitting outside, thoroughly enjoying eating his green beans, and telling us that he had allowed some other tourists to take the room that had been booked for us because he had decided we were not coming! We were irate and told him so, but that made no difference. Ian called the agent, but that made no difference, either. The town was packed, but despite this, luckily, we did manage to find a room for the night – tiny, noisy, and uncomfortable, as it was. In the morning, we set off to find the boat and discovered that the agent had booked us on a small yacht! This had not been Ian's intention, but it all turned out very well indeed. We shared the yacht with two other passengers. There was so little wind that our captain motored across rather than sailed. It was an unusual way to get to Turkey from Greece but the trip turned out to be a treat. We had blue skies, calm blue sea, sun, and the company of dolphins most of the way.

We had a superb holiday in Turkey. Firstly, we stayed in a small hotel in Kusadasi. There was a Genoese fortress up on a promontory in Kusadasi, which looked dramatic lit up at night. We would wander into town each evening, eat well, drink tea from large samovars, and enjoy quantities of delicious mulberry ice cream.

We hired a car and initially used this town as a base for visits to many places in the surrounding area. We went for the day to the large national coastal park south of Kusadasi where the countryside and coastline were protected. The sea was crystal clear. Alex, despite being on a lilo, narrowly missed being bitten by a scorpion. Our impression was that the Turks were taking considerable care at that time, to regulate and control development.

Now, over thirty years later, Turkey has (obviously) changed immeasurably. Cities, in particular, Istanbul, are now vast and prosperous. High rise buildings and billionaires abound, although I believe that recently, the tourism industry has suffered considerably.

We visited many ancient sites, most of which, apart from Ephesus, were not much visited by tourists. There were some places which were just as we imagined Greece must have been well before the days of tourism.

Ian had left us for a couple of days, so I took the children on an expedition north of Kusadasi, to the small ancient site of Claros, which was completely off the beaten track. The Doric ruins were down a dirt road and there was nobody there at all. The remains of a Temple of Apollo with a huge cult statue of Apollo and a subterranean chamber of the oracle were just below the level of the water table and water had collected in some places, creating tank-like ponds. The fragments of the cult-statue of Apollo were gigantic. The atmosphere of the place was almost sinister: it was remote; oppressively quiet; very hot indeed, with the sun beating down; the only sign of life being the large terrapins living in the ponds.

Later, we visited many major sites: Ephesus, Priene, Miletos, Didyma and others, all fascinating in their own ways. On a few of these sites, some ruins had been partly reconstructed by archaeologists, but in the main, they remained as excavated, some, such as Priene, in particularly beautiful locations.

Euromos was a little different, and a delight – a much lesser known site at that time. Olive trees surrounded and grew among the ruins, giving it a wonderfully romantic atmosphere. There was nobody there except for a very old man, who decided to wander around with us and show us the remains of the ancient buildings. There is a Corinthian temple (16 columns still standing) and other remains, including an ancient theatre, which was particularly appealing, with olive trees growing out of the seating here and there.

We had three whole weeks in Turkey for our holiday. We set out on our road trip, which involved driving due east from Kusadasi to the white mineral covered hillsides of Pamukkale; south to Antalya; and then west, along the southern coast and on to Kas and Fethiye; up to Izmir; and all the way north to Istanbul; staying in pensions along the way – a journey of around 2000 km. It was wonderful.

The road going east from Kusadasi was very busy, with large lorries pounding along it belching dirty exhaust fumes. There were quite a few camels in the fields, though, and at one point, we stopped for the children to have a ride. Apart from that, however, it was a pleasure to drive on the impressive and well maintained roads, especially down to and around the southern coast.

Unfortunately, Kate became ill for a couple of days on the journey, with a high temperature. The museum at Aphrodisias was modern, cool and calm and we took it in turns to rest in there with Kate lying on some cool marble out of the sun. When we reached Pamukkale, we found pensions and hotels of all sizes and varieties and almost all of them with a swimming pool, filled with the natural spring water containing the mineral salts which turn the hillsides white. This was a small but popular place so, unfortunately, for the first night, we were unable to find a pension with a pool, but the following morning, we moved into a rather smart hotel with an infinity pool. This was wonderful, particularly for Kate, who, feeling unwell, found it soothing to relax in the warm water. We stayed for a couple of nights and she recovered quickly. It was a strange experience, venturing on to the bright white hillsides, our experience telling us that the ground should be icy cold, only to find it warm under our bare feet.

In many areas the land was green and fertile, with tobacco fields and sophisticated irrigation systems. The drive south through Turkey's thickly forested and dramatic mountains was stunning, with magnificent views as we dropped, twisting and turning, down to the coast.

We found the Turkish people charming and friendly and noticeably calm, in contrast to the Greeks! Our days of driving, looking and visiting, were punctuated by stops for delicious lunches and evening meals. The food in Turkey was very good almost everywhere, although we did see people ordering plates of raw chillies to go with their food and thought that was probably a step too far for us.

We visited many ancient sites: Aphrodisias; Hierapolis; Xanthus; Aspendos; the rock-cut tombs of the south, including Myra (home of St Nicholas/Father Christmas); and others. We completed the large circle we had decided to drive and went north to Izmir (previously known as Smyrna). We had not planned to stop for any time in Izmir, despite Ian's family history, but we did stop for a drink at the uninspiring seafront, before continuing on our route. The road took us behind the city, through an unpleasant wasteland area filled with lakes of polluted standing water; stinking tanneries and smoke from the charcoal makers' burners. Hopefully, it has changed for the better, since then.

From Izmir, we briefly went east to Sardis (the richest city in the world at one time, and the home of Croesus) and then headed north, stopping at Pergamum. The ancient theatre at Pergamum had the steepest seating of any known theatre in the ancient world, 122 ft above the orchestra. It was dramatic and on reaching the top and looking down, Ian suddenly had vertigo, making him feel ill and unsure as to how he would reach the bottom again. Very slowly, however, he managed to make it down, much to our relief.

Our journey continued north to the historic city of Bursa, where the Ottoman Turks had established their capital in the fourteenth century. There are mosques, mausoleums, a market, and grand old Ottoman houses with their upper floors projecting out over the street. I understand that the city is now the fourth largest city in Turkey, so must have changed a great deal since then. We visited a couple of mosques and stayed one night, but sadly did not stay long enough to do it justice, excited as we were at the prospect of reaching Istanbul.

Driving over the Bosphorus Bridge from Asia to Europe was spectacular. At that time it was the fourth longest suspension bridge in the world and the views from the car were vast. It was exciting to be in a large, exotic and, for us, new city. We visited some of the major sights – the magnificent Haghia Sophia and the Blue Mosque – and enjoyed wandering around looking at the hugely colourful and lively markets and street cafés, which were in such contrast to the calm countryside of the last couple of weeks. We took a ferry from the Galata Bridge early one evening, where we struggled to find a way through chaotic throngs of people, to finally board the ferry we wanted. It was lovely to be out on the water in a very uncrowded ferry – taking a trip up the Bosphorus. The ferry took us north past the 19th century Palace of the Sweet Waters of Asia. There was a jump on and off arrangement, so we stopped to have a meal, returning to the city centre later.

Sadly, it soon became time to return to Athens, from where Alex, Kate and I would be returning to London and where Ian would remain.

We flew from Istanbul to Athens and stayed for two nights in an expensive and rather luxurious hotel in the centre of the city. There was an outdoor swimming pool in the courtyard of the hotel, where we swam in hot sunshine. To me, it was a strange thing to be doing in the very centre of a large built-up city – something I had not done before. It was quite a good way, however, to go out with a bang and to bid farewell to the city in which, despite our oddly fractured family set-up, we had enjoyed three wonderful years.

CHAPTER 10

Knocked Sideways

* * *

We Were Back

MUSWELL HILL, WHEN WE GOT BACK, was just as it had been when we left. It was almost as if we had not been away at all. Everything looked the same and friends and neighbours were doing all the usual things. This was to be expected I suppose, but not having given it a thought, I was surprised. Our house had been well looked after by our tenants and our belongings arrived from Athens in good time, so we settled in quickly. It was very good to see old friends again.

So, it was in early September 1986, that Alex and Kate started at their new schools. Initially, Kate joined Rhodes Avenue Primary School but after not too long, moved to Highfield School, a small mixed primary school, not far from Alex, who was at the all boys (at that time) day school: Highgate School.

Not long afterwards, I started looking for work, something I had always planned to do once we got back. I was soon interviewed for a job at University College London and was offered a post. I was to work as the part-time departmental secretary in UCL's very small Department of Classical Archaeology, where they seemed to think my knowledge of Greece and Greek would be useful. I had confirmed in the interview, that I thought I would be able to type in Greek without too much difficulty, which proved to be the case. The working hours were as if made for me, since the job was a term time only one, plus a couple of additional weeks, before and after the beginning and end of each term. My working weeks were full-time, so effectively, I worked for about three quarters of the year. This meant that I did not have to worry about how I was going to look after Alex and Kate in the school holidays.

I decided that the way to deal with my new single parent status in relation to work, was to find help with the children by taking on an au pair. I registered with a small agency and very soon a young Swedish woman joined us at home. Anniken turned out to be a responsible and sensible young woman and the au pair arrangement worked extremely well. She already had a driving licence, but I paid for her to have some extra lessons, to get her used to driving our car in London. This enabled her to collect both Kate and Alex from school, after which, she would give them tea, help with homework, and wait for me to return home from work. She was treated as a member of the family and we all got on well together – occasionally, she would bake a cake for us all. Anniken also went on holiday with us to Ireland one year. The elderly and very small Mini I had was full, with four passengers and luggage on the roof, for the long journey.

I found my new job interesting and fun. I had my own small office and was visited by students and staff from other departments as well as my own, particularly from the Institute of Archaeology and the Greek and Latin Departments, since our Department contributed to interdisciplinary courses. There were only two academic staff in the Department, a Professor and a Senior Lecturer (later to become a Reader), and I respected and got on very well with both of them. I enjoyed my work, which was nicely varied and even included opening and looking after the Department's Museum on Friday afternoons; even, occasionally, handling ancient pottery objects from the ancient Mediterranean, which was a real treat.

Because I was officially a part-time employee, I was not included in UCL's pension scheme. However, the EU introduced a new ruling in 2000 that all part-time employees should be given the statutory right to be treated equally regarding pension schemes, and stated that these rights could be back-dated. Later on in my working life at UCL, I claimed these rights for the four year period in which I had worked as a so-called part-timer. I had to chase my request over a very long period, since it was not an automatic right, but eventually, my request was granted, and my final pension calculation included my four years of part-time work.

It was less than six months later, that Ian returned to the UK, having resigned from his job in Athens. Initially, he seemed to expect that he would be able to move in with us again, which surprised me, since it had not occurred to me that this was an option. Unsurprisingly, I turned down the idea and Ian went to live with his girlfriend.

Ian had inherited some money on his father's death and decided that he would use this to set up and run a geriatric nursing home in Muswell Hill. He proposed to raise further funds by re-mortgaging our jointly owned house. Unwisely, I agreed to this arrangement and The First National Bank advanced him the sum of £126,000. Ian also borrowed £20,000 from his sister, Patty (which she had inherited from her parents), and all this enabled him to buy a property in Church Crescent, Muswell Hill, which he converted into a new and well designed nursing home. This went well to start with, and I understood that Ian built up a reputation for running a high quality nursing home.

However, the house next door to Ian's nursing home soon came on the market, so he bought this too, knocking the two houses together, and extending the nursing home across the two properties. Sometime later, the third property in the row also came on to the market and Ian went ahead and bought this too.

Kate and Alex adapted very quickly to our new lives which, importantly, included them making new friends at school. Alex had a small group of new friends, but found himself at times, in an environment where bullying was not uncommon. He found himself at the sharp end of this for a while, and was being physically beaten up by one particular boy – something I felt sure would not have happened in the school playground in Athens. However, with the help of the headmaster, who talked to the parents of the bully, and friend David in Salisbury, who advised on exactly where to punch someone on the arm without damaging them (how did he know this?!); and his form teacher, who agreed to look the other way if Alex retaliated – which he did – the bullying stopped overnight. After a while, this boy left London, but bizarrely, then wrote to Alex as if he was his best friend. Alex's school work went well and he made good progress in playing the violin, with a new teacher who lived not far from us. He also took up the flute for a while. Although by using the Suzuki Method, Alex took no violin exams, he became remarkably accomplished.

In 1988, Alex's school arranged a cricket tour in Kenya and Alex was lucky enough to be included in the group. The Headmaster of the Junior

School was a keen and enthusiastic geographer and, with other teachers, went with them. This was an enormous bonus, given the places they visited (including the Rift Valley) and, I suspect, helped to encourage Alex's interest in the subject. He continued to enjoy geography, achieving an A grade in his A level exam; studying environmental science at university and going on to becoming a geography teacher himself!

Kate settled into her new school and started to play the recorder and the violin. She also made new friends, Georgina becoming her best school friend. This led to us getting to know Georgina's family: Angelique, Freddie and Pablo (younger than Georgina and Kate), with whom we became, and remain, close.

All the usual family things took place in our lives over the next few years and we enjoyed ourselves. Everyday life was fairly well organised. We had four different au pair girls in total over the years, three of whom were good and one who was not. . . The children went to school and I went to work; I did a large 'shop' once a week in the evening after work, and weekends were a time for relaxing. Alex and Kate would see their friends and Ian would visit sometimes. We had great weekends and holidays with Judy, and with Elizabeth, Jeffrey and Eli, who visited us from Canada, and with whom we went on holiday to Burgundy. Also, we used to stay with David, Sarah, Eddie, Laura, Sophie and Alec in Salisbury, at Christmas and/or New Year. And Max used to come up to London for work occasionally, and I would meet him for a meal sometimes. I also started going on regular theatre outings with Henley, which we took it in turns to organise. We had the most wonderful holidays in Ireland Italy and Greece, with Maggie, Jules, Mia and Miranda, and in Greece with Janette, Thanos, Lisa and Daphne. We took a driving trip around Scotland in 1987, visiting the west coast, dodging midges, herding sheep in the mountains and visiting Skye. We also visited my brother, David, and his family in Mallaig, and spent a week in Edinburgh, where we rented a flat. On a couple of occasions, Alex and Kate went on holiday with Ian and on one of these, I had the liberating experience of going on my own to Paris for a few days.

However, serious financial stresses and strains emerged and developed. In 1989, First National Bank issued a summons for repossession of our house (claim to be heard on 11 September 1989). This claim was adjourned; then restored (to be heard on 22 March 1990); and then adjourned again. This was very stressful. Ian was giving us considerable financial support: paying the increased mortgage and the children's school fees. However, his payments were becoming increasingly erratic and cheques were bouncing. I began to dread the arrival of the post and was so fearful, that I could not bring myself to open my bank statements. Money was very tight and every time one of Ian's cheques bounced, I was charged yet another fee.

In early 1990, Ian told me that he was struggling with his new business (he was not and had never been a businessman, after all) and wanted to borrow further funds for his business (Macdonald Medical Ltd), by securing a further loan against our house. I was hugely reluctant to agree to this but he put me under great pressure, telling me that if I did not go along with this idea (which I resisted for some time), his nursing home business would collapse and he would be unable to support us, financially. I also felt (naively, I later realised) that half the house was his and that I should 'do the decent thing' and allow him to use this asset.

In early 1990, therefore, after many discussions and arguments, and despite my doubts, he persuaded me to agree to his taking out a further mortgage on our Cecil Road house.

* * *

1991

1991 was a tumultuous and challenging year for Alex, Kate and me, during which several major life-changing events took place, some of which threatened to overwhelm us.

In early 1991, I suddenly recognised, not having noticed until then, that Kate was extremely thin – far too thin. I was sitting at the kitchen table when Kate came out of our walk-in larder, with the bright light from inside, shining directly on to her. I was shocked and amazed that I had noticed nothing previously. An urgent trip to the GP resulted in her being diagnosed with diabetes type1 and being hospitalised the same day. I rang Ian to tell him the diagnosis and he came to join us in the Whittington Hospital. I remember giving Angelique the news outside the girls' school and Freddie being Kate's first visitor, taking her a television, which she could watch in bed. It was at this time that Kate was sitting her entrance exams for secondary school and despite being an in-patient, she was allowed (to my enormous regret afterwards, when I realised how awful this had been for her) to sit the last exam, after only a couple of days in hospital – returning to hospital again afterwards.

The care Kate received from the paediatric diabetes department at the hospital was excellent, the lead consultant, specialist diabetes nurses and dieticians, and later the outpatients clinic, all providing her with excellent care and support. When she came home, Kate had already learned a great deal about managing her diabetes. She was eleven years old and had to deal with regularly pricking a finger to test her blood sugar, plus the very tricky procedure of filling her syringes from two separate small bottles of insulin before injecting herself (there was no such thing as a an insulin pen for children then). Many was the occasion when, to do this, we had to go to the women's lavatories wherever we were, trying to maintain hygiene whilst doing so. It was difficult for her in many ways.

Kate returned to school after not too long an absence, and the very good news was that she was happy and continued to do well at school. She continued to play violin and recorder, both of which she enjoyed. She decided after a while, however, to drop the violin and concentrate on the recorder. Unusually, she took her recorder lessons (instrumental and theory) as far as it is possible to go: both to Grade 5 – when her teacher said she was a 'natural' to learn the oboe and recommended an oboe teacher. Sure enough, Kate took the oboe up to Distinction at Grade 8.

Soon after returning to Highfield, the school decided to run a skiing trip to Switzerland. Georgina (a relatively experienced skier), was due to go, but there was a question mark as to whether Kate should go, given her very newly diagnosed diabetes, although she was keen to do so. However, Freddie (a very keen skier) stepped in, offering to join the group as a parent helper, with special responsibility for Kate. He made an appointment to see Kate's consultant to ask for an opinion on the idea, and for advice as to Kate's needs and also how she would need to be helped to cope with the extreme cold. The school accepted this arrangement and we were all, unsurprisingly, very pleased. Kate, Georgina and Freddie all had a terrific holiday.

More good news came along when Kate was offered a couple of school places for September, accepting one at South Hampstead High School – a girls' day school at the bottom of Fitzjohn's Avenue, close to Swiss Cottage.

By this time, I had decided that I wanted to start working full-time, so I applied and was interviewed for the post of PA to the Dean of the Institute of Child Health, the research institute connected with Great Ormond Street Hospital. This was a specialist postgraduate medical institute at that time, one of several similar institutes which made up the British Postgraduate Medical Federation, part of the University of London. The

Dean was Roland Levinsky, a brilliant Professor of Paediatric Immunology and Consultant Paediatric Immunologist. After a very unconventional and amusing interview, I was delighted to be offered the job. My job offer was hand delivered to my house by Roland (I was out) because there had been a power cut at the Institute and the phones were not working. It emerged that Roland lived a few roads away from us, in Dukes Avenue.

In the summer, Alex joined a Suzuki violin music camp, held at Highnam Court in Gloucestershire. He had been there before, when Kate and I had stayed with him, but this time, he stayed on his own. The weather was glorious and Kate and I went to visit Judy, with whom we had a wonderful weekend. We drove back home from Bath but had not been in the house long, before the phone rang.

It was my neighbour, Margaret, who was ringing to break the shocking news that Ian had died suddenly of a heart attack the day before. I shook all over at the news and continued to shake for some time, such was the shock. I decided not to tell Kate the news until the next morning, so she got ready for bed in the usual way. I rang Judy to tell her and she drove up to join us in London. I also rang Sally, who came round immediately with a bottle of whisky. Angelique arrived the following evening, with a large cooler box absolutely full of delicious food and drink.

Ian died on Saturday 13 July 1991. He was born on 30 July 1940, so he was not quite 52. I was told that he had collapsed on an airport bus at Heathrow. I understand that he had been on his way to Athens, to arrange for the last of his furniture to be sent back to the UK.

I had the horrendous job of having to tell Kate about her dad. She was, understandably, extremely upset. I then had to make the journey to Gloucestershire to collect Alex and tell him. I drove there with Kate, and Judy went with us. Ian had been due to collect Alex at the end of the summer camp, so when we arrived, Alex asked again and again and again, why Ian was not there to collect him. I could not tell him until we had said our goodbyes to everyone, so had to keep hedging. Once we were en route, however, I stopped in a country road at the edge of a field and while Judy stayed with Kate in the car, I walked around the edge of the field with Alex and told him the tragic news. Kate and Alex cried all the way back to London.

Ian had been under enormous stress and it was only once he died that the full extent of his financial troubles emerged. The Mercantile Credit Company (I discovered after his death from papers I was sent) had advanced

Ian's company £760,000 against the security of numbers 8, 10 & 12 Church Crescent. On 22 May 1991 they had asked for repossession and did so again on 10 July 1991 (three days before Ian died), claiming a sum of £940,830.41p owing. There were many other debtors, too, including the Bradford & Bingley Building Society with whom our house had been re-mortgaged, and who, having started possession proceedings, also put in a Possession Order – on our house – just after Ian died. Ian had mortgages on at least one flat in Muswell Hill and on a house in East Anglia, which he had recently bought for his new family, which were also re-possessed. Patty also lost her £20,000.

Ian died insolvent and intestate. Given the timings of the financial deadlines, and his highly demanding lifestyle, it seems more than likely that the financial and family stress he was under, played a major part in his untimely death. Not only did he die owing money, but he had not kept up any insurance payments either. . .

Later, I wrote to two separate life insurance companies not involved in the funding of the nursing home and received a sum of approx £5,500 from one of them. I also wrote to Ian's German employer to enquire whether Ian had had any pension rights, but they replied in the negative, since he had not worked for the company for long enough.

I had to come to terms with the fact, very fast, that we were likely to be homeless very soon.

I did several things very quickly: I had only just started my new job, so, firstly, I went to Roland's house one evening to tell him and his wife, Beth, that Ian had died and in what circumstances. Roland reacted in the most supportive way. He told me that he would expect me at work after a couple of days (later, he told me that he would not have been surprised if I had resigned) but, when I got there, he also said, and meant it: "do what you have to do". This meant that I worked very hard, but was able to make arrangements, phone calls and visits as and whenever necessary, during the day, while I was at work. What an attitude! It was brilliant. This was one of the good features of this dreadful year: I had found and just started a new full-time job, and I had a boss whose flexibility allowed me to try and sort out our family crisis at the same time as working. My work and having a full-time job was fundamentally what saved the entire situation for us.

Ian's funeral was arranged by his girlfriend and the manager of the nursing home. Patty chose some Greek Orthodox religious music sung by a Greek male voice choir and I suggested that Kate and Alex might play an

Irish jig "The Irish Washerwoman", to remind us of our wonderful holidays in Ireland. They played a duet – Kate on her recorder and Alex on his violin. It was very moving.

I was not consulted about the decision to bury Ian rather than have his body cremated (which would have been my choice), so he was buried in East Finchley Cemetery and the wake was held in the flat of the nursing home manager. Unfortunately, when the undertakers presented their bill to her (she had commissioned them), they were told that there was no money to pay it. I received a phone call at work from her, asking me if I could pay it! When I responded that not only did I have no money, but very soon I would have no house either, I was told that Ian would be looking down on me from above, upset that I was not paying for his funeral. . . However, (rather kindly, I think, looking back) I wrote an explanatory letter for her to send to the funeral directors.

Coincidentally and not long after this, Alex, Kate and I were booked to take a holiday in Cape Cod, Massachusetts, where Elizabeth and Jeffrey had rented a house and had generously invited us to join them. The fares had already been paid, but I needed to decide whether or not to continue as planned. I thought that it would probably do us all good to go, especially since we would be with close friends. It turned out to be a wonderful holiday and certainly did a lot for us. We flew to Boston and took a coach to Cape Cod, where Elizabeth, Jeffrey and Eli met us in their car. The large Massachusetts style wooden house we were in was very comfortable. It was hot, and on some days, very humid – there was a dehumidifier in each room, which needed to be emptied every day. We were introduced to the delights of toasted bagels, and we barbecued outside on the decking. We had a choice in terms of swimming: the long exposed, windy and sandy beaches on the Atlantic side of the Cape Cod peninsula; the more sheltered beaches on the western side of the peninsula; or the multitude of fresh water ponds inland. These were all very different and all a lot of fun. We went to Provincetown where we took a boat out to sea and watched blue whales – an amazing experience. Alex went on a day's fishing trip too, on his own, not only winning the small lottery on the boat, but catching a couple of blue fish, which we barbecued for dinner (it was fairly horrible, but we were tactful – there was a lot left over!). We visited the Audubon Wildlife Sanctuary on a day when there was no breeze at all, and where the humidity was almost as high as it had been in Papua New Guinea. We also ate legendary East coast seafood in the famous crab shacks. We were so well looked after by Elizabeth and Jeffrey and returned to London well prepared to face the difficulties ahead.

The owners of Kate's school contacted me to inform me that Ian's cheque for the previous term's fees had bounced, so after speaking to them on the phone, I wrote to confirm what had happened, and to apologise, which of course, was of no real help, but they handled the situation with kindness and discretion.

The second urgent item on my list was to see what I could do to keep both children at the schools they expected to attend in September. My reasoning was that they had lost their father and would lose their home; and that I should at least try to keep some continuity in their lives by keeping to their school plans. I visited my local library and found an enormous tome listing most of the UK's charitable institutions. I soon discovered that each institution had letters beside its name to indicate the areas they supported. I was therefore able to find out which charities made funding available to support education and I wrote to all of them, setting out our situation and asking for help. Some replied and some did not – one way or another, I had no luck at all.

I was talking to Angelique about this when she suggested (brilliantly, as it turned out) that the British Medical Association (BMA) might be able to help. The BMA is the trade union and professional body for doctors in the UK. I rang them and immediately met with a positive response. There was an office within the BMA which ran some charitable trusts, available for doctors and/or their families in need of help in a financial crisis. I had a long conversation over the phone with a sympathetic and very well-informed Case Officer, and was then sent an application form for assistance from the Dain Fund for Alex, and was put in touch with the Royal Medical Foundation for assistance for Kate. Two separate funds were involved because the criteria for each fund were different – the children differed in age and also in the stage they had reached in their education. Alex was just about to start his two year GCSE course, and Kate had not even started at her new secondary school. I completed the forms as quickly as possible and sent them off.

In the meantime, I had also written to the Heads of both Highgate School and South Hampstead High School (SHHS) informing them of our difficulties and letting them know that I had applied to the BMA for financial help with school fees, but would not immediately know the outcome of my applications. I asked whether they, too, might be able to provide financial help.

All this was in the first week of August. School terms were due to start very soon, so there was enormous pressure to act quickly. There was no certainty as to what may or may not happen, nor where Alex and Kate would be going to school – in just a few weeks.

The Head of Highgate School passed my letter to 'The Friends of Highgate School Society' and on 12 August I received a letter from the Honorary Secretary (who later taught Alex biology 'A' level) to let me know that 'The Friends' would make an award covering Alex's tuition fees for the first term of the academic year and would review the situation in December. This was wonderful news, and when I received a letter dated 29 October from the BMA, letting me know that the Dain Fund would cover the following two terms' fees, we were more than pleased.

I had to apply in detail each year for funding from the Dain Fund to cover Alex's school fees, and I was warned that there was no certainty that these applications would be successful, since assets were decreasing in value and funds were limited. In the end, however, the Dain Fund paid Alex's fees in full for four whole years, including his two year 'A' level course. This was absolutely brilliant and Alex pleased the BMA fund; the school; himself; and Kate and me; by achieving excellent 'A' level results. The Head of Highgate School wrote to thank the Dain Fund for their support, as of course, did I, and I also wrote to the Head to thank him for his personal help (he had written letters of support) and for the help from 'The Friends'. Quite an astonishing outcome.

The Head of SHHS was still away on holiday and the phone response I received when I rang, was not at all encouraging: there was a shortage of funds due to most awards having already been made for the year. However, on her return, the Head herself rang me, told me that a child who had been awarded a Government Assisted Place had had to turn it down, and she would like to offer this place to Kate. She was very kind. I was sent a form on 2 September and posted it the next day. On 16 October, I received the excellent news that Kate had been awarded an Assisted Place. On 8 November I heard from the Royal Medical Foundation that they would also make a contribution towards the remaining fees! This would leave one third of Kate's school fees to be paid by me. In order to pay this, I arranged to take out a loan from a friend, and this covered my share of the payments over the next three years. Again, to say we were pleased is an understatement.

In 1993, it emerged that an error had been made in the school office's calculations concerning Kate's Assisted Place in 1992 and 1993, and my contributions should have been changed to take account of my slowly increasing income. This was a blow, but I managed to find the extra money needed.

The other major problem I had to deal with was the question of where we were going to live. I visited the Bradford & Bingley Building Society at their nearest branch in Edmonton Green, to enquire whether there was anything I could do to forestall the repossession of our house. However, since the amount owing was large, there was no possibility of my being able to pay off the mortgage, and they were not at all helpful, confirming that the house would be re-possessed, and that I would receive a Bailiff's appointment for 4 November 1991.

I therefore registered with the London Borough of Haringey that we would be homeless very soon – and in need of emergency accommodation. This was surprisingly difficult. First of all, it was almost impossible to get through to the right department on the phone to make an appointment for an interview. As there are now, there were many homeless people at that time. In the past, it had been possible to visit the special registration centre without an appointment, but I was informed that the Council had been so overwhelmed by people queuing down the street that they had made it compulsory for people to phone for an appointment before going there. While I had the good fortune to be sitting at my desk waiting for someone to answer the phone, I had visions of women with small babies, queuing outside telephone boxes, desperately ringing and ringing, trying to get a reply – an appalling situation. Eventually, not on the first day of trying, I got through, and was given an appointment. I was told to bring various documents with me, including several forms of ID and, of course, the notice from the building society confirming the date by which we had to move out of our house.

I think this appointment took place in a building which has since been refurbished or rebuilt, in Station Road, Wood Green. I arrived at a large warehouse-like building which was locked, with a queue of people waiting outside. The situation was bizarre. Every now and again, a tiny man would unlock the door from the inside, open the door a crack and peer out at us, before letting the next person with an appointment inside the building. The large space inside was divided up temporarily into cubicles and there were notices all over the walls, warning against threatening behaviour. The atmosphere was not reassuring.

I was interviewed and my documents were inspected and copied. I was subsequently visited at home, too, when two women wandered around the house, apparently struck by how nice my furniture was. . . I was soon informed that I and my two children were now officially registered as 'homeless' and that I would receive a letter offering me a further appointment.

In due course I received an appointment to visit the Metropolitan Housing Association offices in Mayes Road, Wood Green, where I was again interviewed, and all the same documents were inspected and copied once more. I understood that the criteria used to find appropriate accommodation for us would take into account the fact that I had two children above a certain age and of different genders, who, accordingly, would need to have their own bedrooms, and also not be too far from their schools. In addition, the fact that I had my own furniture would also need to be taken into account. I was then told that I would be offered London Borough of Haringey emergency accommodation before the date by which we had to leave our house; and that I would soon receive a letter informing me of its address.

Since Haringey is a large London Borough, I was worried that we might be accommodated far from Kate's and Alex's schools. I therefore wrote to two local Councillors, asking them to support my request to be accommodated within a reasonable distance of the two schools and of the Whittington Hospital. Both of them replied positively to me and wrote to Haringey in support. I had done everything I could think of and I now had to 'wait and see'.

It was a nerve-wracking time. I had no idea where we would be living, nor what the accommodation would be like. However, a letter from Haringey Council did arrive, dated 15 October 1991. It offered us accommodation under the Private Sector Leasing Scheme, on the basis that "the council has a duty to secure that temporary accommodation is available for you". The accommodation offered was at 55A Tottenham Lane, London N8, and I was informed that the tenancy would begin on 28 October 1991, at a rent of £49.88 per week, plus water rates. I was also informed that if I refused this offer, I would not be offered any other alternative temporary accommodation. The letter said that I would be able to collect the keys on 23 October 1991.

I looked up the address right away and was astounded to see that the accommodation we had been offered, was a five minute walk from Angelique and Freddie's house. I phoned Angelique immediately and she went out to take a look, quickly ringing me back. She reported that the accommodation was located above a café, with its front door on Tottenham

Lane, Hornsey, and looked quite decent. I was vastly relieved and felt confident in confirming to Haringey that I would collect the keys and sign the sub-tenancy agreement.

I was told that the maisonette was furnished, so I particularly reminded the Council that the furniture needed to be removed, so that I could move in my own furniture. This was arranged and their furniture was placed in Haringey's storage facility.

The next thing to think about was what I should do with our furniture, as much as possible of which I would keep, but some of which, especially the larger items, I would not. I managed to sell the larger items at auction, and a friend of a friend offered to store my enormous old loom for me and sold it for me later. I contacted most of my men friends, who, quite brilliantly, agreed to help me move my furniture out of the house and into our new home. David came up from Salisbury, Jules from Tunbridge Wells, and Henley, Nick and Richard from around London. Alex, who had been excused from a school rugby match, helped too, of course.

The job involved driving the two vans I had hired and also heavy lifting, both down the stairs from Cecil Road's second and first floors and up the three flights of stairs in our new home – a maisonette on the first and second floors. It was a Saturday, the day of a big rugby match, so Alex went down the road to our local butcher and bought ham and other goodies, from which we made sandwiches for everyone's lunch, eaten in front of the television watching the rugby.

At the end of the day, everyone was tired but the mission had been accomplished. Our friends had been more than fantastic. We made our beds and fell into them.

We had been very lucky indeed and Haringey had looked after us well. We found ourselves in a three-bedroomed maisonette with a kitchen, bathroom and a good sized living room, whereas we could have found ourselves in temporary bed and breakfast accommodation. It seemed that the genders and ages of my two children and the fact that I had furniture of my own, had been crucial in the decision making process, as to what size and type of accommodation we would be given. I felt lucky and grateful and it was not long before I registered on the Council's waiting list for permanent accommodation. I was told that the waiting period at that time was about four years.

We had taken our two cats with us to our new home – all black Noodles and tortoiseshell Toots. We followed instructions and did not let the cats out for three days to get them used to their new surroundings but unfortunately, on finally letting them out of the window on to the lower flat roof, Noodles disappeared. Despite making calls to a number of cat rescue organisations and displaying notices in the neighbourhood, sadly, we never saw him again.

A few days after moving in, it was Guy Fawkes Night and we were very excited that we could watch the Alexandra Palace fireworks from my bedroom window!

We had various property difficulties to deal with – the boiler needed to be fixed and serviced, which in the end, I paid for, since Haringey did not manage, ever, to get the landlord of the property to deal with this. The lavatory/bathroom door could not be completely closed and we had a major drama one day when the roof covering over Kate's bedroom literally blew off, causing water to pour into her room. This happened on a Sunday, but Council workmen turned up and in due course the roof was properly fixed. In addition, almost immediately outside Alex's bedroom, there was a huge flue from the 'greasy spoon' below us, as a result of which, some of the fumes from this flue would inevitably get into his room. This was unpleasant but must have been unhealthy too. Otherwise, we were comfortable, and having our own furniture around us, made the place surprisingly homely.

All in all, 1991 could be called an eventful year for us. There was certainly no shortage of events! The bad news was that Kate was found to have type1 diabetes; Ian died of a heart attack at the same time as going bankrupt; we became homeless; and we had no hope of further help with our finances, over and above my modest salary. The good news, however, was that Kate responded to and managed her diabetes treatment well; Kate was offered places at two schools; amazingly, funding was found for both Alex and Kate to continue with their schooling as planned; we had a great holiday in Massachusetts; Haringey rescued us by providing us with decent temporary emergency accommodation in Hornsey (five minutes from Angelique and Freddie's house); a friend, out of the blue, gave me a £1,000 Marks & Spencer voucher; and I started a full-time job, which became the stepping stone to my career in the years ahead and thus enabled me to support my family. However, I could have managed none of this without all my wonderful friends, who provided loving, strong and unwavering support.

* * *

Moving On...

We settled into an astonishingly normal lifestyle fairly rapidly, although we were all shell-shocked and things were not always smooth. In the mornings, Alex would take the bus (and later, ride his bike) to school, and I would take Kate to her school bus and then walk the short distance down the road to Hornsey overground station, to catch a train to King's Cross, from where it was a short walk to work. Angelique and Freddie were wonderful and helped beyond measure. Both Georgina and Kate travelled to and from school on their school buses. On the return journey, stops for the two buses were very close to each other. Freddie, who collected Georgina from her bus every day, offered to collect Kate as well and take her back to their house, where she could unwind, have some tea and watch TV with Georgina until I was able to collect her. It was a fantastic arrangement and Kate was very happy. Alex would get back home after school and let himself in, and I would go straight to Freddie and Angelique's house when I got back from work, collect Kate and take her home. I'm really not sure how things would have worked out without their help.

I had landed on my feet in terms of my job. Roland turned out not only to be a wonderful and thoughtful boss, always encouraging me to take on new roles and responsibilities and to progress in my career, but he also became a firm friend. I worked hard, climbed the promotion ladder, and very quickly became one of those very lucky people who love their work. My colleagues were great fun and the atmosphere in the office and at the Institute was hugely positive. I got to know Roland's family, particularly his wife Beth, and was invited to their house, and later, to stay with them, once they had moved to Devon. I also sailed with Roland and Beth on a couple of occasions along the south coast, including doing an over-nighter, when, among other things, I helped Roland (who was colour blind) to distinguish between the red and green lights of oncoming vessels. . .!

After nearly three years in temporary accommodation, I received letters warning me that I would receive one offer and one offer only of local authority permanent accommodation, and that if I turned this offer down, I would be well and truly homeless. Two women from Haringey, who did not mince their words, made an appointment to visit me, to ensure that I had fully understood this message.

I again visited and wrote to local Councillors, asking for their support in trying to make sure that our permanent housing offer would be within reach of both Alex and Kate's schools and the Whittington Hospital for Kate's diabetes care. I also asked Freddie, as a consultant psychiatrist, to write to Haringey concerning the importance of Kate remaining at her school (given everything that had happened to her) which he very kindly did, on 14 Feb 1994. Our GP also provided a letter confirming Alex's asthma, since I needed to ensure we were not housed somewhere with flight after flight of stairs.

Haringey seemed to take all this on board and we were offered a flat in August 1994 in Finsbury Park. I went with Angelique one afternoon to see it. The flat was filthy, and had a family of cats in residence. I was told it would be cleaned up, but had my doubts. The estate itself was run down and depressing. The sheds were covered in graffiti and there were several people standing on their small balconies staring into space. It was sad, dirty, gloomy, and looked unsafe, and I was very unhappy at the prospect of Kate returning home there on her own after school. I discussed the situation with Angelique and decided, despite everything, and taking a big risk, to turn down the offer. I decided to try and buy a property.

The Council wrote to me on 5 August 1994, noting my refusal to accept their offer of accommodation and discharging themselves of their duty to provide me with accommodation forthwith. However, they advised me that the accommodation would be kept available for me should I wish to reconsider, until 12th August. The letter finished by saying "If you are occupying temporary accommodation arranged by the Council, appropriate steps will be taken to terminate your occupation as soon as possible".

My rent had risen periodically during my tenancy. In March 1992 it was increased to £60.15 and then again to £72.57.

On 23 Jan 1995, however, after I had refused Haringey's offer of accommodation, it was suddenly put up to £208 and then to £210.53. I wrote to a solicitor asking whether Haringey was within its rights to give me only 9 days' notice of any increase in rent, let alone such a huge one. He confirmed that no court would uphold an increase in rent with only 9 days' notice, let alone one of this proportion. On 1 March 1995, it went up again to £212.85. . . .

When I rang Haringey, I was told not to worry and that I would not have to pay this! We discussed Housing Benefit, for which I applied. As a result, I was awarded £58.44 per week, meaning that I would need to pay £152.09 in rent per week. On 23 March 1995 this was adjusted slightly and I was asked for £151.09 per week.

Haringey's somewhat shambolic (and illegal) behaviour was clearly designed to intimidate me and to put pressure on me to move out. It certainly scared me . . . my blood ran cold every time I received yet another letter. It is true, however, that I had been warned, so perhaps their behaviour should be interpreted as taking "appropriate steps". . .

However, I had not been kicking my heels since turning down Haringey's offer of permanent accommodation. I had not known whether I would qualify for a mortgage, given the debts left on our house in Cecil Road, so I investigated; and was happy to discover there was a good chance that I would. Fortunately, none of the debts relating to the house and Ian's business had been logged against my name, since despite the house being in our joint names, the debts had had nothing whatsoever to do with me. My financial record was clear. This was encouraging.

I had also investigated the "Do it Yourself Home Ownership Scheme" – a scheme where the purchaser buys a proportion of a property, with the DIYSO organisation owning the rest. The purchaser under this arrangement would take out a mortgage on an agreed percentage of the property, which s/he would own, and pay rent on the percentage owned by DIYSO. This did not seem to me to be value for money, and when I discovered that if the purchaser were to improve the property, the costs of any improvement and therefore the increased value of the property, would not be taken into account when the property was sold, I decided that the arrangement was unfair and not for me.

However, we suddenly met with success, when – as part of our search for a flat – Kate, who had been assiduous in looking through each copy of the free newspaper "Loot" saw an advertisement for a flat in Muswell Hill – towards the bottom of Colney Hatch Lane. It was an ex-local authority flat, had three bedrooms and was priced at £62,500. We went to see it and offered the asking price straight away. This was accepted, and the purchase was completed for us by the bemusingly named solicitor: Mr Fidler, on 1 March 1995. I hired two men and a van plus a professional piano remover, and we moved into 14 Monkswell Court, Pembroke Road, London N10 2JH. It was a brilliant move.

Having done everything necessary to inform Haringey of when we would be moving out and our new address, I was surprised to receive a letter from the Hornsey Area Office telling me that on visiting the property, they had found it empty of furniture. The Housing Manager wrote, "We shall have to make arrangements for collection of this furniture, and if necessary inform the police." I responded by suggesting that a letter of enquiry might have been more appropriate; that it seemed that because we had been homeless, we were automatically assumed to have been criminals; and I also pointed out how unlikely it would have been for me to openly leave a forwarding address if I had intended to abscond with the furniture!! I provided them with the name and address of Haringey's own storage facility. . . I received fulsome apologies from her, her senior Manager, and the local Councillor!

We had been in temporary accommodation for approximately three and a half years. I received my final bill from Haringey, which I was expecting. When it arrived, it was a notification of oustanding rent arrears of £629.22p. I responded with a detailed outline of the figures involved which indicated that I owed them £167.28p and sent them a cheque for that amount. I am glad to report that I heard nothing further.

Another new stage in our lives was about to begin.

* * *

A New Start

Monkswell Court, on the corner of Pembroke Road and Colney Hatch Lane, provided us with a very comfortable home, where we lived for six years from March 1995. The flat was part of a small three block low-rise1930s estate, the blocks arranged in a semi-circle, slightly above the road. The grounds were not extensive, but grassed over, front and back, with a semi-circular driveway at the front. It was wonderfully located for all of us in terms of getting to and from work and schools.

Our flat was one of the few larger ones and was surprisingly spacious, located on the first floor, in the central block of the three. The walls of the main stairwell were decorated all over with white 'Artex' and each room in the flat had a differently patterned textured wallpaper. The whole flat was painted cream and the synthetic carpeting, which even extended into the bathroom and the loo, was beige. Fortunately, it was all in reasonable condition and no work was necessary. The rooms were all of a good size and since it was on the first floor and the estate was on the side of a hill, we had wonderfully wide, open, and far-reaching views from the sitting room, of the sky and the sunsets.

I was a Leaseholder with a long lease; the Freeholder was the London Borough of Barnet; and I had to pay an annual maintenance charge and ground rent. It suited us down to the ground.

Big changes were also happening in the lives of Alex and Kate at this time.

* * *

Alex's Gap Year and Uni

At some point, probably towards the end of his school career, Alex had a small number of his friends over to our flat when Kate and I were away . . . and I returned home to find the front door open and the flat not quite in the state in which I had left it. . . Luckily, no strangers had taken advantage of the open front door and there was no damage. Luckily. . .

Alex finished school at the end of the summer of 1995. He had done very well in his 'A' levels (Geography, Biology and Ancient History) and had been offered a place at the University of East Anglia to study Environmental Science. He accepted this offer, but before joining UEA, decided to take a gap year and through the organisation GAP, arranged to join the Australian Trust for Conservation Volunteers (ATCV) for six months. He applied to the 'Friends of Highgate School Society' – the same fund that had provided him with one term's fees back in 1991 – for one of their travel scholarships, and was successful. He needed to earn some money as well, however, and found a somewhat unusual job, working in a small sword factory on the North Circular Road! The company produced fencing swords mainly; was clearly very basic in terms of the conditions in the workshop (which I once visited); and from what Alex said, safety was not their prime issue. He was not paid a lot, but still managed to save some money, and together with a financial gift from Aunt Olga had enough funding to make the trip.

When the time came, Kate and I took Alex to Heathrow for his flight to Oz. All went well until I heard from Alex (not long into his trip) that he had just come out of hospital in the north of the country, where he had been treated for meningitis. He had had a lumbar puncture from which it had been confirmed that he (very fortunately) had the viral rather than the bacterial variety. The ATCV group was living in tents at this point and he was convalescing in a tent. . . I was anxious and rang GAP, who had no knowledge of his situation. GAP investigated, and rang me back to tell me of their discoveries. Since Alex had told the ATCV that he absolutely did not want them to advise me, nor GAP, of his illness, and since he was over 18 years of age, the ATCV had respected his wishes. This had put GAP (which in theory was *'in loco parentis'*) in a difficult position. They apologised profusely and undertook a review of their responsibilities in such situations. They felt that, at the least, the ATCV should have informed them. Alex had imagined me flying to Oz immediately I heard the news, which he did not want, but in reality, our friend, Sal, a doctor, lived in Melbourne and said she would have flown up to Brisbane to check on him immediately, had she been asked. The most I managed was to get the ATCV to agree to put him on light duties for a few days – peeling potatoes, among other things! Later on, he managed to cut into his leg with an axe, but survived that too. . .

Alex continued to enjoy his adventures in Australia. All the members of his ATCV group were given a break and encouraged to go off on their own for a while, which he found a little lonely, but he went out to one of the offshore islands and also did a couple of bungee jumps in the jungle (of which there is a DVD) all of which I heard about later. At the end of the trip, he bought an ancient and decrepit camper van which he drove down to Melbourne, where he got some work, painting a corrugated iron roof, and sometimes clearing tables in a café. It was in Melbourne that his friend Adam visited him on his way to the west coast of the USA, where he was planning to meet up with their great friend Will in Los Angeles. Alex had a 'round-the-world' air ticket and had planned to come home via the USA, so this was an opportunity not to be missed.

Meeting up with Adam and Will took a few days, with Alex loafing around in a hostel waiting for them to return to LA, but they managed to meet up – and he was collected, much to his delight, in Will's brother's scarlet Mustang! I did get a few phone calls, while he was waiting. Will's mother, Adam's mother and I had a telephone network going, too. Will's brother had a small and by now quite crowded flat, so Alex went to stay with my mother's brother, my Uncle Peter, who lived in Santa Barbara. It seems that the family was very taken aback by this scruffy individual who by now had huge dyed blonde hair and no decent clothes. My mad Uncle started taking notes about Alex's behaviour, even noting the time Alex turned his light off at night. It seems that he very quickly came to the conclusion that Alex was a drug addict – and when Alex for the second time (because he preferred to be with his mates, rather than visiting properties(!) with his real estate uncle) – only gave them short notice that he would not be turning up for an evening meal, Peter erupted. He told Alex over the phone, to meet him in downtown LA, where he dumped Alex's belongings on the pavement and drove off. This incident caused a huge rift between my mother and her brother which was never really repaired. He wrote a long crazed letter to her, listing in minute and mad detail, all Alex's movements, and she replied with a staggeringly angry letter accusing him of abandoning her grandson with nowhere to go, no food, and no money. It was a heartening read and I still have the letter. Of course, Alex was put up by Will's brother along with the other two but it was not long before I received a phone call at work from Will's mother, telling me that Will had been in touch to describe these events and to say that Alex had been upset by them, was a bit depressed and rather than crossing the USA on a Greyhound Bus as planned, wanted to come home sooner, especially since Will and Adam were returning and they were all sitting round and talking about Muswell Hill! I rang Alex and reassured him. He took an internal flight to New York, and then flew back to London.

I went with Will and another of Alex's friends, to meet him at Heathrow. It was lovely to see him again. He had developed an Australian accent, a very loud laugh and his dark eyes looked darker than ever in contrast to his huge blonde Afro hairstyle! He had lost almost everything on his travels but still had two important items in his possession: his passport and his sleeping bag.

It was not long before Alex went off to university. In Year 1 (from autumn 1997) he lived in university halls, in Year 2, he shared a house with friends and in Year 3 he reportedly lived in a cupboard under the stairs in yet another house. He had very little money indeed but still managed to buy significant amounts of beer. At one stage, he took a telephone sales job, trying to sell advertising space in the 'Auto Trader' magazine. I understand that he lived mainly on potatoes, onions and carrots. Occasionally, I managed to speak to him on the phone (no mobiles then) and he re-joined us at home in the vacations. I used to drive him up to uni at the beginning of each year and enjoyed visiting Norwich and, particularly, the Sainsbury Gallery, in the grounds of UEA.

One particular incident remains with me: I was woken up in the middle of the night, by the phone. It was Alex, ringing to tell me that he had been arrested and was in a cell in Norwich police station! I tremulously asked if this was the one phone call he was allowed. It was. I was worried and rang the police station immediately after his call. I was assured by a friendly sounding policeman that Alex was fine – that he had been arrested for being drunk and disorderly and would be released in the morning, by which time he would hopefully be sober. This was in fact what happened, so all was well. However, Alex had been a passenger in a Mini being driven by a drunk friend. The friend had crashed his car into a parked car in a residential area, and Alex had been very lucky indeed not to have been hurt. The police were called and Alex was arrested for swearing at the car owners, and for being drunk and disorderly, despite being warned. Alex's friend was banned from driving and dropped out of university. Alex, fortunately, had survived and had not (seriously) broken the law.

Somehow or other, in 2000, Alex managed to graduate. However, had I not opened a letter addressed to him at home, telling him that unless he paid his Library fine, he would not be able to graduate (at which point, I paid the tiny fine), he might not have done so! Kate, Patty, and I went to his very enjoyable graduation ceremony.

* * *

Kate's New School and Gap Year

Kate decided that she wanted to move to another school for her 'A' levels and received conditional offers from Latymer School in Enfield and Woodhouse College – a sixth form College in the Borough of Barnet. She did very well in her GCSEs, and was able to start at Latymer in Sept 1996, which, at that time, had an excellent reputation for its music. Both these were state institutions, which meant that after three years of applying for and receiving help towards paying Kate's school fees, this help was no longer needed. Both institutions took boys as well as girls and Kate's academic and social life shifted its axis from South Hampstead to Enfield.

Kate settled in at Latymer, taking the local bus there and back every day. She had started out doing Chemistry as a fourth subject, but soon dropped that. Her subjects were Biology, French and Geography. She played lots of music, continuing with her oboe lessons and playing in school orchestras and concerts, excelling on her oboe. Her other interest now was her social life. I spent a lot of time and drove many miles up and down the A10 road, taking Kate and sometimes her friends Vicky and Emily to various gatherings, particularly to Vicky's house, but also to the huge and horrendous looking nightclub called 'Eros' that was on one of the industrial estates on the A10! They loved it. I insisted always, on collecting Kate from wherever she was, regardless of the time of night. I think I was considered eccentric, but I preferred it that way, and Kate always rang me for a lift, which was reassuring. Before I knew it, however, Kate and Vicky were celebrating their 18th birthdays with a joint party and then school was over.

Kate took a gap year. She decided not to travel, but to work for a while (finding temporary office work quite easily) and then concentrate on setting up a girl band with Maggie and Jules' daughter Mia and two others. Since the other three all came from Tunbridge Wells, Kate spent a great deal of time staying at Maggie and Jules' house. The band even had two managers – Bob and Mick, who had a van, drove the girls around, and arranged practice sessions, gigs and recordings. The band was terrific. Kate was the lead singer and Mia played bass guitar. There were two other players as well – a guitarist and a drummer. All four girls were talented and very musical and they sounded great. Maggie, Jules, Miranda, Alex and I went to several of their gigs. Initially, Bob and Mick wrote the songs, when the band was called "Gender". The band performed at various venues: 'The Forum' in Tunbridge Wells; a small music venue just off Tottenham Court Road; and the 'Rock Garden' in Covent Garden. The CD they recorded was great too and I still have a copy. After a while, they decided to leave their managers, write all the songs themselves, and rename the band "Derotchka". In the end, however, time ran out and university beckoned.

* * *

A Couple More Battles

Barnet

I was one of several leaseholders at Monkswell Court, the freeholder being the London Borough of Barnet. The small estate (three 3-storey buildings) had previously been council housing and the elderly couple from whom I had bought the flat had exercised their 'right to buy' and then sold up.

The service charges levied were based on estimates for the year ahead and this led to endless arguments about amounts being charged and amounts owed. The way the system was run was highly inefficient and there were frequent errors. The paperwork involved in all this ran to several files. The final details were only settled when we left.

Barnet had announced in late 1994 that they planned to carry out an 'External Redecoration and Repairs Programme' in 1995/96, and advised, in due course, that this would include replacement of all windows. I decided against being part of Barnet's window replacement programme and therefore, in October 1996, applied for a Deed of Variation, which allowed me to take responsibility for this work myself (as long as I did replace my windows, ensuring that they were in exactly the same style as Barnet's, with matching materials). This was a lengthy bureaucratic process involving the London Borough of Barnet and Barnet County Court, which cost me £350. However, I received confirmation finally, in July 1997 that this had been registered at the Land Registry. Subsequently, I requested quotations from several companies, informed my neighbours, some of whom followed suit, and I had a full set of new windows installed and my front door painted, at a significantly lower cost than that proposed by Barnet!

The next problem was a much larger one and involved the rest of the building works. In view of the fact that all the leaseholders (not the Council tenants) would be charged large amounts for this work, I thought it would be a good idea to set up a recognised Residents' Association to fight the plan, which looked far too expensive. The rules for the recognition of such associations stated that both tenants and leaseholders had to be represented. I therefore called a meeting of all occupiers and booked the local church hall. A number of those who would be most affected (the leaseholders) wanted to join and by some miracle, I managed to persuade a couple of tenants to join as well. I was therefore able, not only to get the association recognised by Barnet, but I was even able to apply for and receive, a small amount of funding from Barnet to pay for the hire of the hall and tea and biscuits! We met for the first time and appointed a Chair and a Treasurer; I was appointed as Secretary; and a couple of people made tea. Arranging the meetings, which involved booking the nearby church hall, writing, printing and distributing flyers to each flat in advance, and writing and distributing the Agendas and Minutes of the meetings, kept me busy. It was through this association, however, that we were able to object officially, to Barnet's refurbishment plans for the estate, when they were presented.

In June 1998, I received two letters from Barnet, informing me of the nature of the work involved in their works project at Monkswell Court, and the estimated cost. A quotation for the work had been accepted from a company called Crook Bros(!) in the sum of £145,645. The first letter is addressed to me as a resident, informing me of my contribution towards this (excluding the windows). The second is addressed to me as Secretary of the Monkswell Court Residents Association (MCRA) and the letter says: "As a recognised residents' association you have the right to be consulted formally on the cost and nature of this work. Please send any observations you have to me at the above address within one month."

A number of meetings were called by Barnet involving members of their Surveyor's Department, other Council representatives and our association. The meetings were held in the evenings and were usually well attended. After various discussions and requests, the Council provided me with all the quotations they had received. I then made an appointment to visit Barnet Town Hall to inspect the plans. On exclaiming at the high costs of the project, and the extent of the works, I was asked in a mild way what I expected, since there was a reason for the Freemasons being called masons. . . I was told that the contractors would meet up at the pub and share out the local authority contracts amongst themselves, ie: "you have Barnet, you have Camden, you have Islington . . . etc".

We (the residents) challenged the tendering process, as a consequence of which, the project was put out to tender for a second time. The price for the project was still too high, so we demanded to see a full detailed Schedule of Works for the project, from which it became clear that the schedule included works that were entirely unnecessary. . .

I had already found a strong ally in the son of an elderly couple who lived on the estate as leaseholders. His name was Jason and he was a Surveyor . . . not only that, but his brother was a Solicitor. Lucky indeed.

As soon as I received the Schedule of Works, I sent a copy to Jason and we independently went round the estate inspecting every item listed in it. It became plain very quickly that the schedule included work that did not need doing at all (roofing, painting, etc) and exaggerated some of the work that did. The Schedule was a shocking document. It included, for example, the replacement of all the small 1930s bevelled window panes in all the (14) front doors, when not one of them was even cracked or in any way in bad condition. This would certainly be described by many, as fraud. I incorporated our notes into one document and sent it to Jason with a draft letter, who forwarded these to his brother. Jason's brother then wrote a warning letter to Barnet, including all this information and threatening to report them to the Local Authority Ombudsman.

This produced results! The Deputy Borough Surveyor called an urgent meeting of residents. The first thing he did at the meeting was to put his hands in the air and declare "Mea Culpa". We never saw nor heard from or of him again. . .

A new schedule of works was written, based on Jason's draft, and the project was put out to tender again. Appropriate works were finally carried out and we all paid our shares. My final contribution, excluding windows and doors was £1675.21p. It had been a great deal of work but the outcome was, at last, appropriate and fair. Excellent!

* * *

The Bradford & Bingley

All was going well at Monkswell Court, until another bombshell arrived out of the blue and hit us.

Three and a half years after moving into Monkswell Court, ie nearly seven years after the Bradford & Bingley Building Society had repossessed our house in Cecil Road on 4 November 1991, I received a letter dated 29 September 1998 from the Bradford & Bingley (B&B), advising me that: "following completion of the sale of the above property, the proceeds of sale were insufficient to repay the outstanding mortgage in full. The property was sold for £150,000, leaving a shortfall of £96,272. The Society would therefore like to enter into discussions with you to see how this sum may be repaid as you remain liable for the full extent of the debt". I read the letter, shaking all over, in total shock and disbelief.

However, yet again, friends were at the ready to come to my aid. Thanos (a lawyer) and Janette, who were living in Athens, recommended a Muswell Hill friend of theirs, a solicitor, who, it turned out, not only worked from a practice in Lincoln's Inn, but worked in an environment where clients were not overcharged. He was perfect – an intelligent, gentle and delightful man. We met and went over the case. Correspondence went back and forth between the solicitor and Bradford & Bingley, and with me. The solicitor then proposed that we seek advice from Counsel – a barrister specialising in property matters of this kind, with whom we also met. By then, it was May 1999 and the B&B had withdrawn its original deadline. The barrister was impressive and, after some time, a letter was drafted by the offices of the two lawyers with minor corrections from me.

By coincidence, I had read an article in 'The Guardian' dated 15 May 1999 entitled "Hope for the repossessed". It described various scenarios similar to mine (but involving lesser sums) and then reported a Court of Appeal decision which "could mean that lenders have only six years to chase a debt". I sent a copy of this article to the solicitor immediately, who confirmed that it was helpful and that he would discuss it with Counsel.

The upshot of all this was that an absolutely brilliant letter, based on the advice of Counsel, was sent to B&B by the solicitor, dated 21 June 1999. This set out the various reasons why they did not have a leg to stand on, and said "Mrs Macdonald has no proposals for settlement to make and at this stage is not prepared to make any voluntary disclosure of her financial means". This letter summed up a real David and Goliath story. In response, on 13 August 1999 (nearly one year after their original letter) B&B wrote, briefly, denying some of the points made, but saying "That aside however, the Society is also mindful of Mrs MacDonald's circumstances and on this occasion, purely as a gesture of good will and without any admission of liability on the part of the Society, any employee or representative of the Society, we are prepared to close the file and take no further action".

Result! The episode cost me £2,449.38p which, although a lot of money for me at the time, was not a great deal in the grand scheme of things, and was money extremely well spent. The consequences, had I not taken legal action, do not bear thinking about. . .

* * *

Kate at Uni

Kate was offered an interview at Aberdeen University to study French and Psychology. She travelled to Aberdeen by train on a day when the weather was glorious and she told me how wonderful the sea looked from the train. She very much liked the look of the university and accepted their offer of a place on a Scottish four year degree course. After a year, she dropped the psychology and concentrated on French.

In Year 1 Kate lived in Halls, in Year 2, in a flat in a tenement style building and later in a shared house. As part of her course, Kate was expected to spend six months at a French University. There was a choice and Kate chose Grenoble. She was a little late in starting because she had been unwell, and the accommodation arrangements were vague, but finally, it was all sorted out. I went with Kate to settle her in. We flew to Geneva, took the train to Grenoble and then took a taxi to the student residences. The taxi took us over the river and up the very steep winding mountain road until we emerged through the cloud to find several halls of residence overlooking the city below, with views far into the distance, to the snow covered mountains. It was beautiful. The boules of the téléphérique which went up to the Bastille at the very top of the mountain, passed by quite close to Kate's window. I stayed for a couple of days only. After some searching, we managed to find and buy a very small fridge for Kate's room, by which time, she was all set up. Kate sent me a postcard when I got home, telling me how free she felt. It worked out very well and Kate enjoyed herself living with many international as well as French students. At the end of her time there, I drove our Vauxhall Astra to Grenoble to collect her and her belongings. Before leaving, we took a trip further along the mountain, which was just a bit much for the car which so seriously overheated, that after a rest, we stuck as much as possible, to the downhills. . . We drove back home through France, enjoying ourselves and visiting places en route. One evening, the boot of the car simply refused to lock, with all Kate's things inside. . .

I drove Kate up to Aberdeen at the beginning of each year and collected her at the end of each year. Whenever I did this, I usually took a couple of days' holiday and would explore some new town or city. On one of these occasions, I was driving from Aberdeen to London on 9/11 – Tuesday 11 September 2001 – the day the World Trade Center Twin Towers in New York were attacked and destroyed. The car radio was on non-stop and I watched the television reports late into the night at the motel I stayed in en route.

Kate graduated in 2003 with an MA in French. Alex and I went to her graduation ceremony, where Kate wore a slinky black woollen dress that had once belonged to me! She had officially objected to the university about the fact that women were required to wear skirts for the ceremony, but when the university relented, she decided not to wear trousers after all! I took the three of us for a wonderful celebratory dinner at 'The Silver Darling' in Aberdeen.

* * *

UCL

At about the same time that Kate went to Aberdeen, my boss, Roland, having turned the Institute of Child Health into a 5* research institute, was appointed as Vice-Provost for Biomedicine at University College London (ICH had merged with UCL in 1996). This involved moving to the main UCL campus on Gower Street. Roland asked me if I would like to go with him and I agreed – back to where I had started out. Roland was also asked to take on the Headship of UCL's Graduate School. Apart from very smart farewell dinners arranged for Roland, one at the Middle Temple, with highly distinguished guests, to which I was also invited, a brilliant farewell party was organised for me at ICH, where Kate was asked to join us to play the piano. We left ICH in 1999.

Things at UCL were a little rocky for me to begin with – I soon became worried and depressed. I thought I had made a big mistake in moving from the Institute because my role was unclear and did not carry enough responsibility. After a while, however, things changed, and I took on the more senior role of manager of the Graduate School – the team supporting UCL's postgraduate community, especially research students and their supervisors. Everything went from strength to strength from then on as we recruited more staff members to the Graduate School. I was very busy but got great satisfaction from my work and felt very privileged to be managing such a talented team.

Roland left UCL to become the Vice-Chancellor of Plymouth University. He asked me whether I would like to go with him, but I decided against the idea – it would have been too far away from family, friends and London. Tragically, Roland was killed in an accident on New Year's Day 2007. A power cable had blown down in a high wind and he was electrocuted by it when he was out for a walk on a footpath near his house with Beth and a friend. He is sorely missed by me and many others. I was one of several people who spoke at UCL's memorial event, held to remember and honour him. It took place in the impressive main lecture theatre of the Institute of Child Health, in the new building he had been responsible for creating. The great and the good of UCL, ICH and GOS turned out in force, including the UCL Provost. Beth and family were also there. Roland was a wonderful friend and mentor to me, as well as being my boss.

Once Roland had left UCL, I was lucky enough to have two further Heads of Graduate School (a 50% post), who both turned out to be great bosses. I even visited one of them in New York after she had left UCL.

The UCL Graduate School, with its closely-knit team and numerous achievements, became highly regarded, both within UCL and outside the university. Other universities borrowed from us; visited us; and wanted to emulate us. The UCL Graduate School consistently received high ratings from research students, and from the Quality Assurance Agency for Higher Education.

* * *

The Next Move

We had lived in Monkswell Court for six years and I yearned to have a garden. I thought that if I moved to another area, I might be able to afford a small house with a garden, so I started to house hunt.

I searched methodically, and narrowed down the areas that I could afford and that would be pleasant to live in. Trini and Peter, friends of Angelique, and later me, suggested that I should look in the area East of Turnpike Lane, where they live. One of the offers I made fell through, and so I waited for a while. I also waited until I had a firm offer to purchase our flat. I soon accepted an offer of £167,000. Then, on the very first day of visiting properties by appointment – which I did with Alex on a beautiful day with blue skies – I put in an offer for a small house with a delightful garden backing on to the park. The offer was accepted immediately. However, in view of the estimates I received for essential works that would need to be done, a revised offer of £160,000, was accepted in due course and we moved in. This was 29 November 2001.

Kate was still at university in Aberdeen but Alex was at home and unclear as to what sort of career to take up. He had had a couple of reasonable but boring jobs and had decided they were not for him. Once I had completed the purchase of a new house, however, which was in need of complete refurbishment, he became very interested in learning various aspects of the building trade. As a result of acting as mate to the various tradesmen who came to work on the house, he quickly became very skilled; among other achievements, tiling the entire bathroom and building a large raised patio.

However, he also began a Master's course in IT at Middlesex University. After this, he decided on teaching as a career and in September 2005, registered for a Postgraduate Certificate of Education (PGCE), also at Middlesex University. At that time, to address the shortage of teachers, the government was offering to pay PGCE tuition fees and also offering student loans. With no rent to pay, this was an excellent package for Alex.

Kate had stayed on in Aberdeen. She had found jobs in the human resources departments of a couple of oil companies and one of her employers funded her to study for two years part-time, for the Chartered Institute of Personnel Development's Postgraduate Diploma (CIPD) at the Robert Gordon University, which she was awarded in 2006, and which set her on her career path.

Kate's decision to leave Aberdeen and return to London became complicated and difficult. She and her ex-boyfriend had split up and the flat that they co-owned did not sell for a very long time. Her ex-boyfriend refused to take responsibility for any payments once he had moved out, and stupidly, refused to accept offers from potential purchasers because he thought they could get more if they waited. All this time, Kate was having to pay the mortgage, and also the payments on a loan taken out specifically for him. Kate was forced to the edge of bankruptcy, and completed all the bankruptcy application papers in readiness for submitting them on our return from a short holiday that she and I took in Cornwall. However, walking along a sunny and blowy cliff top on the coastal path, Kate received a phone call. This was an offer (by this time, her ex-boyfriend had finally been brought to his senses over the figures involved), and was an offer she could accept. This 'at the absolutely last minute' development, not only solved the problem, but meant that, after final calculations, Kate, fortunately, did not make a loss.

For years, I had been visiting my mother in Sanderstead, south of Croydon, every two weeks. Sadly, she eventually had a fall and died in hospital on 5 March 2008. Both my brother and I had managed to visit her very shortly before this.

The task of clearing out my mother's flat was no small matter and Alex and Kate helped me. Firstly, I spent a couple of days sorting everything out and then Alex drove us all in a large hired van to the flat, where we loaded it to the brim. It was a tiring job and we made it to the dump just as it was closing. I tried everything to find a charitable organisation that would take the teak 1970s furniture, mostly from Heals, to give to anyone who could use it, but south London just did not have any organisations doing this. I therefore had to pay a clearance company to smash up all the furniture and take it away, which was depressing and an appalling waste. Back at our house, over the next few days, Kate helped me to sort out the mountains and mountains of papers, which we eventually boiled down into a reasonable file to give to the solicitor. The flat was in a poor state and was finally sold for very little. The solicitor took two years and charged significant fees, to sort out what was a simple and certainly not very valuable estate.

* * *

Onwards and Upwards

Our lives continued in their usual highly turbulent way:

> The 'Downs' were that Alex, who had been diagnosed with diabetes type 1 when we were still at Monkswell Court, was diagnosed with testicular cancer.
> Kate was already ill when I collected her from Aberdeen and was diagnosed a couple of months later with sarcoidosis. Maggie was an extraordinary support during this period and many later times, too.
> Kate lost her right eye in an operation to try to save her detached retina.
> Later, due to the sarcoidosis having attacked her kidneys, Kate's kidneys started to fail and over time, she was extremely ill more and more frequently. Eventually, dialysis loomed and I realised that maybe I could help out.

* * *

However, the many wonderful 'Ups', which totally eclipsed and continue to eclipse what went before, were (in no particular order):

> Both Alex and Kate were treated at the Royal Free Hospital and both recovered. Alex had surgery followed by chemotherapy. Kate was hospitalised and treated with a medley of drugs. She had, unbelievably, managed to hold down a part-time job while she was ill, but for some

time had to recover at home with nothing to do, which, given the side-effects of the drugs, was difficult. But the treatment worked!

Kate was fitted at Moorfields Eye Hospital with an ocular prosthetic. The prosthetic was handpainted and fitted in front of her. It was made by the ocularist, David Carpenter, at Moorfields Eye Hospital, whose 'eyes' featured in an exhibition of crafts at the Victoria & Albert Museum, to which Kate and I happened to go later. It is a brilliant piece of craftsmanship and she looks as lovely as ever.

Kate, despite still receiving treatment, started to work part-time again, and also enrolled for a Master's in Employment Law at Middlesex University.

On 28th May 2012, after immensely efficient and speedy arrangements by the hospital to test both of us, a kidney transplant operation was carried out at the Royal Free Hospital, and in what seemed like no time at all, Kate was in possession of and using one of my kidneys and her health was transformed. We both stayed with Alex and Anne in Potters Bar afterwards, to recuperate – by a lucky chance, it was their half-term.

Alex was awarded a Diploma in IT and later, a PGCE. He then got his first job as a secondary level geography teacher and is now a Head of Department at a large comprehensive school.

Kate was awarded a Distinction in her Master's (the Graduation Ceremony was on 16 July 2012, to which Alex, Paul and I went), and, in due course, she started working again full-time. This led to her current role, which, she tells me, is busy and challenging, provides her with great job satisfaction, a good salary, and where she is happy.

Our house refurbishment was completed and continues to provide stability, comfort and enormous pleasure.

* * *

In writing this account, far from thinking too much about the difficulties we have faced as a family, I have been slightly overwhelmed by the sheer number and variety of positive experiences I have had – and continue to have.

Despite having lived in various countries in the Far East as a child, and having lived in France, Papua New Guinea, Australia and Greece as an adult, I can still get so much pleasure from sitting under the apple tree in my garden on a sunny summer's day, listening to the birdsong and reading my book, or just being with my Gang of 4.

I am setting out some of the more recent highlights and things I have not included before, hoping that I will be forgiven for repeating myself, or for forgetting or overlooking things that should have been included elsewhere:

A holiday with Kate on the Greek island of Lefkas for a couple of weeks, soon after her return to London, and holidays together in Paris, Rome, Barcelona, Marrakesh and Madeira.

Taking part in the 'Million' anti Iraq war protest march in London and incredibly, meeting Caroline and Geoff in the enormous crowd, and marching along with them.

Great holidays with Judy in Sicily, Venice, travelling around southern Spain and visiting the Scottish island of Mull.

Three weeks living on my own in a flat in central Nice in the south of France.

Two great holidays with Alex and Anne, together with Anne's mum and dad, Gladys and John, and the rest of the family, near Avignon and in Normandy; and visiting them in their cottage in the Lake District.

Staying with Max and Jenny in Caerleon, Wales, a couple of times, once recently to attend a Jesus College event in Abergavenny when David and Sarah also stayed with them and we all met up with Maggie and Jules. Max had been involved in organising a ceremony, held to honour the first Principal of Jesus College Oxford (appointed by Queen Elizabeth in 1571). There's even a photo of us all.[133]

Maggie and Jules had taken the opportunity of being in South Wales to hunt for traces of Maggie's ancestors, by visiting the nearby grand house in which they had lived. Not long afterwards, I discovered that Maggie, who is descended from the Lenox family of Brown Lenox & Co, were also wealthy ironmasters who lived and operated in South Wales, and bought the lease of the Ynysangharad iron-works from the Llanover Estate in 1908! The Lenox family must therefore have known my family as well as Sarah's back in the day! Extraordinary. . .

Hundreds(? – yes, probably hundreds) of theatre trips and meals out with Henley.

And even more gallery, museum and concert visits, sometimes with friends, often on my own.

---

133 http://www.southwalesargus.co.uk/news/14625180.Plaque_honours_Abergavenny_man_who_founded_Oxford_college/#gallery0

Countless gatherings of family and friends for meals around many different dining tables.

Walking with Sally, particularly the 50 miles of the River Lea (in short bursts!) from Bedfordshire to the Thames, plus a recent trip to Paris and a couple of short breaks in England.

Making new friends.

A trip down memory lane with Maggie, when we visited Malvern for a few days and sneaked into the rear quadrangle of our old school, from where we could see (up high) the window of our infamous two-dorm!

Being called urgently in the middle of the night to help my neighbour give birth to her first child, Aruna (an amazing experience) which she did, unexpectedly, at home – and then watching Aruna and her younger sister, Ushma, growing up next door.

Visiting Maggie and Jules' new grandchildren just after they were born; Mia and Lawrence having become the parents of triplets! – three tiny little wrapped up bundles: Corinna, Hana and Miriam. Mia asked me to be the MC at the triplets' naming ceremony three years later, on 27 July 2014 – a lovely occasion held in Maggie and Jules' garden.

All five of us going to Lisa and Tom's wedding in Whitstable very soon after Kate and I had come out of hospital, and to Daphne and Gareth's wedding on Hydra, both brilliant occasions. We stayed on in Hydra for a week and had such a good time (Alex and Kate re-visiting old memories of Greece), after which I visited Meteora in central Greece and also stayed with Janette and Thanos in Athens. Not so long ago, visiting Lisa and Tom in Kentish Town, where they now live with their two small children Marina and Alexander.

In 2013 staying with Elizabeth and Jeffrey in Toronto where I had a fantastic two weeks with wonderful weather, exploring the city, and also travelling by bus one day to the magnificent Niagara Falls. The three of us went on to spend a week in New York together, where their son Eli lives and where Jeffrey's brother, Robbie, also lived at the time. The trip got off to a wonderful start. We flew from Toronto in the early evening, and I had a window seat on the left hand side of the aircraft. As we approached NY, the plane flew south (quite low by then) above the middle of the Hudson River, following it down to the southern tip of Manhattan, then turning north up the East River (with a view of the other side of Manhattan), to La Guardia airport. It was dark by then, and the view of Manhattan, with all its lit up skyscrapers with lines of red tail lights between them, was spectacular

– it was genuinely as if I was being given my own special flight to see the sights – I thanked the pilot accordingly! We had a great time, being shown around by Eli, being hosted by him to a meal at his house, and being driven around by Robbie and taken to eat out in Queens. All the food we ate was delicious and visiting a traditional NY deli/sandwich and coffee place in Manhattan was great too. I took the ferry out to Staten Island one day, passing the Statue of Liberty, of course, and also visited my ex-boss and her husband in Brooklyn, who took me out for dinner. We also visited the very moving Ground Zero Monument.

* * *

Both my wonderful children are in firm relationships with wonderful partners. Alex and Anne found each other and married at a moving wedding ceremony on 6 August 2010. Firstly, they bought a flat very near me, but later bought a house in Potters Bar. Kate and Paul found each other not long before Kate's kidney transplant, lived together in South London for some time and then bought a flat together in Walthamstow in 2014, staying with me for 5 months while the flat was gutted and refurbished. Both couples live not too far away from me, which is a huge plus for me.

I retired from UCL when I was 65, when I was treated to a farewell dinner with a group of a dozen people from UCL. These included Graduate School staff and several academics associated with the Graduate School, including my ex-boss, who timed a planned visit to London to coincide with the date. I received many very generous presents from across the university.

However, I thought I would hold a party myself. I wanted to celebrate my 65th birthday; my retirement; and the fact that I had (quite incredibly) paid off my mortgage. Very kindly, Angelique suggested that I could hold the party at their house in Crouch End and Freddie, also very kindly, agreed. I sent out invitations for 4 June 2011. I hired a marquee and a French caterer with helpers, and the day turned out to be beautiful, with sun and bright blue skies. It was a fantastic occasion for me. As well as my family, almost all my friends were there, barring those few living in other parts of the world.

Two years later, on 1 June 2013, tragically, suddenly, and unexpectedly, Freddie died, which was a massive blow for all of us and we still miss him a great deal. He was a very important, caring and supportive figure, not just in my life but also in the lives of Alex and Kate.

On my 69th birthday, my Gang of 4 and I took a ride in the new London cable car across the Thames to the London Dome, where we had booked a climb up to the top of the roof. We followed this with lunch outside in a pub on the river.

On my 70th birthday, we went for a long weekend to Sussex where we rented a small house with a garden; spent a day doing falconry; had a marvellous evening meal out; had tea, cake and presents in the garden and also visited a well-known garden. We had a similar long weekend in Yorkshire for my 71st birthday, which included a visit to the National Coal Mining Museum, where we took a tour led by an ex-miner, deep (140m) underground into a coal mine, and later had dinner at the Old Bell Inn, with its Gin Emporium, which stocks and displays all its 600 gins! And in 2017, Elizabeth and Jeffrey visited.

And on it goes. . .

How lucky am I?

I have had some extraordinary and fascinating holidays in the recent past, too: in the Outer Hebrides in June 2016, and the Orkneys in June 2017 (when our B&B hostess said she knew someone with the surname Gaudie!); both fantastic trips with Angelique. And in September 2016, Sally and I toured around south western USA for 18 days.

However, when Maggie suggested that she and I should take a holiday to Myanmar (Burma), which we did in January 2015, I was brought full circle – back to the beginning – where all this started. . .

Kate & Alex on holiday. In Edinburgh. 1993?

Anne with her Mother Valerie (Granny). 1990s

*Alex, suited and booted. 1998.
Monkswell Court, Muswell Hill, London*

*Kate ready to go out for her 18th
birthday party. Monkswell Court,
Muswell Hill, London. 1998*

*Alex's Graduation,
University of East Anglia, 2000*

*Kate's Graduation,
University of Aberdeen, 2003*

Anne Flook and Alex Macdonald in the Lake District. 2009

*Alex and Anne (née Flook) Macdonald at their wedding
6 August 2010*

FROM THE ESK AND THE USK: OUT EAST AND BACK HOME

Kate Macdonald & Paul Barrow in Mexico. 2012

Kate & Paul on holiday with Anne. Nice, France. 2013

Anne's birthday outing to the Dome, London, with Paul, Kate, Anne and Alex. 2014

Patty Macdonald's 70th birthday, at Higham Road, London. With Anne, Kate, Alex and Paul. 2017

*My children: Alex Macdonald and Kate Macdonald.
Hydra, Greece, for Daphne's wedding. 2015*

*My children's partners: Paul Barrow and Anne Macdonald (née Flook).
Hydra, Greece for Daphne's wedding. 2015*

Anne's 70th birthday weekend with Alex, Anne, Kate and Paul. In Sussex. 2016

Anne's 70th birthday weekend with family. In Sussex. 2016

CHAPTER 11

Myanmar

BURMA BECAME MYANMAR IN 1989 – its name changed by the military government to "Union of Myanmar" and later to "Republic of the Union of Myanmar". Rangoon, the former capital of Myanmar became Yangon, and a new capital was created in Naypitaw. Other cities were also given new names.

Aung San Suu Kyi, the Burmese pro-democracy leader, approved the return of tourism in November 2010 and I decided that Maggie's idea of a trip to Myanmar was fantastic. Having booked the holiday for 17 January 2015, I started to think about trying to visit some key sites in Yangon where my family had lived, worked, and stayed. Other towns and cities lived in by them at different times were too far away from our tour and in any case, the British Foreign Office was advising against all but essential travel to some of these.

It took a considerable amount of research to find the various locations because not only had the street names changed, but they were now in the Myanmar language and script. In addition, some of the buildings were being used differently. Once I had found the information I needed, however, I printed an A4 size map of central Yangon, on which I marked the main places I would like to visit, numbering them and providing a key[134]. Almost as soon as we arrived at our hotel in Yangon, where we met the other fourteen members of our group, I asked our Myanmar guide, Za Za, how I should go about trying to find these sites and when. She was very

---

134 See page 326.

helpful, and when she saw the marked up map, realised that it would not be too difficult to find them. She suggested that there would be time on our return to Yangon at the end of our trip.

The next morning, after setting out by bus[135] for some sight-seeing in Yangon, including passing the famous gates of Aung San Suu Kyi's house (where she was held under house arrest for a total of 15 years and where she addressed the people on her release) and visiting the Shwedagon Pagoda; we took a short flight to Heho and drove to Nyaung Shwe, on the shores of the enormous and beautiful Inle Lake on the Shan Plateau. We explored the lake in long flat bottomed boats, visiting many villages built on stilts at the edges of the lake, with their picturesque floating vegetable gardens. We visited a number of craft workshops in these villages, and also a big local market. The lake people and fishermen are famous for their style of rowing, which involves standing at the stern of the boat on one leg whilst wrapping the other leg around the only oar and paddling with it! We also travelled up small creeks to Indein village, where we wandered around the overgrown and picturesque ruins of hundreds of stupas built between the 17th and 18th centuries.

Two days later, we took a local train (a dilapidated relic of British colonial times) and a bus, to Kalaw (a popular hill station for the British). The next morning, we took a gentle four hour trek though the entirely unspoilt countryside, climbing up to pine forest and then down to red soil fields, where villagers were working on their farms.

After that, it was a long day's bus ride to Mandalay where we made a number of visits to several sites. These included a seven mile boat ride up river, where we saw a couple of the protected (and rare) Irrawaddy dolphins. The next day involved taking a pony and trap along bumpy dirt roads on the other bank of the river, to visit a couple of monasteries and have lunch in a local restaurant, ending the day at the famous teakwood U Bein bridge as sunset approached. This was the first place we had seen a lot of tourists

---

135 Most vehicles in Myanmar have right hand steering and yet drive on the right hand side of the road! The bus driver always had a 'helper' standing to his left, who kept an eye on the traffic for him. This is because many vehicles continue to have right hand steering (from British colonial times) but in 1970, General Ne Win ordered that traffic should move to the right (apparently his wife's astrologer advised that the country would be better off driving on the right hand side of the road!). Myanmar has the second highest road accident death toll in South East Asia, but luckily for us, our journeys by road in both city and countryside were surprisingly safe.

and tourist coaches, which spoilt it somewhat, but Maggie and I walked all the way across the bridge and back again, and, on the whole, avoided them.

The tour notes say that on the following day, we would be taking the "express boat service" down the Ayerwaddy (Irrawaddy) River to Bagan. From April/May to September, water levels are too low for this boat trip, so we were in luck. It was an all day and very enjoyable trip down the river, and we arrived in Bagan at sunset with clouds and clouds of bats flying towards us, silhouetted against the sky as they set out on their night time hunt.

Bagan, which was the capital of the Kingdom of Pagan from the 9th to the 13th centuries, is set on a huge plain, which was covered in thousands of 1,000 year-old temples and stupas. Of the 10,000 or so buildings which were constructed there, earthquakes and fires had put paid to many, but around 2000 survive. We took horse-drawn traps through the maze of temples, to see and visit the most remarkable ones.

It was then time to fly back to Yangon, where Za Za, who had turned out to be the most delightful, friendly, efficient and well informed guide, said she would take me and Maggie around the city herself, to find the sites that I had marked on my map.

On our first day in Yangon, we had visited the Strand Hotel – a beautifully refurbished old colonial hotel. I cannot be sure, but I suspect that my parents would have visited this hotel, even if only for a drink at sundown. Even though, later on, my parents always drank whisky with a lot of water, gin was apparently the drink at the time.

My mother's birth was registered at the Central Plague Depot in Rangoon, but it is unclear where this was – possibly at the Yangon General Hospital, where she was born – and also, it transpired, where Za Za was born! This information emerged when we were on our bus travelling though the city and passed the hospital.

Both my mother and I were baptised at The Cathedral of the Holy Trinity[136], my mother on 19 June 1921 and me on 8 February 1947. It was our first port of call after a visit to the large covered Bogyoke Market. The cathedral, which Ian and I had visited when we were in Yangon in 1973, still has the same name and looks just the same. It was rather extraordinary to go inside and walk up to the font where my mother and I had both been baptised, half a world away from 'Home'.

---

136 http://en.wikipedia.org/wiki/Holy_Trinity_Cathedral,_Yangon

Next, we walked to the address on my mother's birth certificate, which was where my maternal grandparents had lived. We found the street, which had been York Road, but unfortunately, the building concerned (number 26) had been demolished (as have many buildings in Yangon) and a modern building had been put up in its place.

I had trawled the internet for any trace of the Steel Bros. Ltd 'chummery' where my father had lived and was amazed and delighted when I came, by chance, across a blog written by some visitors to Yangon, who had stayed in the Yuzana Garden Hotel, which they wrote: "is the former Steel Brothers 'chummery'". What a stroke of luck![137] We made our way there, where Za's Za's smile ensured that the staff were very welcoming. There is a plaque which confirms that the building was indeed the Steel Bros. chummery and we were shown around the hotel, even going upstairs. The overall 1920s/1930s style of the building had not been changed and the original bar was there, alongside the restaurant which had obviously been the refectory. The lift was the original one, too, with a plaque showing the name of the English company that had made it and the date of manufacture. It was fascinating to imagine my father living there as a young man and my mother (having just arrived in Rangoon with her small baby), being refused accommodation until my father returned from 'up-river'. She managed to find accommodation for us in the YWCA.

Almost immediately opposite the chummery, we found the site of what had been the "Scots Kirk". The original church had been built in 1875 and was where my father was baptised on 14 June 1914, but this had been replaced in 1928, with a new but very similar church, now called, among other things, the English Methodist Church[138].

The book "Calling to Mind", about my father's company, Steel Bros., includes a photograph, taken in 1945, of my father's office building in Yangon. I spent a very long time trawling through photos on the internet, when suddenly, out of the blue, I found it – a picture of the same building! I was very excited, found the current street name and marked it on the map. Za Za thought she knew the building[139], which is now used as a bank. When we arrived, the bank was closed, but Za Za's smile, which invariably did the trick, meant that we were allowed in through a side door, where friendly

---

137 http://www.wright-photo.com/yangon2.htm
138 https://www.flickr.com/photos/23268776@N03/3812885515
139 See photo

staff were working and also smiling. It was clear that the interior had not been changed since it was the head office of Steel Bros. & Co. Ltd., and this was where, when he was not in the field, my father had worked from 1934!

The YWCA[140] in Yangon is completely unchanged outside and is in a street with many original buildings. We were told that there had been a recent awakening in Yangon, to the fact that too many beautiful old colonial style buildings were being demolished and that this street was to be preserved. This was where my mother had stayed, with me, in 1946, when I was eight weeks old. We went inside, where the interior had also not changed; we were welcomed, and allowed to climb to the top of the wooden staircase.

I was extremely pleased with my successful trip down memory lane. It had been an exciting and moving experience, adding an extra dimension to all the information and material I was gathering, and it had been fun doing it.

The following morning, we visited the Yangon Museum before taking our flight to Singapore and then home. I had read that the Museum, among many artefacts, owns some paintings by M. T. Hla, the Burmese painter I mentioned in Chapter 1, a couple of whose watercolours I inherited. I was keen to see these, but sadly, the art gallery section of the Museum was closed for refurbishment. I enquired whether it would be possible for me to be allowed into the gallery but unfortunately, this was out of the question. It would have been interesting. . .

However, there is one final Burmese story that should be mentioned. This is that Za Za came to stay with me in London in the spring of 2016. She had won a tour guide prize from her company and the prize was a visit to the UK. She was an unusual guest: despite her sophistication and mature approach to her job, her education, financial training and language skills, she still checked, with some bewilderment, whether I really lived in my (relatively small) house on my own. Relatively small, that is, in this country. . . She adored the big magnolia tree outside her bedroom window which was in full flower, and hurried down the garden to pick a bright red camellia, which she put, Myanmar style, behind her ear. It was fun and I felt rather lucky. I turned the tables on her and, acting as her guide, took her sight-seeing around London.

---

140 See photo on page 14.

Myanmar has been in the news a great deal in recent times due to the government's horrifying ongoing persecution of its Muslim Rohingya people and Aung San Suu Kyi's refusal to acknowledge that this is happening. The UN Assistant Secretary General for Human Rights has said that "acts of genocide may have taken place against Muslim Rohingyas in Myanmar's northern Rakhine state" and in March 2018 also said "the ethnic cleansing of Rohingya continues". Hundreds of thousands of Rohingya people have fled in terror to neighbouring Bangladesh, where they are living in appalling conditions in what is, I understand, one of the largest refugee encampments in the world.

Despite this, it seems that some tourists are still visiting the country and Za Za, from whom I still hear once a year, told me by email at the end of 2017 that she is still managing to earn a living for herself and her family. I was aware of anti-Muslim sentiment in a couple of the conversations I had while in Myanmar, but this was well hidden apart from occasional incidents and outbursts from right wing Buddhist extremists.[141] It does seem, however, that the racism against Muslims is widespread. Paradoxically, Maggie and I were struck again and again by the natural friendliness and charm of the Myanmar people. What next for Myanmar?

May 2018

---

141 I read the news online at times while in Myanmar, and saw a Reuters report that an extremist Buddhist monk had said publicly to Yanghee Lee, the U.N. special rapporteur on human rights in Myanmar: "Just because you hold a position in the United Nations doesn't make you an honourable woman. In our country, you are just a whore."

FROM THE ESK AND THE USK: OUT EAST AND BACK HOME

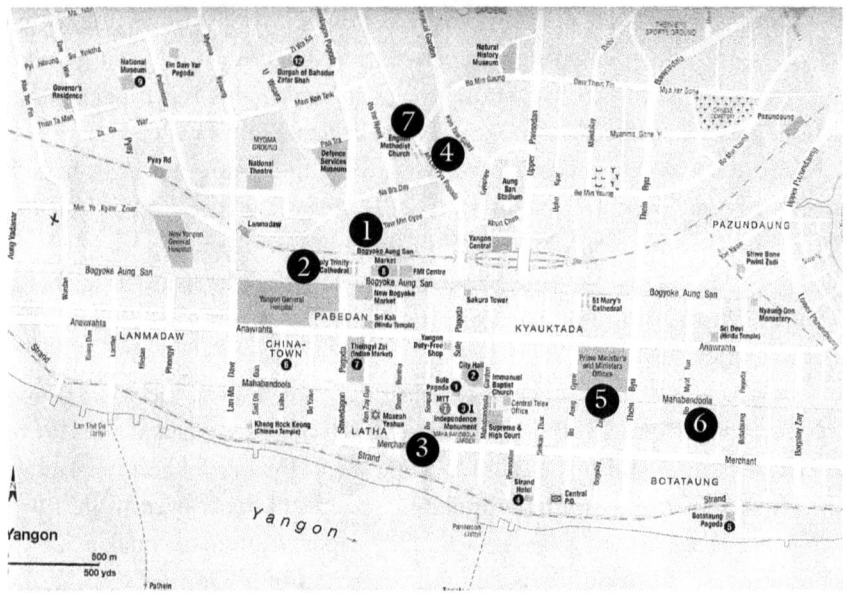

Southern part of Yangon city, Myanmar

Gaudie/Berrington sites in Yangon:

1. My mother was born on 8 August 1920. Her birth certificate gives her address at the time as: **26 York Road, Rangoon**

    This is now: **Yaw Min Gyee (just north of Bogyoke Aung San Market and Holy Trinity Cathedral)**

    The Registrar's Office was given as the Central Plague Depot. Perhaps this was in the Yangon General Hospital or perhaps in City Hall?

2. My mother and I were both baptised in **The Cathedral of the Holy Trinity**, Rangoon. My mother on 19 June 1921 and me on 8 February 1947.

    This still has the same name and is located **on the corner of Bogyoke Aung San and Shwedagon Pagoda Road – almost next to Bogyoke Aung San Market.**

3. **Steel Bros Ltd office** (my father's firm) was at:

    The **corner of Merchant Street and** Maung Taulay Street. This is now known as **Bo Sonpat Street**. Major building works on the next door corner, but I found a photo of this building online in 2014, so may still exist. The book about Steel Bros has a photo of the building taken in 1945.

4. Steel Bros Ltd 'Chummery' where my father lived.

   This was originally 'Kandawaalay House. It is now the Yuzana Garden Hotel – see print-out.

   Its address is **44 Alan Pya Pagoda Street** (which is parallel to Kan Taw Galay Street).

5. **YWCA** where my mother stayed on her arrival. Ian and I stayed at the 'Y' on our visit in November 1973, but probably at the YMCA since married accommodation was more likely to have been there (see point no. 6).

   Boogalay Zay Street – north of Merchant Street and South of Mahabandoola Road (just south of Prime Minister's and Ministers' Offices).

6. **YMCA International House** is four streets along from YWCA on **45th Street just south of Maha Bandula Road**. I think we must have stayed here, rather than the YWCA, since the YWCA may not have had married accommodation. Usually this was available at one or the other, but not both.

7. The **"Scots Kirk"** where my father was baptised. This is now called the English Methodist Church. The address was Signal Pagoda Road, Rangoon. This is now **Ah Lan Pya Pagoda Road** and is **almost opposite the 'Chummery'.**

   "The Presbyterian Church was established in Rangoon in 1873 through the efforts of Rev G Fordyce. This red brick church was built in 1928 and replaced an earlier church built in 1875." **So my father (baptised on 14 June 1914) would not have been baptised in this building.**

   My paternal grandparents, who were in Burma for 28 years, lived in Akyab (now Sittwe).

   My father worked briefly in Moulmein (now Mawlamyine) in 1935 and in Thaton in the 'jungle buying section'. In 1939 he went to Maymo (now Pyin-u-Lwin) for army training (completed in February 1940) before joining the Bhamo Battalion.

   We all lived in in Bassein (now Pathein) in a house called 'Middle Mill'. Pathein is approx 155 miles west of Yangon.

Bibliography

Books:

Holy Bible (1845): with family details first entered by hand by my Paternal Great Great Grandfather William Gaudie (1808-1881)

The Burkes Peerage World Book of Gaudies – a present from my mother, undated.

Berrington, M. D: *Stones of Fire* (July 1958)

Black, G.F: *The Surnames of Scotland. Their Origin, Meaning and History* (1946) New York Public Library

Braund, H E W: *Calling to Mind – An Account of the first hundred years of Steel Bros. & Co Ltd.* (1975)

Charney, Michael W: *A History of Modern Burma* (2009)

Davies-Berrington, Peter: *Davies Berrington.* Compiled and written by my maternal uncle in Pacific Palisades, California (1997)

Eugenides, Jeffrey: *Middlesex* (2002)

Hembry, Phyllis May: *British spas from 1815 to the Present Day* (1997)

Housepian Dobkin, Marjorie: *Smyrna 1922. The Destruction of a City* (1971)

Khin Muang Nyunt et al: *Myanmar Painting: From Worship to Self-Imaging.* EvoHeritage (2006)

Kurkjian, Vahan M: *A History of Armenia* (1958)

Mansel, Philip: *Constantinople City of the World's Desire, 1453-1924* (1995)

Marr, Phebe: The Modern History of Iraq (2004)

Marsden, Philip: *The Crossing Place: A Journey among the Armenians* (1993)

Maxtone Graham, Ysenda: Terms & Conditions: Life in Girls' Boarding Schools 1939-1979 (2016)

Milton, Giles: *Paradise Lost: The Destruction of Islam's City of Tolerance: Smyrna 1922* (2009)
Morris, Chris: *The New Turkey. The Quiet Revolution on the Edge of Europe* (2005)
Muthiah, S: *Madras Rediscovered* (ebook 2015)
Ranard, A: *Burmese Painting: A Linear and Lateral History.* Silkworm Books (2009)
Thompson, Julian: *Forgotten Voices of Burma. A New History of the Second World War's Forgotten Conflict in the Words of Those Who Were There* (2009)

DVD:

ΣΜΥΡΝΗ (Smyrna). Benaki Museum Athens (2012)

Records and Papers:

A 'Family Tree' of the Gaudie family created by David, my brother, in 2002, using, amongst other things, information from the Censuses of 1841, 1851, 1861, 1878 and 1881, together with information on the origin of the name Gaudie from the on-line records of the local history section of Dundee Central Library.
My mother's collection of certificates, documents, letters, photos, newspaper cuttings and objects.
National Archives: Shipping Passenger Lists
National Archives: London Gazette: 2 May 1939, 6 February 1940, 2 July 1940
Marshall, Harry I: Burma Research Society: *Burma Pamphlets No. 8: The Karens of Burma (May 1945)*
Sunday Empire News: 17 September1950
Daily Express: Monday 22 January 1951
Empire News: 28 January, 4 February, 11 February 1951
Hansard: 26 November 1956 vol 561 cc30-3
'Liberty' (Liberty, the National Council for Civil Liberties) Newsletter (Spring 2014)

Websites:

Dictionary of National Biography: Cadwalader Vendigaid: https://en.wikisource.org/wiki/Dictionary_of_National_Biography,_1885-1900
Holy Trinity Cathedral, Yangon: http://en.wikipedia.org/wiki/Holy_Trinity_Cathedral,_Yangon

"Scots Kirk", Yangon: http://www.flickr.com/photos/23268776@N03/3812885515/
Yazuna Garden Hotel: http://www.wright-photo.com/yangon2.htm
Nicholas, Thomas: *Annals and Antiquities of the Counties and County Families of Wales:* https://archive.org/details/annalsantiquitie02nichuoft
National Library of Wales Journal XIV: http://wbo.llgc.org.uk/en/s3-EVAN-CAS-1844.html
"Statistical Accounts of Scotland" Jisc-designated national data centre at University of Edinburgh
The University of Aberdeen: http://www.abdn.ac.uk/alumni/connected/gaudie-95.php
Gower: Clyne Castle: http://www.ggat.org.uk/cadw/historic_landscape/gower/english/Gower_078.htm
Pant-Y-Goitre House: http://www.rightmove.co.uk/property-for-sale/property-37216639.html
Peace Pledge Union: http://www.ppu.org.uk/coproject/cotestimony1.html
The Anglo-African who's who and biographical sketch-book": http://archive.org/stream/angloafricanwhos00will/angloafricanwhos00will_djvu.txt
Imperial Airways: https://en.wikipedia.org/wiki/Imperial_Airways
British Airways: https://en.wikipedia.org/wiki/British_Airways
St Hilda's School: http://www.sthildasooty.com
The Anglo-Burmese Library: http://www.angloburmeselibrary.com/the-war-against-japan.html
Arbroath Smokie: https://en.wikipedia.org/wiki/Arbroath_smokie
Dooars online: http://www.dooarsonline.com
Discovering Tea: http://www.discoveringtea.com/tag/longview-tea-estate/
BBC Asia: 'Thailand Profile': http://www.bbc.co.uk/news/world-asia-15641745
Bangkok Snake Farm: http://www.renegadetravels.com/bangkok-snake-farm-at-queen-saovabha-memorial-institute/
Mount Lavinia Hotel: www.mountlaviniahotel.com/
Malvern St James (MSJ): http://www.malvernstjames.co.uk/
Malvern Girls College: https://www.google.com/search?site=imghp&tbm=isch&source=hp&biw=1004&bih=500&q=malvern+girls+college&oq=malvern+gir&gs_l=img.1.0.0j0i24l9.172357.180053.2.181641.17.8.9.0.0.0.156.768.5j3.8.0....0...1ac.1.36.img..4.24.1993.m_O9hVemZW4
Homme House: http://www.hommehouse.co.uk/
Westons Cider: http://www.westons-cider.co.uk/
Treaty of Peace with Turkey: http://treaties.fco.gov.uk/docs/pdf/1920/TS0011.pdf
A History of Greece: Venizelos and the Asia Minor Catastrophe: http://www.ahistoryofgreece.com/venizelos.htm

Polish Order of the Virtuti Militari Recipients: http://feefhs.org/resource/poland-virtuti-militari-recipients

Bodleian Library, University of Oxford: *The Suez Crisis*: http://www.odl.ox.ac.uk/digitalimagelibrary/

BBC History – History in depth: "*The Suez Crisis*": http://www.bbc.co.uk/history/british/modern/suez_01.shtml

The Guardian.com: Derek Brown, 14 March 2001: "*1956: Suez and the end of empire*" https://www.theguardian.com/politics/2001/mar/14/past.education1

The Economist, 27 July 2006: "*The Suez Crisis, An Affair to Remember*": http://www.economist.com/node/7218678

YouTube: Sagar Rana: Interview by the Nepali Times about his book "Singha Durbar: Rise and Fall of the Rana Regime of Nepal": (2017): https://www.youtube.com/watch?v=-0masX9G7ok

Arthur Nortje: https://en.wikipedia.org/wiki/Arthur_Nortje

Weatherbase.com: http://www.weatherbase.com/weather/weather.php3?s=58049

Papua New Guinea: https://en.wikipedia.org/wiki/Papua_New_Guinea

Kea, Greece: https://www.greektravel.com/greekislands/kea/ioulis.html

South Wales Argus: http://www.southwalesargus.co.uk/news/14625180.Plaque_honours_Abergavenny_man_who_founded_Oxford_college/#gallery0

Reuters: Myanmar monk's U.N. whore rant 'could hurt Buddhism': https://www.reuters.com/article/us-myanmar-religion-idUSKBN0KU0Q420150121

www.ingramcontent.com/pod-product-compliance
Lightning Source LLC
Chambersburg PA
CBHW070136100426
42743CB00013B/2724